Leonora Chestnutt

**Changing
and welfa**

Related titles from Open University Press:

Social Work and Social Welfare Yearbook 3   (1991)
Edited by Pam Carter, Tony Jeffs and Mark Smith
ISBN 0–335–09795–2 (paperback)   0–335–09796–0 (hardback)

Social Work and Social Welfare Yearbook 2   (1990)
Edited by Pam Carter, Tony Jeffs and Mark Smith
ISBN 0–335–09423–6 (paperback)   0–335–09424–4 (hardback)

Social Work and Social Welfare Yearbook 1   (1989)
Edited by Pam Carter, Tony Jeffs and Mark Smith
ISBN 0–335–15875–7 (paperback)   0–335–15876–5 (hardback)

Changing social work and welfare

Edited by
Pam Carter,
Tony Jeffs and
Mark K. Smith

Open University Press
Buckingham · Philadelphia

Open University Press
Celtic Court
22 Ballmoor
Buckingham MK18 1XW

and
1900 Frost Road, Suite 101
Bristol, PA 19007, USA

First Published 1992

Copyright © The Editors and Contributors 1992

All rights reserved. No part of this publication may be reproduced, stored in a retrieval system or transmitted in any form or by any means, without written permission from the publisher.

A catalogue record of this book is available from the British Library

Library of Congress Cataloging-in-Publication Data
Changing social work and welfare/edited by Pam Carter, Tony Jeffs, and Mark Smith.
  p.   cm.
  ISBN 0–335–15757–2 (hb)   ISBN 0–335–15756–4 (pb)
  1. Social service.   2. Social service—Great Britain.
3. Public welfare.   4. Public welfare—Great Britain.
I. Carter, Pam, 1949– . II. Jeffs, Tony.
III. Smith, Mark K., 1950 June 25– .
HV37.C37   1992
361—dc20   91–46235
                                                  CIP

Typeset by Type Study, Scarborough
Printed in Great Britain by Billings Limited, Worcester

Contents

	Notes on editors and contributors	vii
	Introduction	ix
1	Implementing the Children Act 1989 in a hostile climate *Nick Frost*	1
2	'The family': changes, challenges and contradictions *Fiona Williams*	14
3	Guidelines for public service management: lessons not to be learnt from the private sector *John Stewart*	26
4	Competence and contradiction *Mary Issitt and Maureen Woodward*	40
5	Personal mobility and social inequality *Michael Cahill*	55
6	Managing the poorest: the Social Fund in context *Gary Craig*	65
7	Housing issues in social work *Gill Stewart and John Stewart*	81
8	Social welfare developments in Eastern Europe and the future for socialist welfare *Bob Deacon*	94
9	Countdown to 1992: preparing social work for the single market *Hugh Barr*	108

10	The future of education welfare: evolution or extinction? Arnold Dry	120
11	Sexuality and social work organizations Elizabeth Harlow, Jeff Hearn and Wendy Parkin	131
12	Community work: current realities, contemporary trends Hugh Butcher	144
13	The Community Development Project revisited Judith Green	159
14	Professional practice and public controversy: discourse and transracial adoption Derek Kirton	179
15	Trust in the future: an examination of the changing nature of charitable trusts Alison Harker	192
16	Policy-making in the probation service: a view from the probation committee Simon Holdaway and Greg Mantle	203
17	Force for change or optional extra? The impact of research on policy in social work and social welfare Jan Pahl	215
18	The hidden curriculum: sexuality in professional education Pam Carter and Tony Jeffs	231

Notes on editors and contributors

Hugh Barr	Director of the Centre for Inter-Professional Studies in the School of Social Studies at Nottingham University; formerly an Assistant Director for CCETSW
Hugh Butcher	Head of Community Studies at Bradford and Ilkely College
Michael Cahill	Senior Lecturer in Social Policy at Brighton Polytechnic
Pam Carter	Department of Economics and Government, and Social Welfare Research Unit, Newcastle Polytechnic
Gary Craig	Research Fellow, Social Policy Research Unit, University of York
Bob Deacon	Reader in Social Policy at Leeds Polytechnic
Arnold Dry	Senior Education Welfare Officer
Nick Frost	Development Officer for Child Care Services for Wakefield Community and Social Services Department
Judith Green	Local Government Officer, Newcastle City Council; formerly Research Fellow, Durham University, based at Benwell Community Development Project
Alison Harker	Field Officer, City Parochial Foundation, London
Elizabeth Harlow	Lecturer in Social Work, Department of Applied Social Studies, University of Bradford
Jeff Hearn	Senior Lecturer, Department of Applied Social Studies, University of Bradford
Simon Holdaway	Senior Lecturer in Sociology and Head of the Department of Sociological Studies at Sheffield University
Mary Issitt	Youth and Community Work Tutor at Crewe and Alsager College of Higher Education

Tony Jeffs	Department of Applied Social Sciences and Social Welfare Research Unit, Newcastle Polytechnic
Derek Kirton	Senior Lecturer in Social Work at the Polytechnic of East London
Greg Mantle	Lecturer in Social Work at Anglia Polytechnic with special responsibility for probation studies
Jan Pahl	Director of Research at the National Institute for Social Work
Wendy Parkin	Senior Lecturer in Sociology and Social Work, Huddersfield Polytechnic, and Family Centre Social Worker, Kirklees District Council
Mark K. Smith	Tutor and Research Fellow, Centre for Professional Studies in Informal Education, YMCA National College, London
Gill Stewart and John Stewart	Lecturer in Social Work and Social Policy, Department of Applied Social Science, Lancaster University; Lecturer in Social Policy, Department of Applied Social Science, Lancaster University
John Stewart	Head of the School of Public Policy at the University of Birmingham
Fiona Williams	Lecturer at the Open University
Maureen Woodward	Professional Tutor, Tile Hill College of Further Education, Coventry

The views expressed are those of the contributors and should in no way be taken to represent those of their employers or other agencies with which they are connected.

Introduction

The purpose of this book is to bring together a collection of accessible material which will address certain aspects of current practice and thinking. It also seeks to provide a more limited number of contributors with the opportunity to reflect on earlier initiatives. Space does not allow comprehensive updates and reviews of current and potential practice developments and research. Rather we seek to encourage critical debate in a limited number of areas. We hope that this book, like its predecessors,* achieves this balance, ranging over detailed analysis of legislation, policy changes and forms of practice while visiting debates about wider welfare questions. In all cases we hope the contributions will provoke argument and dialogue.

Our thanks go to the contributors to this book. They have had to work to very tight deadlines and have been amazingly prompt with their delivery. Our thanks to all those at the Open University Press and at the typesetters and printers for the fast turnaround they achieved on this book.

Pam Carter
Tony Jeffs
Mark K. Smith

---

* *Social Work and Social Welfare Yearbooks 1, 2* and *3* (Open University Press).

1
Implementing the Children Act 1989 in a hostile climate

Nick Frost

The Children Act 1989 has been widely welcomed as a progressive piece of legislation which modernizes and improves an extremely complex area of law – that regulating the relationship between the state and families. The Act itself was hailed by the Lord Chancellor as the 'most comprehensive and far-reaching reform of child care law which has come before Parliament this century' (*Hansard* HL vol. 502, col. 488). The Act laid down a major challenge for local authorities throughout England and Wales, who were given around two years between the passage of the Act and its implementation date of 14 October 1991 to gear up for a total reform of all their child-care practice and policy.

This chapter aims to review the experience of local authorities in facing up to that challenge. This is of particular interest, because the Children Act is unusual in terms of the social policy of the Thatcher era in as much as it was broadly welcomed by local authorities and their associations – thus providing a sharp contrast with housing, education and local government finance legislation of the 1979–90 period. It will be argued here that, while aspects of the Children Act are flawed, in general it represents a positive step forward for children, young people and their families. However, it will also be argued that the Children Act is at variance with the major thrust of the remainder of the government's social policy. It therefore exists in a hostile climate in which it could not possibly meet its stated policy objectives. This was the real challenge for local authorities in their implementation process.

The key themes

In order to facilitate a discussion of the policy issues emerging from the Act it is important to identify some key themes that can be found in the Children Act.

2   Changing social work and welfare

Theme A: unification of the legislation

The Act brings together the bulk of child-care legislation as a coherent piece of legislation. This is significant in itself as it simplifies the legislative basis of child-care. More fundamentally, the Act brings together what was previously identified as the 'public' law (that concerning state intervention in the family) and the 'private' law (that concerning disputes within families, usually following matrimonial breakdown), and also integrates provision for children with disabilities with 'mainstream' provision.

Theme B: the paramountcy of the child's welfare

Section 1 of the Act requires a court, when considering any question in relation to the upbringing of a child, or in relation to administration of the child's property, to ensure that the child's welfare is the paramount consideration. This strengthens previous terminology, and the Act also lays down a 'welfare checklist' for courts to ensure that the principle is applied in reality.

Theme C: the effective protection of children from abuse and neglect

It is not surprising that child protection was identified by government ministers as a key theme, given that much of the developmental work for the Act took place in the aftermath of a number of significant child abuse inquiries (London Boroughs of Brent 1985; Greenwich 1987; Lambeth 1987). The government saw the Act as removing outdated powers, such as the Place of Safety Order, and creating an effective framework for state intervention in family life.

Theme D: the promotion of family life

One of the impacts of the Cleveland inquiry was to strengthen the theme of promoting family life, one which built on Margaret Thatcher's speeches on the centrality of the family (see Frost 1990 for a critique). There is clearly a key tension here between themes C and D – how can we protect children and promote family life? A new concept of parental responsibilities is created by the Act, responsibilities that can only be revoked following the adoption of a child. A principle of 'non-intervention' by the courts is also established, unless the outcome of any intervention is clearly beneficial to the child.

Theme E: the enhancement of partnership with parents

In a development from theme D, local authorities are asked to work together with parents wherever possible, the concept of partnership being strongly promoted in the background documentation to the Act. Part Three of the Act requires local authorities to safeguard and promote the welfare of children in

Implementing the Children Act 1989 in a hostile climate

need in their area, and to promote the upbringing of such children by their families through the provision of services.

Theme F: the improvement of court proceedings

The Act reforms the operation of the courts, making them more flexible in their response to child welfare issues and creating a presumption that delays are likely to prejudice the welfare of children.

These key themes summarize a long and complex Act (HMSO 1989a), which itself rewards reading in full. However, these themes give us a benchmark against which we can measure the reality of implementation.

The political context

The Children Act falls clearly outside the mainstream of Thatcherite social policy of the 1980s – it is not a charter for privatization or an attack on local government. It even contains a fair smattering of 'social democratic' thinking, particularly in promoting 'preventive' interventions. Of course, the imprint of Thatcherism is to be found, particularly in the contentious concept of 'children in need', a concept I shall return to in some detail later. Nevertheless, the 'progressive' social services manager, or even the Labour-controlled local authority, could approach the Act with a degree of enthusiasm, at least regarding the bulk of its content. The resource implications, of course, were not so welcome – again I shall return to this later.

The opportunity for modernizing and reforming child-care has been offered to us about every twenty years this century (1908, 1933, 1948, 1969). The last such opportunity, the Children and Young Persons Act, 1969, represented the high watermark of welfarism (Clarke 1979), but disappointment lay around the corner as an incoming Conservative government did not implement or fund the Act to the full.

By 1984 the general dissatisfaction with child-care law and practice was expressed by the House of Commons Social Services Committee (HMSO 1984). Two significant elements emerge from this: first, there was an all-party consensus around particular aspects of reform, a consensus that remained largely intact through the legislative process; second, the process of reform had a civil service lead, which was to leave a strong imprint on the entire reform process. The civil service role was epitomized by the *Review of Child Care Law* (HMSO 1985), which formed the basis of the White Paper that appeared early in 1987.

The politics of child welfare was particularly vibrant in the period during which the Children Act was conceived. Significantly, inquiries into the deaths of Jasmine Beckford, Tyra Henry and Kimberley Carlile had a major impact on state, media, public and professional perceptions of child abuse. The two inquiries chaired by Louis Blom-Cooper (Jasmine and Kimberley) promoted an interventionist model of the social worker as an agent of the law, utilizing a disease model of child abuse (Parton 1986). These reports helped to create a climate that encouraged stronger state interventions around child abuse, a tendency reflected in the increasing use of Place of Safety Orders in the mid and late 1980s.

The high profile of child welfare during this period was maintained by the events in Cleveland in the spring of 1987, which raised the central issue of the sexual abuse of children within their families. These events were widely interpreted as suggesting an over-reaction by state-employed professionals to the issue of child sexual abuse (see the report of Butler-Sloss (HMSO 1988), and Campbell (1988) for an alternative interpretation). The increased awareness of sexual abuse had its roots in the women's movement of the 1970s, which began to have an impact on professional consciousness in the early 1980s. Cleveland acted as a battleground on which this new awareness was tested. The dominant interpretation of Cleveland impacted on the Children Act in the form of increased powers for parents to challenge court and local authority interventions.

In this political context we can see the emergence of two potentially contradictory trends: state intervention was seen as too weak in the cases where children had died and as too strong in Cleveland.

> The tension between these two positions, between child protection and parents' rights, between state intervention and the autonomy of the family, is the primary political relationship which the government has quite explicitly attempted to balance in the Children Act.
> (Frost and Stein 1990: 17–18)

The Children Act was born in this context and it bears the characteristics of the contradictory pressures on it.

While political differences emerged as the Bill passed through the Houses of Parliament, these were largely restricted to the important issues of day-care and family courts. Politically there existed a consensus around the need for reform and support for the general direction of the proposals.

Once the Act was in place local authorities and other relevant organizations were given about two years to plan for implementation. The period 1989–91 became an exciting one for social services departments (SSDs) – the twin challenge of the Children Act and the community care reforms were an opportunity to go into the twenty-first century in some shape to meet the challenges. The spectre of abolition, which hung over education departments, seemed to be avoided by SSDs being asked to accept these new responsibilities.

The policy process

Towards the end of 1989 and the start of 1990 SSDs up and down the country were reading the Children Act and beginning to understand exactly what it meant for them. It became apparent to most that resources would have to be allocated to a policy process that geared up for service changes, policy reviews and an extensive training programme. Importantly, the Children Act required an effective corporate implementation process, involving relevant local authority departments and a range of other voluntary and statutory organizations.

Implementing the Children Act 1989 in a hostile climate

By the spring of 1990 most SSDs had geared up to this challenge to some degree or other. Some had established new 'lead officer' posts, others planning teams, and some asked an existing post-holder to accept responsibility. Already one could detect an unevenness in the process: some SSDs geared up for major structural reform in response to the Act and the community care reforms, others responded piecemeal as the process unfolded.

The dominant model for policy development seemed to be through the now familiar departmental working group – the make-up of such groups varies, although most make at least a nod in the direction of participation from all relevant sections of the department. Some authorities, taking on board the corporate themes of the Act, immediately established working groups across the authority, involving housing, education and other relevant departments. There are fewer examples of involvement of service users – such as parents, children and young people – in this process, although this has occurred (Griffin and Jordan 1991). It should be said that the community care planning process tended to be considerably more successful in this respect.

By the turn of 1990 most local authorities had adopted broad general policy statements which affirmed their strategic approach to the Act. However, local authorities could not act in isolation. They were largely dependent on the Department of Health, who were determined to take an active, guiding role in the implementation process. Thus detailed policy and procedural work had to await the publication of detailed Regulations and Guidance by the Department of Health and other relevant departments. These volumes of regulations (HMSO 1991b) are an extremely mixed bag. Some, such as Volume 1, are lengthy expositions of the Act, while others, such as sections of Volume 2, attempt to specify minimum standards.

The Department of Health has attempted to boost the status of these documents:

> Regulations say 'You must/shall'; codes say 'You ought/should'. When the guidance explains regulations, it reaffirms the 'you must' messages. However, when it goes beyond regulations in setting out good practice, it conveys the message that 'It is highly desirable to . . .' or 'Unless there is a good reason not to, you should . . .' rather than 'You must'.
>
> (HMSO 1989b: 2–3)

While extensive consultation took place on the basis of draft documentation, significantly the attempt to impose these regulations reflects two trends:

1 The general drift of the government to control, through regulation, a process objected to by the Labour Party during the debate on the Bill.
2 The need of the Department of Health to be seen to be regulating, particularly in relation to child protection (see *Working Together*, HMSO 1991c) and residential care, after the Staffordshire 'pindown' controversy.

In this context there is a danger that the Guidance and Regulations will be used as weapons with which to attack local authorities, even when the intention of the volumes is not clear. This has happened in the past when, for example, unclear guidance on parental attendance at case conferences was used to criticize Rochdale (HMSO 1990).

A superficial reading of the Children Act would suggest that it relates mainly to social service departments. Although the Act refers throughout to the 'local authority', Schedule 13(26) points out that these powers are delegated to the social services committee. However, whilst SSDs undoubtedly have a lead role to play, it is clear from certain sections of the Act (Section 27, relating to preventive services, and Section 47, relating to child protection investigations, in particular) that co-ordinated inter-departmental, inter-agency approaches are required if the Act is to be taken seriously.

This represents a major challenge to local authorities who, despite recent moves towards co-ordination, remain largely parochial and 'departmentalized' organizations. While some local authorities adopted a corporate approach to policy development around the Children Act, for a majority this remained a rather *ad hoc* process. There is a clear role in the Children Act for social services departments, education departments, housing, leisure, environmental health and legal sections. The most successful examples of Children Act implementation will be where these departments have planned and co-operated jointly, brought together by a strong lead from the SSD or perhaps from a co-ordination section or the chief executive's office.

Outside of the local authority the Act requires engagement with probation, police, courts and health authorities as well as the voluntary and private sectors. This level of co-ordination and planning has represented a major challenge to SSDs and on occasion the sheer volume of liaison has proved to be too much.

The training implications

The Department of Health took an early and welcome decision to encourage local authorities to fund the training aspects of the Children Act. This was done through an enhancement of the recently initiated Training Support Programme (TSP), which 'ring fences' existing local authority funding and obliges local authorities to submit training programmes, which then attract 70 per cent funding from the TSP. This programme enabled local authorities to get off to an early start in terms of training programmes relating to the Children Act. Additionally, the Department of Health commissioned training materials from organizations such as the Open University, the Family Rights Group and the National Children's Bureau to back up local authority training programmes.

The publication in 1989 of *Training Together* by the Family Law and Child Care Law Training Group was opportune, as it provided a suggested framework for Children Act training. The basic programme was designed around three levels of training;

Foundation: basic training on the key aspects of the legislation.
Comprehensive: aimed at workers involved with children and families, to give them a broad grasp of the Act.

Specialist: more detailed training programmes aimed at staff with specialist responsibilities under the Act.

This basic framework was adopted by a majority of local authorities, who mounted the most extensive training programme that has ever been initiated in any area of social service practice. One advantage of the three-tier model was that the training experience could be seen as a process of learning and development. The Children Act not only requires 'learning what the Act says' but also involves some fundamental changes of attitude, which need to take place over a period of time.

Inevitably the quality and impact of this training programme was uneven, but the training aspects of the Children Act can generally be regarded as a fairly successful area of development into which the Department of Health, voluntary and statutory agencies put a lot of energy and commitment.

Resourcing the Act

The central issue in the implementation of the Act almost inevitably revolves around funding. The Act is indeed a great reform of child-care law and much of it has profound implications for local authority service delivery. The resource implications of Part Three of the Act, which places strong 'preventive' responsibilities on local authorities, and the reforms to child protection will be substantial. Initially I will look at what Part Three says in some detail, and then go on to examine the resource implications.

Part Three of the Act relies on a central concept – 'children in need'. A child in need is defined as:

> he [sic] is unlikely to achieve or maintain, or have the opportunity of achieving or maintaining, a reasonable standard of health or development without the provision for him of services by a local authority under this Part;
>
> his health or development is likely to be significantly impaired, or further impaired, without the provision for him of such services; or
>
> he is disabled.
>
> (Section 17)

This concept is highly problematic. First of all it separates out a group of chidren as 'in need', as if all children do not have needs. This 'targeting' is reminiscent of other Conservative policies of the 1980s, in particular on child benefit (Brown 1988). The problem with such targeting is that some services have a tendency to miss the target, thus excluding those who may require services. It is also in danger of stigmatizing those who are labelled as 'children in need'. It is significant that the phrase echoes the title of the BBC's annual charity appeal! The addition of children with disabilities to this category is also highly problematic. Pressure groups on disability issues have over the past two decades been arguing for 'normalization', that is services for people with disabilities to be part of the mainstream. To add insult to injury the definition of disability in the Act is drawn from the 1948 National Assistance Act, and includes categories such as a child who is 'blind, deaf and dumb' or suffers from 'congenital deformity' – language that most people left behind some years ago.

The concept of 'children in need' is, I would thus argue, fundamentally flawed. Nevertheless, local authorities are obliged to work within this concept and have had to ask how best they could operate using the idea of 'children in need'. The Department of Health soon picked up local authorities' concerns about using this concept and wrote to Chief Executives with the following advice:

> The definition is of course in the Act and an authority cannot lawfully substitute any other definition for the purpose of Part Three. . . . It would not be acceptable for an authority to exclude any of these three, e.g. by confining services to children at risk of significant harm. . . . The decision about what range and level of service is appropriate under S.17 for the children within their area taken to be in need is for local authority to reach.

A local authority treasurer may well respond, 'they would say that wouldn't they', because if the government actually established a minimum level of service they would have to fund it, or at least allow local authorities to fund it.

The children in need definition is open to interpretation and requires some thinking through before it can become a practical concept. Many local authorities have been tempted to adopt a broad working practice in relation to children in need. This has the advantage of allowing socially defined categories (ethnic minority groups, children living in poverty, etc.) to be included in the definition, therefore perhaps making it less stigmatizing. This potentially encourages a corporate approach in attempting to tackle disadvantage on a broad basis. However, this in turn raises the question of whether or not local authorities can resource this approach. If they cannot, the danger is that the aspirations become only paper ones, leading to disillusion and frustration among both staff and the public. A narrower working practice in relation to children in need allows local authorities to deliver services to those within the definition, recognizing the reality of local authority finance. However, this has the disadvantage of individualizing the 'children in need' concept and encouraging a residual model of social services. The key issue for local authorities is whether they should allow their policy in relation to children in need to be resource-led.

The financial backcloth for local authorities before implementation of the Act will be familiar: the abolition of the poll tax had just been announced, charge-capping was still a reality, local authority finance had been subject to almost two decades of attack and restriction (NALGO 1989). This was hardly an encouraging background against which to implement an Act which promoted a pro-active and corporate approach to the provision of services to children and families.

The Department of Health was obviously aware of this problem and pressed the Department of the Environment to increase the Standard Spending Assessment (SSA) in recognition of the demands of the Children Act. As a result the amount estimated for children's services was increased by 23.5 per cent, a figure that has been regularly quoted by the Minister of State, Virginia Bottomley, during the lead up to implementation. Two serious complications emerge from this. First, this money is not 'ring fenced', that is it goes into the general pot of cash for local authorities and is therefore vulnerable to other calls. Second, almost all the local authorities in England and Wales were already spending above their SSA as far as social services are concerned.

> The major reason why the personal social services appear not to have suffered at a time when the rate support grant has fallen from 61% to 43%, and housing subsidies were halved, has been the willingness of local authorities to follow a 'tradition of protection', and increase the proportion of local spending to maintain personal social services levels.
> (NALGO 1989: 10)

Because local authorities were already spending at these levels it effectively meant that there was no new money available for Children Act implementation. Local authority Children Act programmes were therefore struggling to implement the Act through savings, re-direction of already stretched funds or new monies obtained from reluctant finance departments. This is hardly a healthy background for implementing this 'fundamental reform'.

Assessing the Act: a children's charter or a parents' charter?

The Children Act has been described variously as a children's charter and a parents' charter. Not surprisingly, both these arguments have elements of truth in them and a more accurate analysis involves a detailed assessment.

There can be no doubt that elements of the Children Act represent significant advances for the capacity of children to contribute to, or at times to determine, decisions effecting their future. The most developed area of children's rights outlined in the Act is that of participation, the most usual formula being that their views should be taken into consideration. This formulation is to be found in Section 1 of the Act, which states that courts shall have regard to 'the ascertainable wishes and feelings of the child concerned'. A similar formulation is found in relation to the duty of local authorities, in relation to children they are looking after, to 'give due consideration ... to such wishes and feelings of the child as they have been able to ascertain' (S.22). In these examples the child's views are not determinative, but must be taken into account.

In some aspects of the Children Act children and young people are able to make independent decisions, for example to refuse medical examinations when subject to Emergency Protection Orders (S.44(7)), to challenge such orders themselves (S.45(8)) or to be accommodated by the local authority even if their parents object (S.20(11)). However, the Act also contains examples where children lose any sense of power over their lives. The most stark example of this relates to the provision of accommodation for children and young people aged under sixteen, where a parent could remove a child against the child's wishes.

It should be clear that children's rights in the Act do not fall into any one category. The Act in part enhances the ability of children and young people to make determinate decisions effecting their lives, to be listened to and consulted, but also allows them to be overruled by their parents. The Children Act is therefore most accurately described as a cocktail in relation to children's rights, rather than a children's charter in any meaningful sense.

There can be no doubt that parental powers have been strengthened in many respects by the Children Act, and as we have seen this trend was given a boost by the Cleveland Report (HMSO 1988). The idea of parental responsibilities has been seen as increasing the status of parents, in particular as these responsibilities cannot be removed, except by adoption orders. This increases the power of parents in relation to the state, as under previous legislation their parental rights could be removed in certain circumstances. This general approach is reflected in specific aspects of the Act, in particular the right to challenge Emergency Protection Orders and to request the provision of accommodation for children. The 'non-intervention' theme already mentioned can be seen as greatly enhancing the autonomy of the family. This again, however, is a contradictory theme. The abolition of parents' rights as a key concept and the fact that the state still maintains strong powers of intervention in family life both have to be weighed in assessing the impact of the Act.

Any analysis of the Act must carefully weigh the contradictory themes of the Act as it is not amenable to any simplistic sloganizing (see Fox Harding 1990). The political context which was outlined above has impacted on the Act and left its contradictory marks, in relation to state intervention and family autonomy, as well as in relation to children's rights and parents' rights.

'Considering racial groups'

The Children Act lays a duty on local authorities 'to consider racial groups to which children in need belong' (Schedule 2), in relation to foster-care and day-care, and also requires local authorities to give due consideration 'to the child's religious persuasion, racial origin and cultural and linguistic background' (Section 22), in relation to children they are looking after. Some training packs and authors have attempted to argue that this adds up to a 'key theme' in the Children Act. I think that this is wishful thinking rather than reality. While the recognition of race in the Act is welcome, it is actually little more than simply a mention. The Guidance and Regulations do expand this, as one would expect. However, anyone looking for a detailed guide to anti-racist practice would be disappointed. Volume 2 on day-care services, for example, contains three specific paragraphs on issues of equal opportunities and a smattering of other references, in an eighty-four page document. None of the recent publications on anti-racist child-care is included in an otherwise comprehensive bibliography. It is positive that racial needs are mentioned in the Act, but further and more detailed guidance is severely lacking.

This makes the anti-racist aspects of the Children Act very much an area of contestation and development, a challenge that local authorities can rise to. The references in the Act give those arguing for resources, services and training to develop anti-racist practice a boost, but an opportunity to go much further than this has been missed.

A safety net?

I will now examine two particular aspects of the Children Act that relate particularly to other arenas of social policy. It will be argued that both these aspects of the Children Act are positive when read in isolation, but that when seen in the context of a wider analysis it seems that the Children Act has set local authorities an impossible task.

First I will consider the concept of partnership with parents. This idea does not appear explicitly in the Act, but has played a central role in guidance and training materials produced around it. The suggestion is that local authorities should act in partnership with parents in relation to planning the delivery of services to individuals and communities. This work is usually referred to as 'preventive', suggesting services that prevent situations from deteriorating and ultimately triggering court interventions. 'Partnership' has become a term in social work that is difficult to oppose, although is often used in a simplistic way to mask significant power differences between the service providers and recipients.

The ability of parents to act effectively as 'partners' is not enhanced if they are living in poverty and deprivation, which reduces the capacity to make real 'choices'. The impact of social policy in general over the past decade has been to diminish the access of the majority of social work clients to material resources. Research has now established beyond doubt that poverty has increased significantly over the past decade. For example, Oppenheim (1990) identifies 10.5 million people living below the poverty line in 1987, compared with 4.9 million in 1979. The comparable figure for children living in poverty is 3 million in 1987 compared with 1.6 million in 1979. It can therefore be argued that the impact of government policy in general has been to increase the number of people and, more significantly for our argument, the number of children living in poverty (see also NCH 1991). Bebbington and Miles (1989, see also HMSO 1991a), having carried out substantive empirical research, have confirmed the link between poverty and entry into care. 'Deprivation is a common factor among all types of children who enter care' (p. 364).

Thus it seems to be established that poverty has increased in the past decade, and that poverty is linked to entry into care. How can the Children Act's call for partnership with parents operate in this hostile context? It may be possible for personal social services to act as a safety net when social security and employment policies are improving people's ability to cope, but in a situation where these policies are increasing the amount of poverty, it seems to be asking too much for already hard-stretched local authorities to step into the breach on the basis of a well-intentioned, but under-funded, piece of legislation such as the Children Act.

The second example that backs up this general argument relates to homeless young people. Section 20(3) of the Act calls upon local authorities to provide accommodation for sixteen and seventeen year olds whose welfare would otherwise be 'seriously prejudiced'. Again over the past decade local government house-building programmes have been severely and consciously restricted by government. Additionally, young people aged under twenty-five have been particularly harshly treated in relation to social security policy, and in some situations can be disqualified from receiving benefit. Other policies, such as the community charge, have also had a severe impact on young people. The general theme of these aspects of social policy have been to assume that young people would be resident at their parents' home until the age of twenty-five.

As with the previous example we need to ask how the Children Act, under-funded as it is, can possibly respond to this situation. It seems to be asking the impossible. In fact one does not have to be unduly cynical to argue that this is an attempt to take the heat off central government in relation to young homelessness and to turn it on to local authorities.

These examples could be multiplied, but are sufficient to make the point that the Children Act cannot possibly act as a safety net in the context of social policies which clearly contradict its explicit intentions.

Conclusion

In this chapter it has been argued that the Children Act 1989 read independently is largely to be welcomed. I have gone on to explore the challenge set for local authorities in implementing this legislation, in particular looking at the training and development work which took place during 1990 and 1991. Again seen in isolation, while certain criticisms can be made of this process, it appears to have been relatively successful, involving extensive training, multi-agency planning, attitude shifts and service development. The lack of resources for the tasks, however, casts a long shadow over the entire process. My final argument was that the Act sat uncomfortably with the main thrust of social policy of the preceding decade and therefore, regardless of the efforts of local authorities, they were predestined not to achieve many of the highly laudable goals of the Act. A reading of the impact of the Children Act has to be made in a broader social context of developments taking place outside of 'child-care', in the narrow sense of the term.

This argument is not a defeatist one. Local authorities have to operate in the real world and the identifiable achievements they have already made in implementing the Children Act are to be welcome. Many aspects of the Act are still open to development and contestation, for example the interpretation of those aspects of the Act relating to 'racial groups'. The debates over child welfare in England and Wales will no doubt continue. The Children Act has shifted the terms of that debate, but the real test would be for the 'paramountcy of the child's welfare' principle to be applied to all our social policy legislation, so that children's interests are a central concern when decisions are taken about social security or housing, for example. If that was to happen then talk of a 'children's charter' would be more justified than it has been in the past.

Acknowledgements

Thanks are due to Di McNeish and Mike Stein for reading and commenting on early drafts of this chapter and to Paul Stubbs for sharing unpublished material.

References

Bebbington, A. and Miles, J. (1989) 'The background of children who enter local authority care', *British Journal of Social Work* 19: 349–68.
Brown, J. (1988) *Child Benefit: Investing in the Future*, London: CPAG.
Campbell, B. (1988) *Unofficial Secrets. Child Sexual Abuse: the Cleveland Case*, London: Virago.
Clarke, J. (1979) 'Social democratic delinquents and Fabian families: a background to the Children and Young Persons Act', in M. Fitzgerald *et al.* (eds) *Permissiveness and Control*, London: Macmillan.
Family Law and Child Care Law Training Group (1989) *Training Together: a Training and Curriculum Model for the Children Act 1989*, London: LBTC.
Fox Harding, L. (1990) 'Underlying themes and contradictions of the Children Act 1989', *Justice of the Peace* 154: 591–4.
Frost, N. (1990) 'Official intervention and child protection: the relationship between state and family in contemporary Britain', in Violence Against Children Study Group (eds) *Taking Child Abuse Seriously*, London: Unwin Hyman.
Frost, N. and Stein, M. (1990) 'The Politics of the Children Act', *Childright* 16: 17–20.
Griffin, A. and Jordan, B. (1991) 'Support for families', *Children Act Implementation News* 15, May: 9–10.
HMSO (1984) *Second Report of the Social Services Committee: Children In Care*, London: HMSO.
HMSO (1985) *Review of Child Care Law*, London: HMSO.
HMSO (1987) *The Law on Child Care and Family Services*, London: HMSO.
HMSO (1988) *Report of the Inquiry into Child Abuse in Cleveland*, London: HMSO.
HMSO (1989a) *The Children Act*, London: HMSO.
HMSO (1989b) *The Care of Children: Principles and Practice in Regulations and Guidance*, London: HMSO.
HMSO (1990) *Inspection of Child Protection Services in Rochdale*, London: HMSO.
HMSO (1991a) *Patterns and Outcomes in Child Placement*, London: HMSO.
HMSO (1991b) *Guidance and Regulations: the Children Act*: Volume 1, Court Orders; Volume 2, Family Support; Volume 3, Family Placements; Volume 4, Residential Placements; Volume 5, Independent Schools, London: HMSO.
HMSO (1991c) *Working Together*, London: HMSO.
London Borough of Brent (1985) *A Child in Trust*, London: Brent.
London Borough of Greenwich (1987) *A Child in Mind*, London: Greenwich.
London Borough of Lambeth (1987) *Whose Child?*, London: Lambeth.
NALGO (1989) *Social Work in Crisis: a Study of Conditions in Six Local Authorities*, London: NALGO.
NCH (1991) *The NCH Factfile: Children in Danger 1991*, London: NCH.
Oppenheim, C. (1990) *Poverty: the Facts*, London: CPAG.
Parton, N. (1986) 'The Beckford Report: a critical appraisal', *British Journal of Social Work* 16: 511–30.

2
'The family': changes, challenges and contradictions

Fiona Williams

In many different ways 'the family' has, since the late 1970s, been pulled out of the closet of taken-for-grantedness. Just as the Callaghan Labour government was beginning to espouse the values of traditional family care, it was overtaken in 1979 by a New Right government that had already declared itself to be 'the Party of the family'. Particular notions of family life became central to the New Right's social and economic policies of the 1980s and 1990s. Alongside this, feminist writings and campaigns also put 'the family' under a critical microscope, revealing hitherto unspoken patterns of power, inequality and oppression. At the same time, the form and composition of family lives have themselves been undergoing considerable change. The aim of this chapter is to look at feminism and the New Right as two influential yet contrasting positions on the theory and politics of the family.

The problem with 'the family'

One of the main distinctions between New Right and feminist approaches to the family is that while the former understands a particular 'traditional' or patriarchal family form to be both natural (i.e. determined by biology and/or God) and central to the national, economic and moral order, the latter starts by questioning the form, content and naturalness of the family or, more particularly, the 'traditional' family. I start here by looking at the ways in which the notion of the family is seen as problematic and then focus on the insights offered by feminism on the family. That is followed by an examination of the New Right's philosophy and practice in relation to the family. The main area of reference in these discussions will be welfare policy and practice.

One of the ways in which the very notion of 'the family' is held to be problematic is in the commonly held assumptions about the naturalness and universality of the form and content of family life. Thus, in much post-war social and economic policy, in religious institutions, in advertising and popular culture, family life (indeed, social life) is represented by a white, heterosexual, able-bodied, bread-winning man and his dependent but similarly endowed wife and natural children; they live within the privacy of family life, which cares and shares, and supports and protects from the outside world. There are three main problems with such a notion of the family. First, this image of family life is neither universal nor, within Britain today, the predominant form in which people live: family lives are much more diverse and many people live in ways that do not readily fit the description 'family' (for example, people living on their own). Second, patterns of care and resources within families may often be spread unequally, and family life may be experienced as oppressive and even violent, particularly by women, children and other dependants. Third, such assumptions about family life, especially when they underpin social and economic policies, privilege some groups over and above others, reinforce inequalities, and discriminate against, pathologize or marginalize those whose lives do not fit this model.

There is ample evidence for the first problem; that is, the gap between the definitions of what family lives actually are and what they are thought to be, or what we are told they ought to be. In terms of the composition of families, statistics provided by the Family Policy Studies Centre (Kiernan and Wicks 1990) show that there is now increased cohabitation (in 1987, 48 per cent of never previously married women cohabited before marrying), increased divorce (if current trends continue 37 per cent of present marriages are likely to end in divorce, involving one in five children), increased child-bearing outside marriage (25 per cent in 1988), increases in one-parent families (16 per cent in 1988) and reconstituted families (in 1985, 9 per cent of children lived with a step-parent); and an increase in female employment and dual-career families (in 1987, 68 per cent of married women worked). If we add to this ethnic and sexual variations in household forms and an ageing of the population with a consequent increase in households containing only one or two people (36 per cent of women over 65 live alone), then it is clear that the traditional male bread-winner, nuclear family described above accounts for only one of a diverse range of living arrangements in which people may find themselves over their lifetime.

To create policies for 'the family', or even to write about 'the family', runs the risk of excluding the interests of those who, conventionally speaking, do not live in families. For this reason Barrett suggests that since 'the family' is itself an ideological construct it is better to talk of 'households' (Barrett 1980: 201). The following discussion uses the word 'family' as a conceptual construct or specific category (e.g. nuclear family) and otherwise uses the words 'family life/lives' or 'household'.

The second and third issues concern not just the composition of families but the nature of relationships within families and between families and the state. It is in these areas that feminist approaches have made a particular contribution.

Feminist approaches to the family

It is not possible to talk of a single feminist approach to the family. Historically feminism is marked by a variety of political approaches (see Williams 1989: ch. 3) and feminism today is characterized by a fragmentation into specific, often issue- or identity-related perspectives on, for example, racism, disability, sexual orientation, religion, age or peace. Nevertheless, from a general viewpoint, one of the key theoretical and strategic developments of the second wave of twentieth-century feminism was to provide an understanding of the relationship between the public sphere of paid work and politics, inhabited largely by men, and the private sphere of home, family and personal relationships, inhabited largely by women. The slogan 'the personal is political' encapsulated this relationship. Through this focus women's experiences within the family came in for scrutiny and analysis.

A site of oppression?

The articulation of women's experiences of family life revealed processes and patterns of power, inequality, violence and abuse that challenged not only conventional assumptions of the inherently harbouring nature of family life, but also theoretical assumptions about the nature and cause of power in capitalist society, in particular male power. Over the years such work has examined (and campaigned on) violence against women (Brownmiller 1975; National Women's Aid Federation 1978; Hamner and Saunders 1984), female poverty and the unequal access to and distribution of money between men and women in families (Pahl 1980, Glendinning and Miller 1987). It has shown that, in spite of an increase in women's paid employment, women still carry the major responsibilities for household tasks and emotional and physical care (Oakley 1974). The focus on these aspects of family life influenced the claim by a number of feminist writers in the 1970s that the family was the major 'site of oppression' for women in that it controlled and restricted those within it and marginalized and excluded those outside it (Firestone 1970; Millett 1970).

At a theoretical level these studies also raised the issue of patriarchy as a form of social power operating alongside, in tandem with or, as radical feminists argued, over and above capitalist relations of power. Whatever the relationship between capitalism and patriarchy, it was the family that was seen most clearly by earlier feminist writers as the vehicle which absorbed, articulated and reproduced these power relations, to the detriment, above all, of its female members.

Over the past decade this notion of the family as a site of oppression for women has been subject to substantial refinement. Some feminists have balanced it with analyses of other sites of oppression seen as equally significant in women's lives – for example, work (Cockburn 1985; Walby 1986) or state social policies (Wilson 1977; Pascall 1986). In addition, black feminists have argued that for black women the family has not only been a site of female oppression but also a site of resistance against racial oppression – historically against slavery, and today against, for example, police racism or racial harassment (Carby 1982; Lorde 1984). As Moraga and Anzadua (1981: 213) point out: 'We struggle together with Black men against racism, while we also struggle with Black men about sexism.' A comparable point may be made about working-class women: women who supported the miners during the 1984 miners' strike struggled with their partners but, in that process, found themselves challenging the gender relations within their families (Rowbotham 1986). Similarly, as discussed below, some black women and disabled women may have to fight against immigration laws or ableist assumptions about marriage and motherhood for the right to marry and have children. These examples suggest that the theoretical constructs of capitalism and patriarchy alone are not sufficient to explain different women's experiences of family life. In the case of black women, the legacy of imperialism, the operation of an international division of labour, as well as a sexual one, and racist immigration laws play a major role in the formation and experiences of black family lives (Carby 1982; Mama 1989; Williams 1989; Collins 1990).

These arguments mark a move towards a greater acknowledgement of differences between women, as well as a more contradictory and ambiguous role of the family in which women are not simply victims but also central to systems of loving support and social struggle. In some areas of feminism the shift has been towards a celebration of 'women's special values' – caring, sharing, tenderness and intuition – as against 'male values' of competition, aggression, rationality and self-interest. Such a shift is important in rescuing women from a passive victim role, but it comes dangerously near to the biologically determined gender stereotypes that feminism had challenged in the first place. Nevertheless, some recognition of the relationship between women's reproductive capacities, the social conditions in which these take place and the experiential consequences is important. Some of these points are summed up by Ramazanoglu in this way:

> It is not family life as such that gives rise to women's oppression, but the oppressive features of production systems, patriarchal sexuality, men's control of reproduction, and patriarchal ideologies which give rise to male-dominated families. Women who value themselves as mothers, and who identify themselves by their place in the family, would be less threatened by feminism if these connections were made clear. Feminism needs to offer women more than the abolition of the only place in society which is theirs.
>
> (Ramazanoglu 1989: 183)

This contradictoriness of family life raises problems for policy development. There is a tension between acknowledging women's caring role and not wanting to determine women's destinies. Is it possible to recognize, value and reward women for the role they play within households without, at the same time, reinforcing this as women's work or as women's primary work, or without privileging certain forms of 'family life' over and above other ways of living? This points to the relationship between the state, women and the family, to which I now turn.

Women, family and the state

A major contribution of feminist writers and activists has been to challenge the ways in which state policies reinforce assumptions of the traditional nuclear family described earlier. So, for example, an analysis of income maintenance policies reveals the ways in which, historically and today, these define women as economically dependent upon their male partners, and as having primary responsibilities for child-care and housework (Land 1978). In spite of challenges to these assumptions the 1986 Social Security Act still defines households as single-earner units (see Roll 1991). Similarly, feminist analyses of community care focus on the sexual division of labour within families in order to understand the extent to which the welfare state depends upon the unpaid work of women in the home (Finch and Groves 1983; Ungerson 1987). In this way community care policies have been created and developed on the assumption of the availability of women to care for their sick, frail, old or disabled family members. They have also been created on the assumption that sick, frail, old or disabled family members, many of whom are women themselves, want to be cared for by (or be dependent on) their families. Housing policies, too, cater primarily for nuclear family households, marginalizing the needs of single people and single parents, particularly those, often women, who have no access to an independent income.

In these ways, then, social policies reinforce and sometimes privilege household units characterized by female dependency and a particular sexual division of labour. But other assumptions underpin the policies and practices around families – namely, heterosexual coupledom, race, ethnicity and able-bodiedness – in ways that penalize and pathologize. Single parents, for instance, have often been identified as the cause of their children's educational under-achievement, juvenile delinquency or even social decline (Murray 1990 – see next section).

A different form of racialized pathology has been applied to black mothers, as can be seen from the recent history of the state and its relationship to the ideology of familism and motherhood. The post-war state juggled between a need to uphold this ideology and the need to provide cheap labour in the new industries and the growing welfare state (Wilson 1977). The solution for many white working-class women was part-time work, which did not interfere with family responsibilities and also removed the state from any responsibility to provide child-care support. But, as Carby has pointed out, this solution and the state's concern did not extend to the black women (and black men) who were recruited from the Commonwealth to work in the lowest paid jobs – often in the health service – with long unsocial hours. In fact, such a solution was only possible for white families because of the recruitment of black labour. Furthermore, in so far as black mothers worked in such jobs, they were seen to be failing as mothers: 'Rather than a concern to protect or preserve the black family in Britain, the state reproduced commonsense notions of inherent pathology: black women were seen to fail as mothers precisely because of their position as workers' (Carby 1982: 219).

This example demonstrates that black women's labour needs to be understood within the context of the political economy of migrant labour. Views of black mothers or black family life as pathological – which were to be reproduced in different ways for Asian and Afro-Caribbean women in the practices of social work, schooling and health care – were allied to this and to the 'common-sense' racism derived particularly from British imperialism. If we also take into account the fact that immigration policies have split or separated black families (Gordon 1985), that black children are more likely to be taken into care (Dominelli 1988) and that black women have often had their rights to reproduction limited or denied by the use of abortion, sterilization or experimental contraception (Bryan et al. 1985), then we have a qualitatively different view of the relationship of the state to black family life. Indeed, as both Carby (1982) and Collins (1990) have pointed out, the gendered split between the public and private spheres does not operate in the same way for black women – it may be cut across by racialized lines, where black communities feel under threat by white racism, or may be blurred through the greater intervention of the state or the organization of paid work (the public) which disrupts black family life (the private).

Such restrictions and controls have not applied only to black women. The issue of reproductive rights provides an interesting example of who is and is not regarded as suitable for motherhood and family life. As Stanworth (1987: 2) has pointed out, reproductive technologies have 'politicized issues concerning sexuality, reproduction, parenthood and family'. Poor working-class women and disabled women, especially women with learning difficulties, are also subject to medical intervention to limit their fertility, often without their direct consent (Williams 1991). In addition, the Human Fertilisation and Embryology Act 1990 and the Children Act 1989 both dismiss or fail to acknowledge the possibility of motherhood or parenting by lesbians. This is also reflected in the legal practice of denying custody of children to some lesbian mothers in divorce cases. In these examples women's access to and experiences of family life are mediated by differences of class, race, disability and sexuality.

The example of the restrictions to motherhood faced by disabled women raises an interesting angle on the need to have a much wider view of what constitutes family life. Currently policies for people with learning difficulties focus on the strategy of 'normalization' as a way to achieve the rights and opportunities for an 'ordinary life'. However, ironically, if 'normal' family life is conceived of in terms of exclusive and privatized parental rights and responsibilities this in itself excludes those women who may need to live differently and receive a significant amount of support to enable them to care for their children.

In terms of policy and practice around family life how influential have feminist analyses and campaigns been? First, feminism has had an important influence in getting issues of rape, domestic violence and reproductive rights taken seriously within law and social provisions. It has also shaped the nature of some of these provisions, with an emphasis on women-only, non-hierarchical forms of service (Hamner and Statham 1988). Second, it has shed important light on debates on child abuse (*Feminist Review* 1988), old age

(Peace 1986), disability (Campling 1981), social work (Dominelli and McLeod 1989), sexuality (*Feminist Review* 1987) and psychotherapy (Orbach and Eichenbaum 1983). Third, feminism has raised awareness about female poverty, especially among single parents and older women, and about women's caring responsibilities for children and relatives, although these have not been met by increases of state support. Changes to policies in this area have tended to be either single victories, like the extension of the Invalid Care Allowance to married women in 1985, or won through equal opportunities policies in individual workplaces or particular local authorities. Fourth, there has been increasing pressure on policy-makers to create policies that meet the changing conditions of family life and of work. For example, in 1983 Phillips wrote:

> We have to adapt work to fit in with the rest of life and particularly adapt it to fit with children. For the present the adaptation is done by women, the price of having children is paid by mothers. Why not a new approach? If the needs of children do not fit with the demands of full-time work, then the jobs must be changed.
>
> (Phillips 1983: 5)

It is possible to see the influence of a strategy which connects changing conditions of family life to changing conditions of work in some areas of policy research and prescription. For example, the Family Policy Studies Centre document, *Family Change and Future Policy* (Kiernan and Wicks 1990) and *The Family Way* (Coote et al. 1990), a policy paper from the Institute for Public Policy Research, a left-wing think tank, both outline the necessity for supporting women as carers, providing benefits to enable women to maintain employment opportunities, increasing family income, and supporting single and divorced parents and their children. *The Family Way* also focuses on gender relationships: 'Men's reponsibilities as partners should go beyond simply "doing more housework". They must learn to respect – and treat – women as individuals of equal worth' (Coote et al. 1990: 37).

While these documents go a long way in recognizing the way gender inequalities are structured by the relationship between the family and employment and the need for appropriate policies, by concentrating on the needs of women and children in this way do they risk being familist?

In both documents the authors are at pains to demonstrate the need for acceptance of the diversity of family life. However, it is only in relation to single parents that they tie this acceptance into concrete policy changes. There is also the need to reform racist, ableist and heterosexist laws and practices that affect family lives and opportunities. In other words, the conditions of family and work exist within an international and often racialized context, and family diversity exists within differential structures of social power. The significance of these issues becomes clearer when we examine the way in which the New Right's formulation of family life depends on traditional notions of family, work and nation.

The New Right and the family

The New Right's position on the family differs in some respects from that of other anti-collectivists. Neo-liberals like Hayek and Friedman, whose emphasis is on liberty of the individual and freedom of the market, have very little to say about women or the family. The family's existence as a 'natural' and private form is taken for granted – its continuity is possible only when it is protected from state interference. As such the concepts of both 'liberty' and 'the individual' have no relevance for women, for liberty is pursued by individual men in the market.

Mount's book *The Subversive Family* (1982) acts as a bridge between neo-liberal and New Right thought. He spells out the vital historical role of the family as guarantor of liberty in resisting outside interference from church, state or welfare state. However, like both Hayek and Friedman and the New Right, he sees biology and 'natural instincts' as determining gender differences.

By contrast, the New Right's articulation of family life has been central to its social and economic policies. It has elevated the family to a high position of responsibility: first, for the welfare of its members; second, for exercising its consumer role in both the private market and public provision of welfare; third, for responsibility for the transmission of discipline and morality; and fourth, for the maintenance of British cultural values. In its traditional form the family therefore provides a vital link between moral principles and cultural life on the one hand, and market principles and economic life on the other. The cultural values the family is asked to defend are essentially white, British and Christian.

In terms of policy this philosophy has required an attempt to 'break' the family of its dependence on the welfare state and restore its autonomy and responsibility. However, this has involved something of a double paradox. First, rolling back the state has actually required considerable regulatory state intervention. Second, within the context of relatively high unemployment and growing poverty, dependency on state income support has increased (Low Pay Unit 1988).

The shift towards families exercising responsibility for their members can be seen in the extension of children's financial dependence on their parents through the removal of rights to social security to most sixteen and seventeen year olds. It is also reflected in the emphasis on parental responsibility for the discipline of children in the 1990 White Paper on crime (Langan 1991). This notion of parental responsibility has also in some places shifted into an attempt to restore specifically paternal responsibility. The 1990 White Paper on child maintenance proposes to minimize state support for female single parents by making errant fathers accept financial responsibility for their children. This focus is also found in the Children Act 1989, which encourages natural fathers to exercise their parental rights and responsibilities (Langan 1991).

These moves are associated with the identification of female single parents as central to the growth of a 'dependency culture' (i.e. dependent on state benefits), which has gained currency from the writings of Charles Murray (1984, 1990). Murray suggests that welfare benefits have created in the USA and Britain an 'underclass' characterized by high rates of female-headed families, illegitimacy, poverty, crime and unemployment. One solution he proposes is to shift the dependency of mothers away from the state and on to bread-winner fathers. Like the New Right, he sees the ethic of male wage-earning and family responsibility as inextricably linked: 'Young men who don't work don't make good marriage material. Often they don't get married at all; when they do, they don't have the ability to fill their traditional role. In either case, too many of them remain barbarians' (Murray 1990: 23). Murray's focus is on the behaviour and attitudes of poor people and he ignores the structural patterns of class, race and gender inequalities.

Community care policies have also stressed the mobilization of 'families, friends and neighbours' in providing support for older people (Griffiths Report 1988). It is interesting that in these policies, as Finch has pointed out, the government is not working with a model of a nuclear family as much as with the assumed existence of a 'gendered modified extended family' (Finch 1989: 125).

The attempt to limit the influence of non-traditional ways of living can also be seen in Section 28 of the Local Government Act 1988, which prohibits local authorities from promoting homosexuality as a 'pretended family relationship', and in restrictions placed on *in vitro* fertilization (Evans 1989).

Moves to reduce the influence of anti-discriminatory practice in favour of the restoration of 'British' cultural values can be seen in the 1988 Education Act. This also demonstrates the way in which notions of the family are seen as holding together the values of both work and nationhood. The Act introduced a core curriculum and testing and selection processes explicitly to meet the needs of industry and employers. It also emphasized the need for the teaching of traditional morality and British cultural values as against anti-racist and anti-sexist teaching. Finally, it envisaged the family as a consumer shopping wisely in the market place for education to fit the needs of its children. In keeping with the notion of the dependency of children, the consumers are seen here as the parents rather than the pupils. Interestingly, too, parents' rights include the right of parents to choose education appropriate to their own 'culture'. In 1990 a ruling from the Secretary of State for Education said that parental choice included the right of white parents to withdraw their children from schools with a large proportion of Asian children, and that this choice overrode the race relations law.

The changing conditions of work, family and nation all challenge the success of the New Right's family-related policies. Changes in the organization of work processes and in the labour market mean that more women are being pulled into work, but in different ways. Some of these changes have pulled single parents, working-class and black women into the growing 'peripheral' workforce – into the increasing numbers of low-paid, part-time, casual and subcontracted work. On the other hand, the decrease in young workers has drawn qualified women into areas like banking and insurance. In neither case, though, have the needs of these women workers (for child-care or improved maternity provisions, for example) been addressed by state policies. This is partly to do with an ambivalence in response towards this change. There are government ministers who have welcomed women's entry into paid work as necessary for the liberalization of the free market. For example, Norman Fowler when Secretary of State for Employment welcomed the 1990s as the 'decade of the working woman'. Others, like Patrick Jenkin and Douglas Hurd, have seen it as undermining the traditional family and have urged women to put their duties as mothers first. Yet others, like Edwina Currie as Minister for Health, have acknowledged the problems these trends raise but have seen the solution in terms of individual responsibility to choose child-care in the private market, seeing public provision as limited to children in need or at risk (see Langan 1991).

A similar ambivalence exists in relation to the increase in divorce. While the Law Commission recommended dropping the fault grounds in divorce to make divorce a less bitter and expensive process, many in the government felt uncomfortable about a proposal that was seen to make divorce easier and again to undermine the traditional family (see Wicks 1990).

Finally, while the New Right have been emphatic about preserving British cultural identity, this has been within a context of growing awareness of ethnic diversity and also within a context of the shifting and breaking down of national boundaries within Europe and the creation of the EC. This development in itself raises new and contradictory issues for family life. In relation to gender, Britain will be under pressure to conform to European standards of gender equality in, for example, rights for part-time workers, child-care provision and maternity leave (Family Studies Policy Centre 1991). At the same time, this development may also see a standardizing of policies and processes whereby Europe's racialized and migrant communities are denied rights. These include the tightening of immigration controls, denial of family re-union and restricted access to welfare provision (Arnott 1990).

Conclusion

The notion and conditions of the family today are marked by continuity and change, contradiction and challenge. People's experiences and expectations of family life have been affected by social, demographic, economic and political change, which have in turn affected the nature and composition of family life. At the same time, there have been marked continuities: around 79 per cent of men and 83 per cent of women still marry; there has been no dramatic overall change in the domestic roles of men and women; some groups are still subject to discriminatory or exclusionary laws and practices in relation to family life – in particular, black families, single parents, gay and lesbian households, and disabled and old people.

These changes are influencing and influenced by competing discourses over 'the family'. Feminism and the New Right represent two fundamentally different political and philosophical approaches which have themselves been modified by changing conditions. For feminism this has led to an acknowledgement of the different meanings of family life and its component parts for different women and for the same women at different times. Some of these differences may be chosen but they are also shaped by the social relation of power, not only around gender, but around class, race, disability, sexuality and age.

The clarity of the New Right's social, cultural, moral and economic vision of the traditional family has become blurred through the changes that have occurred in the family and its relation to work and nationhood. The result is that social policies, economic and international trends and political discourses are all pulling in different directions. Some of these processes – the diversity in forms of living, in economic organization and in cultural life, the fragmentation of political movements and of the certainties of all-embracing political philosophies – have been described as part of the condition of our times, a condition of postmodernity. However the family is defined, its means that for those who live their lives within or without families and for those who work with families there are no clear lines, no single understandings and no easy solutions.

References

Arnott, H. (1990) 'Fortress Europe', *Poverty* 75: 15–17.
Barrett, M. (1980) *Women's Oppression Today*, London: Verso.
Brownmiller, S. (1975) *Against Our Will: Men, Women and Rape*, New York: Simon and Schuster.
Bryan, B., Dadzie, S. and Scafe, S. (1985) *The Heart of the Race: Black Women's Lives in Britain*, London: Virago.
Campling, J. (1981) *Images of Ourselves: Women with Disabilities Talking*, London: Routledge and Kegan Paul.
Carby, H. (1982) 'White woman listen! Black feminism and the boundaries of sisterhood', in Centre for Contemporary Cultural Studies, *The Empire Strikes Back: Race and Racism in 70s Britain*, London: Hutchinson.
Cockburn, C. (1985) *Machinery of Dominance*, London: Pluto Press.
Collins, P. H. (1990) *Black Feminist Thought*, London: Unwin Hyman.
Coote, A., Harman, H. and Hewitt, P. (1990) *The Family Way*, Social Policy Paper no. 1, London: Institute for Public Policy Research.
Dominelli, L. (1988) *Anti Racist Social Work*, London: Macmillan.
Dominelli, L. and McLeod, E. (1989) *Feminist Social Work*, London: Macmillan.
Evans, D. (1989) 'Section 28: law, myth and paradox', *Critical Social Policy* 27: 73–95.
Family Studies Policy Centre (1991) *Family Policy Bulletin*, August.
Feminist Review (1987) *Sexuality: a Reader*, London: Virago.
Feminist Review (1988) 'Family secrets: child sexual abuse', 28.
Finch, J. (1989) *Family Obligations and Social Change*, Cambridge: Polity Press.
Finch, J. and Groves, D. (1983) *A Labour of Love*, London: Routledge and Kegan Paul.
Firestone, S. (1970) *The Dialectic of Sex: the Case for Feminist Revolution*, New York: Bantam Books.
Glendinning, J. and Miller, J. (eds) (1987) *Women and Poverty in the UK*, Brighton: Wheatsheaf.
Gordon, P. (1985) *Policing Immigration: Britain's Internal Controls*, London: Pluto Press.
Griffiths, R. (1988) *Community Care: Agenda for Action*, London: HMSO.
Hamner, J. and Saunders, S. (1984) *Well Founded Fear*, London: Hutchinson.
Hamner, J. and Statham, D. (1988) *Women and Social Work: Towards Women-centred Practice*, London: Macmillan.

Kiernan, K. and Wicks, M. (1990) *Family Change and Future Policy*, London: Family Policy Studies Centre.
Land, H. (1978) 'Who cares for the family?', *Journal of Social Policy* 7, 3: 257–84.
Langan, M. (1991) 'Who cares? Women in the mixed economy of care', in M. Langan and L. Day (eds) *Women, Oppression and Social Work*, London: Harper Collins.
Lorde, A. (1984) *Sister Outsider: Essays and Speeches*, New York: Crossing Press.
Low Pay Unit (1988) *The Poor Decade: Wage Inequalities in the 1980s*, London: Low Pay Unit.
Mama, A. (1989) 'Violence against black women: gender, race and state responses', *Feminist Review* 32: 30–48.
Millett, K. (1970) *Sexual Politics*, New York: Avon Books.
Moraga, C. and Anzadua, G. (eds) (1981) *Writings by Radical Women of Colour*, Watertown, Massachusetts: Persephone Press.
Mount, F. (1982) *The Subversive Family: an Alternative History of Love and Marriage*, London: Jonathan Cape.
Murray, C. (1984) *Losing Ground: American Social Policy, 1950–1980*, New York: Basic Books.
Murray, C. (1990) *The Emerging British Underclass*, London: Institute for Economic Affairs and Welfare Unit.
National Women's Aid Federation (1978) *Battered Women's Refuges and Women's Aid*, London: National Women's Aid Federation.
Oakley, A. (1974) *The Sociology of Housework*, Oxford: Martin Robertson.
Orbach, S. and Eichenbaum, L. (1983) *What do Women Want?* Glasgow: Fontana.
Pahl, J. (1980) 'Patterns of money management within marriage', *Journal of Social Policy* 9, 3: 313–35.
Pascall, G. (1986) *Social Policy: a Feminist Analysis*, London: Tavistock.
Peace, S. (1986) 'The forgotten female: social policy and older women', in C. Phillipson and A. Walker (eds) *Ageing and Social Policy*, Aldershot: Gower.
Phillips, A. (1983) *Hidden Hands: Women and Economic Policies*, London: Pluto Press.
Ramazanoglu, C. (1989) *Feminism and the Contradictions of Oppression*, London: Routledge.
Roll, J. (1991) *What Is a Family? Benefit Models and Social Realities*, Occasional Paper no. 13, London: Family Studies Policy Centre.
Rowbotham, S. (1986) 'More than just a memory: some policy implications of women's involvement in the miners' strike 1984–5', *Feminist Review* 23: 109–24.
Stanworth, M. (1987) *Reproductive Technologies: Gender, Motherhood and Medicine*, Cambridge: Polity Press.
Ungerson, C. (1987) *Policy is Personal: Sex, Gender and Informal Care*, London: Tavistock.
Walby, S. (1986) *Patriarchy at Work*, Cambridge: Polity Press.
Wicks, M. (1990) 'The battle for the family', *Marxism Today* August: 28–33.
Williams, F. (1989) *Social Policy: a Critical Introduction. Issues of Race, Class and Gender*, Cambridge: Polity Press.
Williams, F. (1991) 'Women with learning difficulties are women too', in M. Langan and L. Day (eds) *Women, Oppression and Social Work*, London: Harper Collins.
Wilson, E. (1977) *Women and the Welfare State*, London: Tavistock.

3
Guidelines for public service management: lessons not to be learnt from the private sector

John Stewart

The new emphasis in social services and in the health services is, as elsewhere in the public sector, upon management. If management is seen as the effective use of resources in the achievement of social purpose, then such a development is to be welcomed. There are dangers, but the dangers lie not in an emphasis on management but in the models on which it is being built. In many instances, the development of management in the public sector is being based upon models drawn from the private sector. The language in which management in the public services is being expressed shows this influence.

Local authorities are preparing 'business plans'. Those who use their services are 'customers' rather than 'clients' or 'citizens'. Local authorities are adopting statements of organizational values, which could be important in guiding action, but which in many instances are based unthinkingly upon the attributes to be found in *In Search of Excellence* (Peters and Waterman 1982):

1 Bias for action
2 Closeness to the customer
3 Autonomy and entrepreneurship
4 Productivity through people
5 Hands on, value driven
6 Stick to the knitting
7 Single form lean staff
8 Simultaneous tight–loose properties.

Prime Minister John Major has said in a lecture on public service management that

> Our approach to the public services is based on the belief that the people

who work in them should, so far as possible, become full participants in the more competitive demanding economy which now surrounds them.

(Major 1989: 8)

The Audit Commission's model of management in local government is entitled *The Competitive Council* (Audit Commission 1988), which, while it may be an appropriate phrase to describe a direct service organization competing with outside contractors for refuse collection or vehicle maintenance, is certainly not appropriate to a social service department determining the need for service or a care manager assessing the package of care required. Nor is it necessarily helpful for the Audit Commission to have used the term 'board member' (Audit Commission 1990) to describe the role of a councillor as a member of a committee, as if that was equivalent to a member of the board of a private company.

The danger is that headteachers, directors of social services or unit general managers will model their behaviour on rather naive assumptions about how businessmen behave. Yet as the distinguished Norwegian political scientist Mancur Olsen has written:

The image presented of the private sector is not based on empirical observations of how this sector actually works. Rather it is taken from how introductory text books in business administration say it *should* work.

Possibly private sector models have had more impact on how we *talk* about the public sector than on how it works. In a period where the private sector is assumed to be modern and the public sector old fashioned, it is tempting for public agencies to change their basis of legitimacy.

(Olsen 1988: 16–17)

The problem is, however, far deeper than the posturing of public sector managers as macho businessmen, although that is problem enough. The real danger is that unthinking adoption of the private sector model prevents the development of an approach to management in the public services in general or to the social services in particular based on their distinctive purposes, conditions and tasks. Even some of those who write about these topics tend to adopt phrases such as management in non-market organizations or not-for-profit management. Such phrases describe what management is not, rather than what it is, surely a strange approach to giving positive direction and enhancing achievement in public organizations.

The mistake is to assume that management should be the same in all forms of organization; that in effect management is undifferentiated, following a common pattern wherever it is found. That is not even true of the private sector. It is a commonplace of organization theory that the way an organization is managed will vary with the technology used. Woodward (1965) found very significant differences between different technologies. Burns and Stalker (1961) distinguished between tasks requiring mechanistic and those requiring organismic approaches. Contingency theory has analysed the factors that determine the nature of management, distinguishing between organizations in, for example, the extent of standardization or centralization

Table 3.1 Private and public sector organizations

Private sector model	Public sector model
Individual choice in the market	Collective choice in the polity
Demand and price	Need for resources
Closure for private action	Openness for public action
The equity of the market	The equity of need
The search for market satisfaction	The search for justice
Customer sovereignty	Citizenship
Competition as the instrument of the market	Collective action as the instrument of the polity
Exit as the stimulus	Voice at the condition

Source: Ranson and Stewart (1988: 15).

required (Lawrence and Lorsch 1967). Such conclusions should not be surprising to anyone concerned with public services. One does not manage a fire service in the same way that one manages social services – and it would be a mistake to do so.

If management varies with technology and the nature of the task then it is not surprising that it should vary with the nature of the organization and with its purposes and conditions. The public services are constituted on a different basis from services in the private sector and that must inevitably affect management. That does not mean that management in the public sector cannot learn from management in the private sector or that management in the private sector cannot learn from management in the public sector. Particular approaches are transferable. What is a mistake is to use the private sector model as the basis for management in the public sector. Table 3.1 attempts to summarize some of the differences between private sector and public sector organizations.

Services are placed in the public sector to be managed in a different way and by a different type of organization from the type of organization found in the private sector. This is not an argument about whether services should be placed in the private sector or in the public sector. That is a different issue. It is, however, an argument that if one wants a service to be managed in the same way as in the private sector, then the appropriate course of action is to place it in the private sector. To attempt to manage a service in the public sector as if it was in the private sector is bad management because it is management contrary to the distinctive purposes, conditions and tasks of the public sector.

Marketing as an example

This point can be illustrated by discussing the extent to which ideas about marketing are transferable from the private sector to the public sector. Marketing has been defined as 'the way in which an organization matches its own human financial and physical resources with the wants of its customers' (Christopher *et al.* 1980: 18). Kotler and Andreason have argued that

> it is only when management realizes that it is the customer who truly determines the long run success of any strategy that the non-profit firm can join the ranks of the sophisticated marketing organization.
> (Kotler and Andreason 1987: 64)

The marketing approaches developed in the private sector focus on the customer, and Kotler and Andreason see that as their importance to organizations outside the private sector, although they were writing largely about voluntary organizations. The focus on the customer has a value in the public sector, where it can easily be assumed too readily that what the public needs is known and that therefore there is no necessity to find out what the users think of the services received. Yet there are limits to the extent to which the language of the customer is adequate in the public sector.

There is no doubt that marketing approaches have a role to play in the public sector and that there are trading activities where the approaches used in the private sector can easily be adopted in the public sector, but there are limitations imposed by the purposes, conditions and tasks of the public sector.

The private sector can define the customer by the sale. When a private sector firm sells a service in the market, it knows who the customer is – the individual or the organization buying the service. It is not so easy to define the customer of a public service because the service is often provided to meet more than the needs of the immediate consumers. Indeed the service may well have been placed in the public sector because there are many customers whose interests have to be balanced. Who is the customer of the education service? The child is the immediate user, but the parents and future employers can also be regarded as customers, as can the local community or the public at large. It cannot be assumed that all affected by a service necessarily have the same interest in the service, and in the public sector those differing interests have to be balanced. The language of the customer has limitations in the public sector if it focuses attention on the immediate individual user at the expense of other interests.

The language of the customer, with its suggestion of an individual, focus does not fit easily into many other activities in the public sector. There is no individual customer for smoke control or for environmental health. In the public sector law and order are enforced and the language of the customer barely fits the restauranteur being prosecuted, or the criminal being charged.

> Resources of the public sector are finite and limited and distributed as an act of political will. This creates an immediate dilemma for the application of consumer principle. One the one hand, the nature of public services suggest they are of the utmost importance to those consumers who want to use them; on the other hand the interests of individual consumers must constantly be juggled against the interest of the

community as a whole, and of other groups who make up the community.

(Potter 1988: 151)

Marketing is concerned with demand, both meeting it and generating it, but in the public services demand may well exceed supply. In the public sector services can be provided not to meet demand but to meet need as determined by criteria established in the political process. If marketing has a role, it has to be marketing for equity, for which the private sector provides little guidance. This may involve demarketing:

> While most marketing experts are in the business of encouraging and building up demand for an organization's products or services, a major task of public managers in these times of scarcity is often to stretch their meagre resources, trying to make sure that there is enough of the shrinking pie to give their clients some amount however reduced. They are not trying to attract consumers for their program. In some other cases (e.g. energy or water conservation . . . emergency calls) the aim is to dampen public demand or limit usage to only 'essential' customers and activities as a matter of public policy. Demarketing – the uses of marketing strategies to reduce demand or channel it to appropriate uses – can be helpful here.
>
> (Goodrich 1983: 101)

Marketing approaches as they have developed in the private sector present another problem for the public sector. They define, as we have seen, the public as customers, but in the public sector the public are not only customers. They are also citizens with a right to know, a right to a voice and a right to be heard about a service – whether or not they are its customers. If marketing is concerned with the relationship between an organization and the public, then in the public sector it has to encompass the relationship with citizens as well as with customers, and for that the private sector model gives no guidance.

Marketing, if it means a concern for relationships with the public, clearly has relevance for management in the public sector, for at least the three reasons set out above:

- in the public sector there can be many customers for a service, not just an individual customer;
- in the public sector services are often provided not to meet demand but to meet need as judged through the political process;
- in the public sector the services provided are of concern to citizens as well as to customers.

These conditions mean that if marketing is to develop in the public sector, in the sense of guiding relationships between public authorities and their publics, it cannot merely be based on approaches developed in the private sector. Indeed it could be argued that the differences are so great that the very word marketing is inappropriate for much of the public sector.

Nor should it be thought that these characteristics of the relationships between a public sector and the public are accidental. They are constitutive conditions that derive from the nature of the public sector and from the reasons why services are placed in the public sector. It is because these differences reflect constitutive conditions that approaches to managing the relationship with the public in the public sector cannot simply draw upon marketing approaches but have to be developed in their own right. For in this respect, as in other respects, it is not that the public services do not require effective management, but rather that they will only be effectively managed if the approaches to be used are grounded in the purposes, conditions and tasks of the public sector. That requires management as rigorous and as well developed as in the private sector, but it is management for public purpose and subject to the political process.

The purposes, conditions and tasks of the public sector

The purposes

Services are provided in the public sector to meet *public or social purposes*. They reflect collective purposes as determined by the political processes. The nature of the public purpose will condition the service to be provided. It may mean that services have to be rationed, or allocated to a specified criteria. It may mean that the public may be compelled to use the service – as when a child is taken into care. The nature of social purpose can condition both the service provided and the nature of its management. The mistake is to assume that public purpose necessarily limits responsiveness or even individual choice – that depends on the nature of public purpose. It is a mistake to see choice as dependent on a market. In the library service, the library ticket gives a right to choose which books to take out because the public purpose is about extending the opportunity to read, for public purpose can be as often about extending opportunities as about restricting possibilities. Public purpose should not be used to justify detailed control or the assertion of professional authority, when that is not required by public purpose.

In the public sector, other purposes can be realized, reflecting values that underlie that sector. The values of *democracy and citizenship* belong to the public domain, i.e. to the arena in which public purposes are contended for and eventually determined. That arena depends upon effective public discourse if democracy is to be achieved and citizenship realized. It is a challenge for management to realize these values through setting the conditions for effective public discourse.

It is in the public domain too that the values of *justice and equity* are realized. It may not be sufficient for management in public sector organizations to be judged by the three Es – economy, efficiency and effectiveness – there may also need to be a fourth – equity. Equity reflects judgements established through the political process, but the requirement to make those judgements should have its impact on management, which should be concerned with the distributive impact of policies made and decisions taken.

The conditions

The basic mode of operation of the public sector is public discourse leading to collective choice based on public consent. That is the mode of operation which underlies the model of perfect public action, as a market mode of operation underlies the model of perfect competition, even though neither model is fully realized in practice. However, the basic mode of operation of the public sector sets constitutive conditions which it is the task of management to realize.

A mistake is often made in considering management in the public sector in that the constitutive conditions are regarded as obstacles to be overcome. Thus in our system of government the basic mode of operation is expressed through *political processes*, whether these political processes are those of party or those of pressure and protest. It is common to regard these as, in some way, obstacles to good management or problems to be overcome. Yet, 'it would be easy to manage if it were not for the political process' is as misleading in the public sector as to say in the private sector, 'it would be easy to manage if we did not have to make a profit'. The political process is not an obstacle to be overcome but a constitutive condition, which it is the task of management to fulfil. The challenge to management is how to support and express the political process.

The basic mode of operation depends upon *public discourse*. It is a distinctive role for management in the public sector to enable public discourse, by sustaining access to the public arena, by supporting learning through openness and by removing barriers to the public. Public accountability is not therefore a condition to be regretted by management, but rather a condition to be fulfilled. Organizations in the public sector give their account in the arena of public discourse. That requires openness from public organizations, for without openness communication is distorted. Inevitably there will be limits to openness, but they have to be justified. Management should not merely accept openness, but should ensure it. The enclosure that belongs to the *private* sector should have no part in the *public* sector. It has to be realized that 'the fish bowl environment presents both problems and opportunities for the public manager' (Perry and Kraemer 1983: 18). The task of management goes deeper:

> When organizations or polities are structured so that their members have no protected recourse to checking the truth, legitimacy, sincerity or clarity of claims made on them by established structures of authority and production, we may find conditions of dogmatism rather than of social learning, tyranny rather than authority, manipulation rather than cooperation and distraction rather than sensitivity.
>
> (Forester 1983: 239–40)

One of the tasks of management is to realize the potential of public discourse.

The arena of public discourse is *unbounded*. Demands can be made for public action by any citizen and for any interest. Concern for the impact of a service is not limited to those directly affected by it. Whereas a private firm is free to act within the law, a public organization operates in the public domain and must be prepared to justify its actions in the arena of public discourse; it is not sufficient to say that a public organization has carried out the law. Debate about public and social purpose is not limited to the direct effects and immediate purposes of public action. The debate about a road line is not limited to its impact on transportation. As one American businessman said, reflecting on his experience in government, 'What impresses me about the government is the fact that the people there have to amalgamate a number of diverse points of view and that they actually succeed in doing so' (Weiss 1983: 48). There are, after all, 'few limits on who can get involved in the decision-making process, who can work on it or who can speak on it' (Perry and Kraemer 1983: 20).

For management in the public sector no decision can ever be judged final or performance be judged successful because it has met its apparent objectives. Other voices can always be raised that challenge that judgement.

The tasks

There are certain tasks that are distinctive to the public sector. Organizations in the public sector provide services, but they also act as *government*: 'The single most important characteristic that separates the public and private sector, particularly at the federal level, involves the concept of sovereignty' (Moe 1987: 435). From this derives (and this applies at levels other than the federal level) 'the use of coercion to impose its will' (Moe 1987: 435). In the public sector law and order is maintained. Taxes are levied. Collective decisions are made which can be imposed even on those who do not agree with the decision. The management of regulation makes its own demands in the public sector.

Underlying the whole of the public sector there is the task of balancing the different interests in society, the different values sought and the different voices raised. Any organization has to balance interests within itself. The distinctive task of organizations in the public sector is to balance interests within society. As we have seen, the private firm can define customers by the sale but the public organization has many customers. The private firm can limit its objectives and its criteria of success, but the public organization can never assume that the limits are fixed.

> Multiple criteria of success are inherent in the government of any political or social unit, however small. For the multiple needs and diverse standards of expectation of people bring together in a place, interact with and limit each other in ways which cannot be ignored.
> (Vickers 1983: 134)

This means that no single criterion of success, no objective and no interest can be assumed to be so dominant that it excludes other criteria, other objectives or other interests. Thus in the public sector the task may be not how to meet a single objective, but how to achieve a balance between differing objectives. This is faced by a planning committee balancing the need for conservation with the need for economic development, but it is also met by a social worker balancing concern for the family with concern for the child.

The cumulative effect

The distinctive purposes, conditions and tasks of the public sector place their own requirements upon management:

Purposes:
- the requirements of social purpose;
- the values of democracy and citizenship;
- the realization of justice and equity.

Conditions:
- the basis in political process;
- the necessity of public discourse;
- the unbounded arena.

Tasks:
- the tasks of government;
- the balancing of values and interests.

These are not obstacles to be overcome, they are purposes to be fulfilled, conditions to be realized and tasks to be carried out. Separately and together they are what make management in the public sector so challenging. Tasks cannot be opted out of – because the market is not favourable. Objectives cannot be limited – to suit the organization's purposes. The public cannot be defined as customers alone – because many voices have to be listened to and interests balanced.

> What makes public management so hard – and so interesting – is that all these players act simultaneously with few clear lines of authority, constantly changing public mandates and frequent turnover of people. Getting the garbage picked up, a child treated for lead poisoning, a subway to the station on time, or an elderly person a social security cheque may not seem Herculean tasks. But when they are multiplied hundreds of times over, and their execution occurs in the context of the manager's environment, the real challenge of government becomes clear. The tasks can be done, and done well by managers who master this world; but such tasks can easily elude managers who are befuddled by the politics around them, disconcerted by the mixed signals they hear and unsure of their own agenda and purpose.
>
> (Chase and Reveal 1983: 15–16)

The purposes, conditions and tasks of the public sector constitute the manager's environment described by Chase and Reveal. That environment is not to be regretted or complained about. It derives from the rationale of the public sector. Nor does that environment alter if, for example, services are contracted out or management establishes a purchaser role. Social purpose remains and may even become clear. Public accountability remains. Interests and values still have to be balanced in the contracts made.

The development of management in the public sector will not be achieved by working against the conditions of the public sector but in working with them. That demands approaches to management that do not deny the rationale of the public sector but seek to realize it, and that requires new thinking on the nature of management. Some of the directions for that new thinking are now illustrated.

Strategic management

It is too readily assumed that strategic management is achieved through the setting of objectives that should guide the activities of public organizations. Underlying this approach are assumptions drawn from organizations that can limit their purposes and ensure that they are consistent with each other. That may be true of the private sector, but it is rarely true of the public sector.

In the public sector objectives may be in conflict with each other, as we have seen in the example given earlier of economic development and conservation. Consideration of the impact of activities cannot be limited to the stated objectives. Different objectives compete with each other in the budget, which in the public sector is an exercise in choice, unlike in the private sector where it is a forecast of sales and the resulting requirements.

Strategic management cannot be about the simple statement of objectives. It is about changing the balance between objectives. For that is what strategic management involves. If a local authority makes its priorities social problems and formulates its key objective around those problems, that does not mean that it eliminates all activities that are not devoted to that objective. If the key task in strategic management is about the balance between objectives, it is surprising that so little attention is paid in management approaches to this issue and to presenting information that highlights choice in strategic balance. Such an approach focuses attention not on the objectives of authorities in isolation from each other but in their interrelationship. That is the direction for advance in strategic management in the public sector.

Performance management

A public organization should monitor its own performance, but should also have its performance monitored. The first is necessary for effective management of the organization but the second is a condition of public accountability. The dilemma of public management is that performance in the public sector is necessarily multi-dimensioned because activities in the public sector reflect not single objectives, but a balance between objectives. This means that there can rarely be simple measures of the impact of a service. Thus it may not be sufficient to know whether a service has met the needs of the users: one also has to know whether it has met the public purposes underlying the service, including, for example, the distributional effect.

Assessing performance will necessarily be a matter of judgement because it reflects the weight given to differing objectives or values. Indeed, performance measures can properly be a matter of political dispute: 'the participants in a political conflict trade upon this variability of the point of focus in a particular context to advance their favoured measure of performance' (Dalton and Dalton 1988: 30). If the Green Party were to gain control over a local authority, it is likely that each set of performance measures used in that authority would be revised to give greater weight to environmental considerations.

The values to be realized in the public sector mean that many additional factors have to be considered.

> While some ways of appraising private sector performance find expression in public sector contexts (for example, productivity, innovation and others), we may characterise an organisation's implementation of public policies as just or unjust, equitable or non-equitable, coercive or non-coercive, or representative or non-representative. While most of these values may be utilised as measures of public performance and embody in varying ways what we consider to be essential to the governance of a democratic state, the exact features of what constitute a 'just' or 'representative' state, for example, remain essentially contested.
> (Dalton and Dalton 1988: 30)

Performance in the public sector is necesssarily a matter of judgement and performance measures can never be final because the arena of public discourse is necessarily unbounded. These considerations mean that the dream of a complete set of performance measures is necessarily an illusion.

None of this makes performance assessment any less important. Rather it makes it more important, because it highlights that judgement of performance is at the heart of the political process that provides the rationale of the public sector and sets the conditions for its management. It shows, however, that for management the question to be answered is never the simple one of how one measures performance, but how one supports judgement on and informs public discourse about performance. The tasks for management are the assessment of multi-dimensioned performance and performance management, when performance can only be finally judged in the political process.

The public service orientation

Rather than attempting to develop a marketing orientation by adapting private sector marketing approaches for the public sector, management in that sector requires a public service orientation which recognizes that services have to meet the needs of the user *and* public purpose, and that this requires public authorities to be close to the public as customer but also close to the public as citizen in determining public purpose.

What is required in the public domain is an orientation that encompasses its distinctive purposes, conditions and tasks. A public service orientation is required that recognizes that:

- public services have both to meet public purpose and to be responsive to those for whom the service is provided;

- the service is only of value if it both meets public purpose and is of value for those to whom it is provided;
- value depends upon the judgement of public purpose by citizens and of service by consumers;
- value can only be realized by public organizations close to the public as citizens and as consumers.

A public service orientation has to be built into the working of the whole organization:

- access, for if there is only limited access there is no basis for the voices of citizens to be heard or of service to be provided for those that need it;
- learning from the public, both as citizen and as consumer;
- informing the public, for the citizens have rights and the consumers have needs;
- involving the citizens as part of the public domain and the consumers as part of public service;
- thinking public beyond the boundaries of the enclosed organization;
- staffing policies and practice for public service, recognizing that a devalued staff cannot provide value for either citizen or consumer;
- organizing for service and for citizenship if a public service orientation is to be expressed in the working of the organization.

Organizational values

It has been argued that it is dangerous for organizations in the public sector to adopt uncritically values pursued by private firms. The public service ethic is not to be regretted. Indeed Sir Robin Butler, the head of the civil service, has raised the issue of how those values can be sustained alongside the management changes being introduced within government.

> But I also believe that, in the course of that development, we must retain the unifying characteristics of the Service which are not only its traditional strengths but its duties – the requirements of equity, accountability, impartiality and a wide view of the public interest. The unity of the Civil Service offers stability and a continuing corpus of tradition, knowledge and experience which is part of the infrastructure of a democratic society.
> In my view there need be no inconsistency between maintaining these long-established assets and virtues and the movement towards more individual responsibilities.
> (Butler 1988: 15)

Statements of organizational values can have an importance to the working of an organization, provided those values are seen as expressed in practice by senior management and not just written into formal statements. They must, however, be worked out for and express the distinctive purposes, conditions and values of the organization. They should not merely be adopted from private sector organizations. Thus the values of a public sector organization can include:

- the basis of government in the democratic process;
- the social purposes the organization is designed to achieve;
- the search for equity and justice as a condition of public life;
- the development of citizenship as a rationale for public organization;
- public accountability, not as an administrative tool, but as a moral principle;
- openness in government as a requirement for undistorted discourse;
- the necessity of listening and learning from the public as consumer and as citizen;
- support for the political process as a condition of government;
- value placed on staff as public servants.

In such values the distinctive purposes, conditions and tasks can be given expression and shape the distinctive nature of public sector management.

Conclusion

In this chapter it has only been possible to indicate some of the directions for public sector management. Effective management is required in the public sector if public resources are to be fully used to achieve public purpose. But effective management will not be achieved through models based on the private sector. What is required is the development of management based on the distinctive purposes, conditions and tasks of the public sector. Some directions for that development have already been indicated. Others are required. Examples include:

- marketing for equity, because relating service to need is the task;
- the management of rationing, for resources are limited in relation to need;
- value grounded policy analysis, for the task is to expose not to resolve the value conflicts;
- learning from protest, recognizing that protest is a constitutive condition of the public domain;
- the conditions of joint action, as inter-organizational relations is the context of public service management;
- community accounting that seeks to relate the costs and benefits of public services;
- the assessment of multi-dimensioned performance, recognizing that public services can rarely be judged by the simplicity of output measures;
- management processes for political choice, building and arraying information;
- the ethics of public service management, recognizing the dilemmas of conflicting values.

In these and other ways public service management has to build its own understanding. The purposes, conditions and tasks of the public domain present their own demands and their own challenges for management thinking.

References

Audit Commission (1988) *The Competitive Council*, London: HMSO.
Audit Commission (1990) *We Can't Go on Meeting Like This*, London: HMSO.
Burns, T. and Stalker, G. (1961) *The Management of Innovation*, London: Tavistock.
Butler, Sir R. (1988) *Government and Good Management – Are They Compatible?* London: Institute of Personnel Management.
Chase, G. and Reveal, E. (1983) *How to Manage in the Public Sector*, Reading, MA: Addison-Wesley.
Christopher, M., Kennedy, S., McDonald, M. and Wills, E. (1980) *Effective Marketing Management*, Aldershot: Gower.
Dalton, T. and Dalton, L. (1988) 'The politics of measuring public sector performance', in R. Kelly (ed.) *Promoting Productivity – the Public Sector*, Basingstoke: Macmillan.
Forester, J. (1983) 'Critical theory and organizational analysis', in G. Hangar (ed.) *Beyond Method: Strategies for Social Research*, Beverly Hills, CA: Sage.
Goodrich, J. (1983) 'Marketing for public managers', in B. Moore (ed.) *The Entrepreneur – Local Government*, Washington, DC: International City Managers Association.
Kotler, P. and Andreason, A. (1987) *Strategic Management for Non-Profit Organizations*, Englewood-Cliffs, NJ: Prentice-Hall.
Lawrence, P. and Lorsch, J. (1967) *Organization and Environment*, Cambridge, MA: Harvard Graduate School of Business.
Major, J. (1989) *Public Service Management: the Revolution in Progress*, London: Audit Commission.
Moe, R. (1987) 'Exploring the limits of privatisation', *Public Administration Review* 47, 6: 453–60.
Olsen, J. (1988) *The Modernisation of Public Administration in the Nordic Countries*, Uppsala: Study of Power and Democracy in Sweden.
Perry, J. and Kraemer, K. (eds) (1983) *Public Management: Public and Private Perspectives*, Irvine: University of California.
Peters, T. and Waterman, R. H. (1982) *In Search of Excellence*, New York: Harper and Row.
Potter, J. (1988) 'Consumerism and the public sector. How well does the coat fit?', *Public Administration* 66, 3: 149–64.
Ranson, S. and Stewart, J. (1988) 'Management in the public domain', *Public Money and Management* 8, 1 and 2: 13–40.
Vickers, Sir G. (1983) *Freedom in a Rocking Boat*, Harmondsworth: Penguin.
Weiss, H. (1983) 'Why business and government exchange executives', in J. Perry and K. Kraemer (eds) *Public Management and Private Perspectives*, Irvine: University of California.
Woodward, J. (1965) *Industrial Organisation: Theory and Practice*, London: Oxford University Press.

4
Competence and contradiction

Mary Issitt and Maureen Woodward

At first sight 'competence', in terms of 'sufficiency of qualification' or 'capacity to deal adequately with a subject' (*Oxford English Dictionary* 1989), seems a sensible starting point for determining not only whether a person can do a particular job, but also to identify the standards he or she should meet. Yet the concept of 'competence' as a measure of occupational capability currently arouses strong feelings, with those who are passionate advocates and others who view the whole matter with extreme caution. In this chapter we are particularly concerned to address its implications for practitioners working in the spheres of youth and community work, social work and teaching, and in so doing to assess to what degree it can facilitate progressive practice. We also explore the contradictions arising from the apparent consensus about the application of competence. We consider both 'top-down' (government-backed policies to restructure vocational education) and grassroots and other initiatives that seek, from the 'bottom up', to widen access to these people-centred professions. We show how the simple concept of competence is being expanded through functional analysis, and how its application causes problems for educators and practitioners.

Competence from the grassroots

As consciousness about structural inequalities has grown, it has been increasingly recognized that the educational system denies access to talented people who do not have a conventional academic background. Knowledge and expertise in education, social work and youth and community work has increasingly been challenged by progressive educators, practitioners and consumers on the receiving end of services (Bailey and Brake 1977; Humphries 1988; Dominelli and McLeod 1989; Knowles 1990).

Community-based self-help initiatives, many of which have sought to tackle inequalities, have led to the discovery of new expertise and knowledge, and to the development of services. While these initiatives often existed outside of direct state provision, the knowledge and methods used have become an increasingly accepted part of the mainstream. The irony of the situation has been that the skills of working-class volunteers and activists within these projects would be informally recognized. They would often be asked to contribute to the training of practitioners, who would eventually become professional youth, community and social workers delivering a service to them. Yet formal recognition of these skills in the form of access to training, paid employment and career progress has often been denied without a paper qualification. Thus to many the demonstration of competence to do the job seems a fairer way to assess who should enter a particular occupation.

Banks (1990) documents and evaluates a range of approaches that have developed through the accreditation of prior learning (APL), which seek to recognize experience gained outside of the formal education system. APL offers those with appropriate experience access to, or exemption from, existing courses. Over a number of years the Federation of Community Work Training Groups have developed a system for appropriate prior learning and experience to stand in its own right as a route to professional community work practice (Federation of Community Work Training Groups 1991). Such a qualification has now been endorsed by the National Youth Agency (NYA), formerly the Council for Education and Training in Youth and Community Work (CETYCW), which itself had researched APL, which it called validating learning from experience, and fostered the portfolio approach to learning.

Inevitably, Banks argues, any process for APL will rely upon assessment standards defined in terms of competence (Banks 1990: 12). For its advocates, the notion of 'competence' offers a concrete way of acknowledging the proven abilities of experienced grassroots practitioners, and also promises that the service they provide and standards defined will be close to the needs of the consumers, rather than being produced in a more remote institutional way. Together APL and competence are seen as a powerful combination for overcoming professional elitism and challenging inequalities from the bottom up.

Competence – streamlining the qualifications system

Competence is a flexible concept. It is not only attractive at the grassroots, it is now also being used as a means of systematizing occupational standards, through the National Council for Vocational Qualifications (NCVQ). This body was established following the publication in 1986 of the White Paper *Education and Training – Working Together*. Jessup (1990) shows how NCVQ was to co-ordinate the development of new forms of vocational qualifications – National Vocational Qualifications (NVQs) – into a new framework. This framework would rationalize the 'qualification jungle', which led to 'numerous awarding bodies competing in the same or overlapping occupational areas, with qualifications with different objectives, size and structure, often with no procedures for recognising each others qualification' (Jessup 1990: 17).

The NCVQ's task was to shift the whole emphasis in vocational standards from 'inputs', which are the 'learning opportunities provided' towards 'outputs', what Jessup describes as the 'standards that need to be achieved at the end of a learning programme'. He shows that this was to lead to 'standards' having a specific meaning, contrasting with the 'generalised and rather loose concept of standards which has prevailed in educational circles in the past'. The output model would require individuals to demonstrate a 'level or standard of performance', which would be set out in a 'statement of competence' (Jessup 1990: 22).

This represents a relatively benign view of the NCVQ, assigning it a demystifying and rationalizing role, which can widen vocational opportunity at the same time as developing a competent and efficient workforce. It might therefore be reasonable to conclude that in reshaping occupational requirements around the notion of competence the interests of 'bottom-up' and 'top-down' approaches seem to coincide. In order to explore this more fully it is necessary to look at the wider social policy context.

Competence and the wider social policy context

The notion of competence is an important ingredient in operationalizing social policy solutions to current economic and political problems in which the lack of competitiveness of British industry and unemployment are two major factors. Davies and Durkin (1991) argue that solutions to these problems have increasingly equated the needs of employers and the market with 'the national interest'. They go on to show how, since the advent of the Manpower Services Commission (MSC) in 1973, training has been shaped to meet employers' needs. Momentum gathered fast during the 1980s through the policies of a Conservative government that 'was determined once and for all to lick British industry into shape. . . . A series of reports emanated from government departments, the CBI, and the (then) MSC, culminating in 1988 with the White Paper *Employment in the 1990s*' (Davies and Durkin 1991: 7).

Policies carried out through the NCVQ not only provide a means of determining a common structure and standards for vocational training, they also exist as part of an overall strategy that puts employers in the forefront of any training system. This point is illustrated by a quotation from the White Paper:

> The system must be planned and led by employers as it is they who are best placed to judge skill needs; it must actively engage individuals, of every age, background and occupation, because they have much to gain from appropriate investment in their own training and skills; it must co-operate with the education service.
>
> (Department of Employment 1988)

Davies and Durkin go on to comment

> Here the allocations of power are unmistakable. In charge – the employer, with his or her needs paramount; next as an unavoidable necessity the

'engagement of the individual worker', in so far as her or his interests are useful to the employer; and finally, very much as a poor relation – the education service.

(Davies and Durkin 1991: 7)

Thus any definition of 'competence' enshrined by NCVQ within a common structure and set of standards for vocational training will reflect this balance of power.

The ascendance of training over education has increasingly been translated into policy and practice as the employers' role in determining vocational competence has developed, and training is seen more clearly to fit the needs of the market. The well-worn debate between education and training has re-emerged, in which 'training tends to convergence and a reliance on established technique, whereas education tends towards divergence and a readiness to break from the confinement of prescribed practices' (Widdowson 1983: 19). In the current climate the dominance of training has led to a reformulated view of education that for the majority becomes less person-centred and more performance-orientated, with employment as the end in view. This shift has now been institutionalized through the setting up of TEED – the Training, Enterprise and Education Directorate (formerly the Training Agency) – which puts education as well as training within the sphere of the Department of Employment.

At all levels the education system itself is being reformed and the vocational and academic are being linked together. In the latest wave of change the government intends even more firmly to marry education with vocational training. The NCVQ will act as a vehicle for the increased development of general NVQs. These will run alongside the more specific vocationally oriented NVQS and 'cover broad occupational areas, and offer opportunities to develop the relevant knowledge and understanding, and to gain an appreciation of how to apply them at work' (Department of Education and Science and Department of Employment 1991: 19). Therefore a complementary path to the traditional A-level route to higher education is provided. This will be for college and school students who have limited opportunities to demonstrate competence in the workplace.

In addition, two new diplomas are being created in an attempt to bridge the academic–vocational gap: the Ordinary Diploma and the Advanced Diploma. Each offers the possibility of combining traditional GCSEs with NVQs. The effect these diplomas will have on access to higher education, on curricular issues and on the nature of higher education itself has yet to be explored in practice but without doubt change is imminent.

On the one hand, attempts to remove artificial divisions between vocational and non-vocational qualifications are to be welcomed, but the initial cost was that adult education would only be funded if it could demonstrate a vocational element. Following publication of the White Paper the government has backtracked on this. Liberal adult education, which has often been the entrance point for intending professionals in teaching and youth, community and social work, faces an uncertain future.

Competence – an all-pervading ideology

The influence of the competency movement has been all-pervasive, and shows clearly the ideological shift that has been engineered away from universal welfare provision to a market-led approach in which services are neatly packaged in terms of 'outcomes' that meet the targets of the contract culture. Efficiency of service output has increasingly been measured in financial terms. The implications are that those responsible for the training of professionals in education and welfare, whose services are largely discharged through the state, have for some time adopted the language and methods of competence. This is occurring even though NCVQ is only beginning to address qualifications at the professional level.

Concrete examples are to be found in social work, youth and community work and teacher education. In 1989 CETYCW rewrote its *Guidelines to Endorsement* for routes to professional training in youth and community work in terms of 'outcomes' and 'core competencies'. In the same year the Central Council for Education and Training in Social Work (CCETSW) regulations for the new Diploma in Social Work 'in the wider arena of training for national vocational and professional qualifications being developed by the National Council for Vocational Qualifications' (CCETSW 1989: 5). The Council set out a statement of requirements for qualification in social work, identifying 'the knowledge, values and skills required to achieve competence in social work practice' (CCETSW 1989: 13).

The Council for National Academic Awards (CNAA) has also begun to consider the application of a competency-based approach in initial teacher training. This approach offers the possibility of conferring qualified status to apprentices working alongside qualified teachers in the classroom who will act as assessors ('mentors') of classroom competence. The licensed teacher schemes are examples of the start of this process. Such moves are in response to government criticism over a long period of the content of some teacher-training courses, which are said to be removed from the practical situations teachers find themselves in on completion of training. Coincidentally this type of training fits in well with the NCVQ remit to improve the quality of training using their outcomes focus. It has further implications that relate to the structural changes presently affecting the status of schools and further education colleges, in relation to local management. As a result individual teachers will be able to negotiate their salaries with the school or college in the privacy of the interview room, creating vast pay differentials between teachers.

Competence – bottom-up and top-down

What emerges from the discussion so far is that in order to understand the concept of competence it is necessary to see that there are two distinct strands coming from different directions, one bottom-up, reflecting the needs and interests of ordinary people, the other enshrined in top-down policies that are part of the restructuring of all of the state's activities in welfare. The former stresses the importance of providing alternative routes to professional competence, with the starting point being the needs of the client group or consumer. The latter prescribes, with all the power of government behind it, what is thought to be required by employers to get Britain out of its present economic morass.

For 1990s social policy there are parallels in the use of 'competence' with the application of the term 'community' in the late 1960s and 1970s. Benington describes the latter as 'an "aerosol" word to be sprayed on to deteriorating institutions' to transform them (Benington 1974: 260). Many of the current approaches to accrediting people's experience have their roots in radical youth and community work, social work and teaching, which began during this period when the state sought to incorporate the involvement of communities into the solution of social problems. In the post-Thatcher 1990s, it is not collective but individualistic solutions that are sought, through 'active citizens' who will find their own routes to the competence required by employers, enabling them to work and provide for themselves.

Over a relatively short space of time, the policy impetus has gathered such momentum that it is difficult to stand back and address fundamental confusions around competence. Little critical analysis has taken place because most of the commentary has focused upon how to put competence into practice at speed, and this has been couched in the language generated, and parameters set, by the implementation of policy through NCVQ. However, notes of caution have been sounded that need to be carefully considered, as they strike at the very heart of the NCVQ programme and question the validity of one of its basic building blocks, namely the very concept of competence.

Competence – towards a definition?

In a seminal article Ashworth and Saxon (1990) argue that there are difficulties with the whole notion of competence that 'do not appear to have been taken on board in any serious way by the competence movement in the UK'. They draw upon work completed in the United States by Grant and Associates (1979), which identifies three main problem areas: the specification of competence, the teaching of competence and the assessment of competence (Ashworth and Saxon 1990: 4). Through close examination of these areas they highlight a number of problems which cast doubt on the validity of the 'output' model as a means of setting standards for the job. They argue that it is difficult to distinguish competence from performance. Outcomes may result from 'diverse processes'. Therefore does the end always justify the means by which a person achieved a particular outcome? Does the person achieving the outcome necessarily have to understand the means by which this outcome is achieved?

In order to establish to what extent the issues raised by these authors are being addressed it is important to examine how the notion of competence is being defined and put into practice. Most of this work has been driven by the motor of the NCVQ and the Training Agency (now TEED). In NVQ terms competence seems to be that which an individual can do in relation to the requirements of a specific work role in an occupational area, which has been identified by a group of employers called a lead body. The assessment of competence is concerned with whether a person can perform the functions necessary for an effective outcome, ideally in the workplace. In NVQ-speak competence is 'the ability to perform work activities to the standards required in employment' (NCVQ 1988).

A more comprehensive definition is provided by the Training Agency:

> Competence is defined as the ability to perform the activities within an occupation. Competence is a wide concept which embodies the ability to transfer skills and knowledge to new situations within the occupational area. It encompasses organisation and planning of work, innovation and coping with non routine activities. It includes those qualities of personal effectiveness that are required in the workplace to deal with co-workers, managers and customers.
>
> (cited in CNAA 1991: 12)

Therefore, the scope of the above definitions covers 'the ability to perform' to a defined standard of performance and 'the ability to transfer' this performance to new work situations; and this is associated with skills, knowledge and personal qualities. The relatively simple concept with which we began is transformed and can be taken to mean quite separate things, namely role competence, transferable competence or personal competence. When viewed in this way there seems to be a notion of qualitative progression in the type of skills and abilities being assessed. This includes skills related to a present role where the person is required to perform immediate tasks; skills related to future roles where the skill of transfer becomes important and necessitates increased levels of knowledge and understanding; and personal effectiveness skills, which imply creativity and the ability to manage people.

The way in which the Training Agency and the NCVQ suggest that competencies are best arrived at is by way of what some would call a form of training needs analysis, namely functional analysis. The Unit for the Development of Adult Continuing Education (UDACE) explains how this approach works:

> Functional analysis is concerned with the key purpose of the occupational role rather than with the process. It begins by examining the whole work role and looking for a key purpose. It then asks what has to happen, what do people have to do, for that purpose to be achieved. At this stage in the analysis, the work role need not relate to an individual: it may relate to a company or a service or a professional function. The question of what has to happen for the key purpose to be achieved begins to divide the work role into a series of activities. Continuing this division eventually yields work roles which are carried out by individuals.
>
> (UDACE 1989: 16–17)

The activities related to the key work role form 'units of competence', each unit further divided into 'elements of competence', which have a set of performance criteria used to assess whether the person can perform the activity to the

Competence and the person-centred professions

The process described above appears to be achieving its objectives of providing a blueprint for defining and assessing competence across the whole range of occupational areas. Yet real problems emerge when the blueprint is applied to person-centred work at professional levels. The difficulty of disaggregating broad, general concepts into ever decreasing elements with specific performance criteria is referred to in the Accreditation of Social Services Experience and Training (ASSET) (Maisch and Winter 1991). Reference is made to the ambiguity of taking what is by its nature unified competence, i.e. professional ability, and dividing this into constituent skills for assessment purposes, then assembling these discrete competencies to recreate a model of professional competence. The essential problem of this is that, at the receiving end, it is the whole interactive performance that is of significance, not bits and pieces assembled or bolted together.

What appears to have happened in the ASSET situation is that, in the very act of reducing a social worker's performance to the micro-skills level, the notion of 'a competent person' able subtlety and uniquely to care for others in a multitude of situational contexts seems to be lost. Additionally there does not appear to be a way of actually assessing the effectiveness of people's performance in relation to their clients' needs.

In the realm of teaching there are similar major difficulties. The CNAA states that:

> Many teacher educators reject the idea of competence-based teacher education on the grounds that it encourages an overemphasis on skills and techniques; that it ignores vital components of teacher education as we currently understand it, that what informs performance is as important as the performance itself.
>
> (CNAA 1991: 2)

Related to this, perhaps the most contentious issue concerning teaching is the causal relationship between teaching and learning. The full intricacies of this process still elude educationalists and cannot be reduced to a means–ends model.

Teacher expectations have a bearing on this relationship, in terms of what they anticipate their students being able to do as a result of the teaching process. This aspect is picked up in a recent piece of research involving higher education lecturers from five subject areas, who were asked to look at, and set out, the learning outcomes they expected of their students. Each group of lecturers developed 'sets of learning outcomes in different ways, beginning at different points and following different routes'. They found difficulty separating out skill, competencies and knowledge, seemingly encountering difficulties in coming to some consensus about what a graduate from each of the five areas should be able finally to do (UDACE 1991: 6).

Questions about the efficacy of the current state of the process identified by those who are relatively new to 'competence' are echoed by those writing in the field of management education and training, whence much of the current application of competence derives. Hirsch and Bevan identify the paucity of the language used in defining the skills required of managers. They suggest that the 'skills language' used at present is superficial. The terminology is similar but at the level of meaning there is discrepancy: 'Some expressions of management skills are used very frequently, but they do not all mean the same thing in different organisations' (Hirsch and Bevan 1991: 98).

The theme of linguistic deficiency is taken up by Pye (1991). She suggests that in describing what makes an effective manager there are some intangible elements that defy close analysis. Management competence

> can be seen and indeed has to be seen in order that others might attribute that behaviour to be competent. Yet it seems to elude our grasp; it can be recognized in the performance of others but somehow seems to defy close analysis.
>
> (Pye 1991: 101)

Some managers just seem to have 'it', the 'it' being indefinable but recognizable by a gut feeling or intuition.

It seems that by breaking down the whole performance into constituent parts, it is impossible to assess the whole person in action, which more accurately demonstrates the interaction of skills, abilities, experience, intuition and knowledge. In Pye's view the language does not adequately define competence, which she shows in management terms to be often based on a 'tacit understanding'. It is no wonder, then, that the Community Work Feasibility Study, undertaken by the Care Sector Consortium of the NCVQ, also highlights similar problems with terminology. They state:

> One of the difficulties encountered in working with the standards methodology, including a strong 'top-down' approach, such as functional analysis, is the way the words have of 'getting in the way'.... Language should be checked for meaning and clarity throughout any future programme. Language must also be accessible to candidates.
>
> (NCVQ 1991: 28)

Competence and contradiction

Thus far we can see a number of contradictions inherent in the whole notion of competence, which are being manifested at a practical level and recognized even by those who are developing competency-based training. These contradictions have not only practical but also political and philosophical dimensions that raise questions about the methods used in developing vocational training around the concept. These questions are of particular significance for those engaged in person-centred occupations. As the competency movement creates it own professional mystique, contradictions about competence cannot be resolved by merely refining the terms used and communicating more efficiently, but have to be understood in relation to fundamental debates about methods and ways of explaining social reality that have been raging within social science for several decades.

Pye (1991) suggests that some of the problems with applying the concept of competence stem from 'our academic tradition'. The current systematizing of competence through the NCVQ draws heavily on an academic tradition that supports behaviourist and positivist explanations of human actions. These assume an objective social reality that can be understood, measured and explained in a scientific way (Stanley and Wise 1983: 108). The definition and subdivision of competence through functional analysis seems to offer clarity and objectivity. On closer examination we find that this apparent clarity is pseudo-scientific.

Even at the level of language used, which has involved increased attempts at precision in specifying competence, we have seen that there can be no common measure of agreement. These problems with the terminology of competence reflect the fact that there is not one 'objective' social reality, but different social realities reflecting the individual organizational context in which the term is applied and who is applying it.

When we come to the question of assessment, functional analysis appears to offer a more standardized system, with competence being broken down into separate elements that can be assessed to agreed common standards. However, what is not recognized is that the apparently 'objective' list still depends upon the subjective judgement of the assessor as to the competence of another human being. In person-centred work this assessment involves a unique set of social circumstances that cannot ever be repeated.

The division of competence, through functional analysis, into a hierarchy of elements that do not necessarily have to be acquired through a sequential period of developmental education and training, relates to the wider debate about 'holism' and 'reductionism'. The problem of managing an understanding of the world is a perennial question for natural and social scientists. Reductionist explanations seek to divide complex phenomena into a series of levels that build upon each other, with the earlier levels having priority. This approach is criticized in both the natural and social sciences as leading to an over-simplification of complex activities that does not fully take account either of the relationships between the levels or of other explanations for the phenomenon (Birke 1986: 57–62). The critique of reductionism has been most often characterized by the phrase 'the whole is greater than the sum of the parts'. This implies that division of a whole into separate components in some way changes and impoverishes it.

In relation to competence the question has to be asked: is a competent worker necessarily the same as a worker who has at different times demonstrated 'elements of competence'? This question is of particular significance when considered in relation to social work, youth and community work and teaching. Because these professions are person-centred, within the realm of practice there has been an acknowledgement that the good practitioner is aware of the holistic nature of his or her tasks.

There is no doubt that certain tasks can be performed in a routine, atomized way. However, what differentiates the good, and often successful, practitioner

50   Changing social work and welfare

from the rest is precisely the ability to integrate action with an empathetic understanding of the person as a whole. Egan describes how Rogers (1980)

> spoke out against what he called the 'appalling consequences' of an over emphasis on the microskills of helping. Instead of being a fully human endeavour, helping was, in his view, being reduced to its bits and pieces. Some helper training programmes focus almost exclusively on these skills. As a result, trainees know how to communicate but not how to help.
> (Egan 1990: 131)

He goes on to show how Hills (1984) advocates 'an integrative rather than a techniques approach to training in communication skills, in which skills and techniques become extensions of the helper's humanity and not just bits of helping technology' (Egan 1990: 109).

Twining, in his discussion of 'the man-made jungle of vocational education and training', refers to the notion of synergy. 'Synergy implies that the whole is greater than the sum of the parts: $1 + 1 + 1 = 5$' (Twining 1991: 9). It seems easy to apply this to Rogers's point above where the 'micro-skills' form the parts and 'helping' the sum of the parts. What seems to happen somewhere in the equation is that the sum assumes added value; this may be because the parts have been put together in a particular way by the right person and that it is this process itself which produces a qualitative difference.

If we move on from the problems of competence that arise from positivist and functionalist/behaviourist models of social reality, we encounter further problems that relate to assumptions about human behaviour that underpin the whole concept of competence. If competence is to be measured by 'output' or outcome, it assumes a mechanism that denies the reality of human experience and behaviour. It does not encompass the notion of 'synergy', which has significance for both the person acquiring competence and the assessor. Emphasis on outcome, which Jessup (1990: 18–19) advocates, minimizes the 'input' and learning process. In training for person-centred work the process of learning, particularly in developing awareness of oppressions and anti-discriminatory practice, requires change at a deep personal level that cannot be reduced merely to 'outcomes'. Neither is it possible, in output terms, to measure the fact that when human beings work with others competence will be mediated by the context in which they are operating, and the values they bring to each situation. In youth and community work, social work and teaching, it may also be difficult to isolate individual competence from teamwork that produces a successful outcome.

Professional practice in this person-centred work involves innovation, artistry, warmth and humanity that defy reduction and description as mere elements of competence. The effective youth and community worker, social worker or teacher is not only a competent technician but also a reflective practitioner (Schon 1983), whose professional judgement is constantly developing to meet new situations, and

> to exert a consistent influence in this spontaneously changing and evolving drama, the practitioner finds guidance not in the pursuit of fixed goals or the certainties of particular known techniques (although these

things may provide some direction). Instead, he or she uses professional judgement responsively, guided by criteria for the process itself: criteria based on experience and learning which distinguish educational processes from non-educational processes and which separate good from indifferent or bad practice.

(Carr and Kemmis 1986: 37)

Competence and anti-oppressive practice

There are also important political contradictions to be considered when discussing competence. There may be real antagonisms around definitions of competence posited by NCVQ that ultimately operate in the 'national' interest of capital, and definitions that are organically developed at the grassroots level. This antagonism is felt particularly acutely by those working within the broad arena of welfare. There is a well developed literature which addresses the problems for radical practitioners in working in a way that does not perpetuate oppressions in society, yet at the same time recognizes the social controlling aspects of their work (Bailey and Brake 1977; London to Edinburgh Weekend Return Group 1980; Dominelli and McLeod 1989).

Increasingly, service provision has been forced to take account of structural inequalities in relation to class, gender, race, disability, age and sexuality. Commitment to anti-discriminatory practice has been incorporated as part of the professional value system, in youth, community and social work. The CETYCW guidelines state that 'the values underpinning the work derive from a clear understanding of, and commitment to, equality of opportunity and the educational importance of choice, freedom, responsibility and justice' (CETYCW 1989: 5). The guidelines go on to spell out how anti-discriminatory practice should be incorporated into any qualification seeking professional endorsement, in line with the Council's equal opportunities policy.

Jordan illustrates how the 'radical agenda' has also been incorporated into CCETSW's *Requirements and Regulations for the Diploma in Social Work*, but is

> put side by side with the traditional agenda of respecting established rights and respecting vulnerable individuals. So power, privilege and prejudice must be effectively challenged, but without upsetting the legal and moral foundations (economic and political individualism) on which they are built.
>
> (Jordan 1991: 5)

He argues that

> value conflict is indeed a central issue for present-day social work, so that the greater prominence given to ethical problems is welcome. The challenge for social work educators is how to present these in ways which empower and enable students, rather than paralyse and confuse them.

This will need clear thinking and good teaching, not just a list of competencies to be assessed.

(Jordan 1991: 5)

As we highlighted earlier, for people from oppressed groupings who may be both consumers and providers of services, competence may have a different meaning from definitions that meet the requirements of government or market place. However, as the market place, in theory, provides an arena in which all may sell their wares, it may be possible for definitions from the bottom up to gain ground. Through a series of regional workshops the Community Work Feasibility Study, undertaken for the NCVQ Care Sector Consortium, arrived at a definition of the key purpose of community work. This was:

to work with people who experience inequality, discrimination and injustice in order that they may take collective action which challenges their oppression, achieves change and improves the quality of their lives.

They state that all the functions following this are underpinned by analysis of 'the nature of inequality, injustice, discrimination and other forms of oppression'. It will be interesting to see how far the NCVQ can live with this definition, to what extent it will become changed and how it can be measured in terms of competence (NCVQ 1991: 15).

If the apparent veil of consensus is drawn aside then the multi-dimensional nature of the contradictions inherent in competence becomes apparent. 'Competence', like 'community', can be used at the level of ideology, policy and practice to blur social divisions on class, race and gender lines. Using competence as a means of defining the requirements for person-centred work obscures the structural divisions that professionals are now required to address.

Competence – the challenge for radical practitioners

Professional practice in person-centred occupations presents major dilemmas and challenges for practitioners. So far we have shown that it requires a holistic approach that cannot be trapped into a mere list of competencies that have the same meaning across occupational boundaries and at all levels of society. However, the qualification process has to be divided up in a way that makes it manageable and meaningful for the learner and the assessor; and that produces good practitioners while being holistic. Furthermore, the process has to be open and accessible to all those who have the potential to succeed. Therefore a path for progressive practice has to be found through the reductionist–holistic impasse.

The question that needs to be addressed is whether competence impedes or facilitates the way forward. Competence at the simplistic level of 'capacity' or 'sufficiency' is essentially a minimalist concept that does not embrace the creative, intuitive and anti-oppressive nature of progressive work with people. Through NCVQ and functional analysis it is being stretched and systematized into the basis for measurement of all qualifications. The top-down approach of functional analysis offers a veneer of objectivity, but when the surface is scratched the problems of 'specification, teaching and assessment' of competence identified by Ashworth and Saxon (1990) still remain. This is because the theoretical basis is flawed and it attempts to resolve problems that cannot be dealt with in this way. There is a danger that the focus will become instrumental and on the employer's terms rather than being consumer- or worker-centred. The paradox is that when it is used in a consumer- or worker-orientated way then it may be one of the tools for helping clarify practice, as the Community Work Feasibility Study shows (NCVQ 1991).

If the notion of competence provides a limited means for radical practitioners more sharply to define their focus, and bring about positive change in terms of widening access to vocational qualifications, then it is important to be aware of the wider political and ideological significance of the concept. We have shown that the contradictions inherent in competence are becoming more pronounced as the NCVQ 'higher' levels are addressed. If this becomes unresolvable then the NCVQ definition of competence may be restricted to the 'lower' levels of qualification, with the 'higher' professional levels determining their own standards as they always have done. Widening access to professional vocational qualifications may prove to be a myth and only go as far as the lower levels. Higher education in a broad sense, that does not pay out in immediate occupational outcomes, will increasingly become a privilege accessible only to those who can pay for it. Radical educators and practitioners should be assertive about their own methods, which take account of the multi-dimensional nature of learning for person-centred work. This will urgently be required to fill the breach when competence is found to be lacking.

References

Ashworth, P. D. and Saxon, J. (1990) 'On competence', *Journal of Further and Higher Education* 14, 2: 3–25.
Bailey, R. and Brake, M. (eds) (1977) *Radical Social Work*, London: Edward Arnold.
Banks, S. (1990) 'Accreditating prior learning: implications for education and training in youth and community work', *Youth and Policy* 31: 8–16.
Benington, J. (1974) 'Strategies for change at the local level: some reflections', in D Jones and M. Mayo (eds) *Community Work: One*, London: Routledge and Kegan Paul.
Birke, J. (1986) *Women, Feminism and Biology: the Feminist Challenge*, Brighton: Wheatsheaf.
Carr, W. and Kemmis, S. (1986) *Becoming Critical: Education, Knowledge and Action Research*, Lewes: Falmer.
CCETSW (1989) *Requirements and Regulations for the Diploma in Social Work*, Paper 30, London: CCETSW.
CETYCW (1989) *Guidelines to Endorsement: Initial Training in Youth and Community Work*, Leicester: CETYCW.
CNAA (1991) *Competence-Based Approaches to Teacher Education*, Committee for Teacher Education, London: CNAA.
Davies, B. and Durkin, M. (1991) 'Skill, competence and competences in youth and community work', *Youth and Policy* 34: 1–11.
Department of Education and Science and Department of Employment (1991)

Education and Training for the 21st Century, Volume 2: the Challenge for Colleges, London: HMSO.
Department of Employment (1988) *Employment in the 1990s*, London: HMSO.
Dominelli, L. and McLeod, E. (1989) *Feminist Social Work*, London: Macmillan.
Egan, G. (1990) *The Skilled Helper: Model, Skills and Methods for Effective Helping*, 4th edn, Pacific Grove, CA: Brooks/Cole.
Federation of Community Work Training Groups (1991) *Community Work Training*, London: AMA.
Grant, G. and Associates (1979) *On Competence*, San Francisco: Jossey-Bass.
Hills, M. D. (1984) 'Improving the learning of parent's communication skills. Providing for the discovery of personal meaning', unpublished doctoral dissertation, University of Victoria, British Columbia, Canada.
Hirsch, W. and Bevan, S. (1991) 'Managerial competences and skill languages', in M. Silver (ed.) *Competent to Manage*, London: Routledge.
Humphries, B. (1988) 'Adult learning in social work education: towards liberation or domestication?', *Critical Social Policy* 23: 4–21.
Jessup, G. (1990) 'National vocational qualifications: implications for further education', in M. Bees and M. Swords (eds) *National Vocational Qualifications and Further Education*, London: Kogan Page.
Jordan, B. (1991) 'Competencies and values', *Social Work Education* 10, 1: 5–11.
Knowles, M. (1990) *The Adult Learner: a Forgotten Species*, 4th edn, Houston, Texas: Gulf Publishing Co.
London to Edinburgh Weekend Return Group (1980) *In and Against the State*, London: Pluto Press.
Maisch, M. and Winter, R. (1991) 'The functional analysis method as applied to the description of professional level practice', Paper presented to the National ASSET Conference, Chelmsford, March.
NCVQ (1988) *The NCVQ Criteria and Related Guidance*, London: NCVQ.
NCVQ (1991) *Care Consortium: Community Work Feasibility Study*, London: NCVQ.
Pye, A. (1991) 'Management competence: "the flower in the mirror and the moon on the water"', in H. Silver (ed.) *Competent to Manage*, London: Routledge.
Rogers, C. R. (1980) *A Way of Being*, Boston: Houghton Mifflin.
Schon, D. A. (1983) *The Reflective Practitioner*, Aldershot: Morris Temple Smith.
Stanley, L. and Wise, S. (1983) *Breaking Out. Feminist Consciousness and Feminist Research*, London: Routledge and Kegan Paul.
Twining, J. (1991) 'Honest men with good intentions', *Educa* February: 8–10.
UDACE (1989) *Understanding Competence*, Leicester: National Institute of Adult Continuing Education.
UDACE (1991) *What Can Graduates Do?* Leicester: National Institute for Adult Continuing Education.
Widdowson, H. G. (1983) *Learning Purpose and Language Use*, Oxford: Oxford University Press.

5
Personal mobility and social inequality

Michael Cahill

Since 1945 mobility has been symbolized by the motor car. In the advanced industrial societies of the world the car has become a cult object and for many a prerequisite of the 'good life'. The 1980s saw these processes exacerbated in our society by a government committed to the private sector whose Prime Minister made it a point of principle never to travel on the train and firmly believed in the virtues of a 'car-owning democracy'. The environmental consequences of this addiction to the motor car around the globe are now being seen in the depletion of the ozone layer and the phenomenon of global warming. The implications for the health of our population of the increase in car usage in this country are becoming more apparent, with increases in childhood asthma and other respiratory disorders being attributed to the pollutants expelled by motor transport (Greenpeace 1991). The social consequences of the hegemony of the car in transport policy have been enormous for our patterns of urban settlement, work and leisure, education, community care; indeed, for almost every aspect of social life. Here the ways in which the commitment to personal mobility by car have affected the independence of carless people will be outlined and the results for access to shopping, a relatively neglected component of community care, will be discussed.

The private world

The motor car as a cultural object is a 'private world' where one can be cocooned in a way that is not open to the user of public transport. Its growing popularity as our principal means of transport is not explained solely by reference to this fact but its dominance can be seen as part of the increasing privatization of our society. Social changes seem set to further intensify trends towards a society in which public discourse is eroded as individuals lose a sense of common identity. There has been a shift from the public to the private in the social and political life of Britain. The home has become more important because of a number of factors: working hours are less so people spend more time there; labour-saving gadgets mean the home is run more easily; consumer purchasing power has greatly increased; there have been great increases in owner occupation; do-it-yourself has become a major hobby; TV has changed male behaviour, with more men spending time at home rather than in the pub; less children mean more room; many homes are better as well as bigger and they have gardens (Saunders 1990). The home is a human construction, it does not exist unless people make it happen and there cannot be an unpeopled home. It is to a certain extent defined by the physical constrictions of space – the building, the house. But the social relationships that are produced there, those between parents and children, between men and women all need to be analysed and studied. There is a mounting body of evidence to suggest that the home has become the centre of many people's aspirations (Marshall *et al.* 1988: 213; Saunders 1990: 270).

Life revolves around the home in our society in ways that were not prevalent in the Victorian era. Homes today have many roles. Clearly they are first and foremost spaces for living in – for getting on with the tasks of everyday life and for pursuing hobbies and recreation. The work of the Henley Centre suggests that increasingly individuals within the home will spend their time in different ways from other household members:

> The Centre's research indicates that over 40 per cent of people in multi-person households watch TV, read a newspaper or magazine or prepare and cook food on their own for over an hour most days a week. In addition, one in four eats a main meal alone on most days.
> (Stewart 1991: 118)

The home is also seen as a retreat from the world outside. Although many experience the home as a place of danger and conflict it is still often regarded as a place of safety where one lives with known people. To this extent it has to be examined alongside trends in modern cities. It is apparent that technological change is going to enhance the role of the home, but will the home then erode the public realm? 'The private, atomized, consumer, receiving messages on a screen is a member of the public only in the sense of sharing with others a passive role of reception' (Mulgan 1991: 247). Information technologies will further strengthen the role of the home in the economy. Home working – made possible by the use of personal computers, the fax and modems – is now with us, although estimates vary as to the extent to which it happens. Henley Centre research indicates that by 1995 twelve million in this country will be in jobs where they could work at home, although they forecast that the actual number will be closer to four million (Stewart 1991: 118). Home shopping using a computer terminal is a technological reality although not, as yet, a commercial proposition.

A positive reaction to the privatization of everyday life is to welcome it as a reinforcement of the individual's power to construct a world that is relatively impervious to the decisions of the state. In the UK the New Right has in the recent past claimed to give more power to the individual through measures that restrict nationalized utilities and local authorities. Cultural critics of Western society are divided in their response to the privatization of individual life, seeing it as a component of modernity: the belief that men and women can control technology and harness nature to their own purposes. Revulsion is an appropriate response for many people because privatization is part of the retreat from the public realm; from the world of public discourse; from viewing politics as the arbiter of relationships between citizens and society, which has been bequeathed to us by the Graeco-Roman inheritance (Sennett 1977). The impact of privatization on the individual citizen is judged to be largely negative, whereas the celebration of the private is to be found in the catalogue of the freedoms made available: the fact that one can choose one's location, live apart from family and friends in the modern society, and, of course, enjoy a range of previously undreamt of pleasures made possible by twentieth-century technology.

Shopping

It is around the private pleasures of the home that retailing has been reorganized in the past decade. Now shops increasingly sell to a lifestyle they do their best to create, having identified what the aspirations of their potential customers are. Aspirational retailing is about the creation of a style by the retailer that will be of appeal to the shopper. In the creation of this lifestyle, market research plays a considerable role in the accumulation of evidence about the tastes and goals of the various segments of the market. Lifestyle reports can be sold at high prices, as the information they contain can be used to good effect by business. The study of consumer wants and preferences and the reorganization of firms to supply this has been one of the outstanding features of the past ten years, so that marketing has been reinforced as a vogue subject. What has become clear is that there is now a variegated array of differing lifestyles and aspirations among the British public and the trick for business people is to identify these. As a result all sorts of market 'segments' have been identified: among the best known are 'yuppies' 'dinkies' and 'woopies'. One of the emphases throughout the 1980s was on design – the look of goods became all-important – and the high street success stories were firms that paid a great deal of attention to this.

One of the major trends in shopping over the past decade has been the move to out-of-town locations by supermarkets and big stores and the associated decline of the high street. This is the result of the mobility that car owners enjoy in our society, and one of the major arguments for these out-of-town stores is that ample parking space can be provided. The trend towards these larger units has major social implications for the poor and other disadvantaged people in our society.

This shift has not been effected only by food retailers but also by other high street multiples. The costs of this are first borne by those who live in the city centres. For them the range of stores narrows as the supermarkets close and the main food outlets for those without transport then become the small (and expensive) grocers. There is also a loss of jobs for those who live in the city centre. The visual look of the city centre changes as well. The sites formerly occupied by Marks and Spencer or Sainsbury's may remain unoccupied for months or years, giving the shopping centre a downbeat look, a form of blight that makes the entire area a less attractive shopping district. Probably the biggest loss is the loss of choice for low-income consumers and those who are without access to private transport. These are often the same people.

The shopping needs of older people

Shopping becomes more difficult with age. The UK General Household Survey (GHS) found that 16 per cent of people over 65 could not do shopping for themselves. Difficulties are acute for very old people, who are likely to have problems walking down the road on their own. The GHS reported that of women aged 80 to 84 one-third could not shop on their own. Of women aged 85 or more two-thirds could not shop on their own (OPCS 1986). Likewise, the GHS found that under half of people in the oldest age groups were likely to travel on public transport and were the most likely group among older people to need help if they did so. The GHS reported that under one-half of people aged 80–84 and only one-third of those 85 or older used public transport (OPCS 1986: 182). In Abrams's survey of the shopping needs of the older population he pointed out that:

> The incidence among elderly shoppers of ill health and health deficits that could affect their shopping behaviour is considerable: over 90 per cent are short-sighted, over half suffered from arthritis/rheumatism, and almost half said they could not walk for half an hour without difficulty; and nearly half are less than 5'4" in height – i.e. well below the height of many top shelves in the supermarkets they use.
>
> (Abrams 1985: 8)

It has been pointed out that modern stores are not designed with older people in mind and that the crowding that takes place in some stores will deter many from shopping there, especially if they are frail. As long ago as 1973 an Age Concern report, *Shopping for Food*, concluded that older people were 'a disadvantaged set of consumers' (Age Concern 1973). Older people interviewed for the Abrams study complained that they got very tired when shopping, had long waits for public transport and found the stores unpleasantly crowded. Even if a store bus is provided there still remains the task of carrying heavy bags from the bus stop to home.

Technology can help with some of these problems. Since 1981 computerized home shopping has been available in the UK. Goods can be ordered from home terminals and delivered to the older person's home. Successful schemes have operated in Gateshead, Bradford and now in a number of London boroughs. Older people report considerable satisfaction with these schemes but there is a high cost in the picking, packing and delivery of the goods. Commentators on the retail sector believe that teleshopping will 'take off' in the 1990s and become a major form of shopping. Keyline, the first major teleshopping operation, promised for 1992, will operate by means of a smart card that will enable goods to be ordered on the terminal screen and then debited automatically from the customer's bank account. Unfortunately, for older and disabled people teleshopping will probably come first in the form of 'weightless' goods and services rather than heavy shopping because of the distribution and delivery problems. France has shown how the costs of introducing a nationwide system can be borne by government with its Minitel system: a home terminal is now in more than five million French homes, which provides access to telephone directory enquiries and a range of shopping and entertainment services.

Shopping and the urban environment

The decline in inner-city shopping is a serious issue for if it continues we could be witnessing the experience of many American cities, in which the inner-city areas have experienced what is termed 'the doughnut effect': where the migration of capital, investment and jobs produces an absent centre. Other problems occur in inner-city shopping areas: these include litter, vandalism and a lack of amenities such as public telephones and toilets. The job losses that come about from the move away from the city centre by retailers can thus be seen as the latest stage of the wider inner-city job losses that have occurred over the past thirty years as firms have relocated on the periphery of cities or in the more attractive locations of small towns. Although there are now a few chains that cater to low-income consumers they do tend to be characterized by a more restricted range of goods.

The job gains associated with the new retail developments are not as great as is claimed. A recent study for Portsmouth City Council showed that of the 200 new jobs claimed for a retail park in the city only fifty were, in fact, new ones, the rest being relocation of staff from other outlets (Test 1989). These stores act as the focal point for a shopping centre, 'the anchor stores', and their closure when they move to out-of-town locations means a fall in trade for the smaller retailers who are left behind. When they also close, as many of them are forced to do, the high streets are in danger of becoming places where one finds only branches of banks, building societies and other nationally controlled organizations. Local business then disappears from the high street. Yet there is another kind of blight, that of graffiti and litter and the problem of those who hang around these centres, particularly when they are closed, and cause vandalism (Davies 1987). The centres of many of our cities have been designated, through past planning policies, as retail and office areas only, so that when these have closed the district is empty (Test 1989). These places are often seen as 'no-go areas' after dark, especially by women, because of the fear of attack.

Vehicles of inequality

If you have not got a car or access to a car in our society then the quality of your life is likely to be inferior to that of others. You may have to pay more for goods in shops because you will not find it easy to travel to the hypermarket in order to obtain lower prices. If you buy a large item it is assumed by many shops that you will have a car to take it home. If an article in your home – the stereo say – breaks down it is assumed that you will be able to bring it along for repair in your car. Many more people now live in villages or small towns that are many miles from their place of work. They like the idea of living in the countryside but in order to do so they are dependent on their car, although if telecommuting were to spread then the car would become less important, as not nearly as many journeys to work would need to be made. The dependency of many people on the car in rural and semi-rural areas is concealed until they are too old to use it. Then they become extremely isolated. Children in rural and semi-rural locations have to be 'ferried' around from home to school, to parties, to their friends. Many journeys are made simply in order to escort children (Hillman et al. 1991).

As is made abundantly clear from innumerable colour magazines and television advertisements, you are what you drive. Motor cars are the products that symbolize the consumer society: they are packaged with reference to their speed, the sexual allure that accompanies a particular make and the emphasis on the individual getting away from society on the wide open roads that only seem to exist in television commercials. They are, then, the ultimate consumer product. The priority given to motor cars has seriously distorted transport policy in this country. But it has also influenced the way in which our social life is organized and always the consequences are most deleterious for the poor and disadvantaged.

For those who cannot drive, or do not have access to a car, out-of-town shopping becomes much more difficult, if not impossible. Many jobs are now barred to people who cannot drive. Various forms of entertainment – theme parks, leisures centres – become very difficult to reach without a motor car. It becomes much more difficult for the carless to visit friends or relations, as bus and train services have declined. Many children's activities are denied to those without cars to ferry the children backwards and forwards. Time is consumed by the use of public transport. It can take an hour for one person to travel to work by bus, as opposed to fifteen minutes by car. There is a growing inequality in travel, with 'distances' for the more affluent becoming shorter and shorter with the use of air travel and high speed motorways, while travel for the poor becomes more difficult with the decline in public transport services. As the range of activities increases for car owners so social life becomes geographically dispersed. Once again it becomes imperative to own a car. All this has ignored the environmental costs associated with the car and the deaths and accidents resulting from our over-dependence on road transport (Hillman 1991). The contribution of car exhausts to global warming is well known but there are many socio-environmental consequences that can be viewed as unwelcome: in South-east England, for example, the prosperous middle class have taken to buying second homes in France, a process that will no doubt be aided by the opening of the Channel Tunnel. One can envisage the Europe of the twenty-first century, where motorways will allow the well off to travel very great distances to socialize or for recreation.

There are serious social disadvantages that result from present policies, which privilege the private car. I have already remarked on how shopping patterns have been altered by the car and how out-of-town shopping seriously disadvantages those who are not mobile. This is a form of deprivation that is as important as those essayed by students of poverty since the turn of the century. Inequalities in transport abound and are connected to wider inequalities. You can be 'transport rich' or 'transport poor' in our society. There is mobility deprivation as well as social deprivation. By and large, the car ownership figures per household in an area are a good indicator of the prosperity of its residents. In Townsend *et al.*'s study of social deprivation in Greater London the most deprived ward, Spitalfields in Tower Hamlets, had 79.64 per cent of households without a car, while the least deprived, Cranham West in Havering, had only 12.42 per cent of households without a car (Townsend *et al.* 1987: 104, 127). Department of Transport statistics show that in the lowest income quarter only 20 per cent of households own a car while in the highest quarter the figure is 93 per cent (Department of Transport 1988: 26).

The distribution and ownership of cars in our society is gender-related. In 1986, 41 per cent of women had driving licences while 74 per cent of men did so (Beuret 1991: 63). This is a marked increase on 1978, when only 30 per cent of women held a driving licence compared with 68 per cent of men (Pickup 1988: 98). If there is only one car in the household then it would appear that often it is gender that determines who will use this vehicle. This can mean that women are constrained in their choice of work because they do not have access to a car. Studies have shown that women's employment is nearer home than men's. This is also connected with the greater role that women play in active parenting, requiring them to be not too far distant from their children (Pickup 1988: 103). The average journey to work for women is shorter than for men: in 1988–9 it was six miles for women and nine miles for men (CSO 1991: 150). Women overwhelmingly predominate in activities such as shopping and school escort journeys, and these can be much more difficult to organize if a car is not available (Pickup 1988: 104).

The car has become a much more popular means of getting to work. Twenty or thirty years ago in our urban centres buses would be packed at rush hours in the morning or evening with 'standing room only'. Outside of London this is much less common today. In 1972–3, 39 per cent of journeys to work by women were made by car whereas in 1985–6 the corresponding figure was 59 per cent. The same trend was, of course, present in journeys made by men. The difference is that men started from a higher percentage of journeys made by car. In 1972–3, 61 per cent of all journeys to work made by men were by car whereas by 1985–6 the car accounted for 72 per cent. Over that period the bus was the transport mode that lost a significant number of passengers, particularly among women. In 1972–3, 38 per cent of journeys to work by women were made by bus whereas by 1985–6 this had fallen to 19 per cent. For both sexes journeys by rail remained constant (CSO 1989: Table 9.5). The transfer from public modes to private has led to increased congestion and longer journey times in certain cities.

Journeys to and from work are often influenced by the employer's policy. In 1982 almost 40 per cent of all car trips to central London were made by company cars. The number of company cars, that is cars bought or, more usually, leased by firms, has greatly increased in the past thirty years to reach a total of 2.4 million (CSO 1991: 150). Companies give staff cars so that they can use them in the course of their work, the most obvious example being the travelling salesperson. But they are often used in lieu of wages for senior executives in a company and are regarded as a 'perk' of the job. They now account for two-thirds of all new cars sold in the UK, so that they have a significant impact on the car industry. Despite recent budgets the government still encourages this practice by tax concessions on the cost of buying these vehicles, treating them as a 'business expense'. It has been argued that this subsidy to the car industry – the latest estimate is that it is worth more than £2 billion a year – has encouraged motor manufacturers to build vehicles for their high performance and speed rather than their safety and reliability (Friends of the Earth 1990: 122). In 1991 the government announced that National Insurance contributions will have to be paid by employers on the estimated addition in salary that the car represents. None the less, there seems to be little sign that companies are thinking again about this 'perk' (Griffiths 1991). Even if employees do not have company cars they may well be paid 'mileage' for the use of their cars while on company business. Often this mileage allowance is generous and is another inducement to use a car rather than public transport while on company business. Another way in which employers can encourage travel to work by car is by providing free parking at the place of work, which in many cities is another extremely valuable 'perk'.

Obviously cars are not used only for transport to and from work. One of their major uses is for social and entertainment purposes: this accounts for 42 per cent of all mileage travelled and 33 per cent of all journeys (CSO 1989, Table 9.4). This refers to going to visit friends and families or entertainment facilities. As the motor car has become the major form of transport in our society so the entertainment industry has had to accommodate to its requirements. Multiplex cinemas on the outskirts of towns, which are really car parks with a cinema attached, provide sufficient parking space to be viable, while inner-city cinemas where parking is difficult or expensive lose customers. A great many people engage in do-it-yourself, and these stores are now usually located on the edges of cities and towns.

Mobility or access?

Transport policy in the UK has been based on personal mobility and has thus ensured the dominance of the motor car. But as we have seen, this has led to travel disadvantages for the carless. Those encountered by older people in relation to shopping have been discussed here although there are many others who face similar problems, children and differently abled people among them. Walking is a daily form of transport for many people but the way in which the government collects travel information ignores the role of walking. The National Travel Survey of the Department of Transport does not count journeys of less than one mile. Pedestrians are second-class citizens in transport policy and this is seen in the dirty and hazardous state of many pavements, the leniency with which pavement parking by motorists is treated and the low priority given to pedestrians at pelican crossings. The increase in personal mobility made possible by motorways, by-passes and priority given to motor cars is one part of what has been termed 'time–space compression' – the erosion of space by time – but this phenomenon is related to class position: the rich and powerful are its major beneficiaries (Massey 1991: 24). The increase in personal mobility for one group can often mean a loss of mobility for another group; for example, the construction of a new motorway near a city can mean that jobs relocate away from the city centre and public transport is reduced.

Retailing and transport are clearly in a process of radical change, which is generating new forms of inequality. The new technologies have been used to accentuate the attractions of private lives, particularly in Thatcher's Britain in the 1980s. There are a variety of responses to the inequalities revealed here. Take the shopping difficulties of older people. One response is to put on a free company bus to an out-of-town store. This is better than no transport at all but limits shoppers to that one store, thereby depriving them of choice. Another more radical response would be to follow the lead of Germany and France and introduce legislation which makes it very difficult to build out-of-town stores. In addition the local taxation that small shops pay could be reduced and in this way the integrity of the high street might be preserved. Teleshopping is one solution for housebound older people but its general introduction, allied to the growth of out-of-town shopping and the decline of the high street, will further increase the social isolation of many older people, for whom a daily trip to the shops is a valuable form of social interaction.

None of these responses challenges the hegemony of the car in transport policy. Rather they adapt to it and provide special facilities for 'transport disadvantaged' groups: in a sense they are 'selective' policies. The transport and shopping difficulties described here have been caused in large part by the commitment to mobility in policy, yet there are always going to be people who cannot use motor cars – at present one-third of households. The alternative to mobility-based transport policies are policies that prioritize the concept of access to places for all members of society. Quite apart from the plight of the transport disadvantaged it can be argued that the dispersal of jobs, hospitals, entertainment and leisure facilities is not in the best interests of the majority of people in our society, the two-thirds of households who run cars. Often the move to small towns and rural locations is a flight from the daily experience of urban problems. Cities need to become places where people want to live and work and where facilities can easily be provided because of the relatively high densities (Sherlock 1990). This will mean the encouragement of walking and cycling, the reduction of danger for cyclists and pedestrians, the improvement of public transport and the reduction of motor car use (Public Health Alliance 1991: 26). In sum, this would lead us towards a more sustainable, low energy future in which the provision of local, accessible services would be a priority.

References

Abrams, M. (1985) *A Survey of the Elderly Shopper*, London: Age Concern.
Age Concern (1973) *Shopping for Food*, Mitcham: Age Concern.

Beuret, K. (1991) 'Women and transport', in M. Maclean and D. Groves (eds) *Women's Issues in Social Policy*, London: Routledge.
CSO (Central Statistical Office) (1989) *Social Trends 19*, London: HMSO.
CSO (1991) *Social Trends 21*, London: HMSO.
Davies, R. L. (1987) *Help for the High Street*, London: Tesco.
Department of Transport (1988) *National Travel Survey 1985/6*, London: HMSO.
Friends of the Earth (1990) *How Green Is Britain?* London: Hutchinson Radius.
Greenpeace (1991) *Air Pollution and Child Health*, London: Greenpeace UK.
Griffiths, J. (1991) 'No such thing as a free ride, but still the best deal going', *Financial Times* 23 March.
Hillman, M. (1991) 'Healthy transport policy', in P. Draper (ed.) *Health through Public Policy: the Greening of Public Health*, London: Green Print.
Hillman, M., Adams, J. and Whitelegg, J. (1991) *One False Move . . . a Study of Children's Independent Mobility*, London: Policy Studies Institute.
Marshall, G., Newby, H., Rose, D. and Vogler, C. (1988) *Social Class in Modern Britain*, London: Hutchinson.
Massey, D. (1991) 'A global sense of place', *Marxism Today* June.
Mulgan, G. J. (1991) *Communication and Control: Networks and the New Economics of Communication*, Cambridge: Polity Press.
Office of Population, Censuses and Surveys (OPCS) (1986) *General Household Survey*, London: HMSO.
Pickup, L. (1988) 'Hard to get around: a study of women's transport mobility', in J. Little, L. Peake and P. Richardson (eds) *Women in Cities*, London: Macmillan.
Public Health Alliance (1991) *Health on the Move: Policies for Health Promoting Transport*, London: Public Health Alliance.
Saunders, P. (1990) *A Nation of Home Owners*, London: Unwin Hyman.
Sennett, R. (1977) *The Fall of Public Man*, London: Faber.
Sherlock, H. (1990) *Cities Are Good for Us*, London: Transport 2000.
Stewart, F. (1991) 'From designer lifestyles to high-tec rustic individualism', *Town and Country Planning* 60, 4: 118–19.
Test (Transport and Environmental Studies) (1989) *Trouble in Store? Retail Locational Policy in Britain and Germany*, London: Anglo-German Foundation.
Townsend, P., Corrigan, P. and Kowarzik, U. (1987) *Poverty in London*, London: Low Pay Unit.

6
Managing the poorest: the Social Fund in context

Gary Craig

Since the social fund (SF) was first introduced in the 1985 Social Security Green Paper (HMSO 1985), critical comment has characterized it as a radical departure from past social assistance one-off payment schemes (Jordan 1985; Meacher 1985). Four aspects of the fund were highlighted: the imposition of cash limits; an emphasis on loans rather than grants; a return to discretionary decision-making; and abolition of the right to appeal against decisions. Some of these features were not new – for example, discretion had been a continuing element from 1934 to 1980 – but it was suggested that, taken together, they moved the fund in a direction quite distinct from the general drift of policy over the past fifty years.

I have previously argued (Craig 1990) that the key to understanding the SF lies not in its financial role (quite marginal within social security expenditure, SF spending being less than 0.5 per cent of total expenditure), but in its ideological role. The argument here is that the SF displays a continuity, in terms of the ideological and economic role set for it by the state, with both social assistance in general and all one-off payment schemes since the creation of the first scheme in 1934 (under the auspices of the Unemployment Assistance Board). The SF is not a radical departure from past practice but a continuation of that practice, within the particular political conditions of the late twentieth century. This continuity was obscured by novel structural features of the fund but exposed more sharply in the highly ideological language of the 1987 Conservative government, which sought to ensure that the SF, and social assistance as a whole (now known as Income Support; IS), contribute to the maintenance of labour discipline just as previous administrations had used earlier assistance schemes. This continuity will be demonstrated through four key features of one-off schemes: (a) the use of discretion; (b) the boundary between one-off payments and the main social assistance weekly benefits (the 'scale rates'), characterized as the distinction between 'essential' and 'exceptional' expenditure; (c) the boundaries between state provision and that of other organizations (particularly charities and local authorities); and (d) the role of appeal tribunals.

The functions of social security

State social security policy has historically been concerned to exercise economic, political and social control of the poor by ameliorating those aspects of poverty that might give rise to political instability, at the smallest financial cost consistent with prevailing political and economic conditions (Novak 1978; Golding and Middleton 1982). As Britain moved from feudalism to capitalism, with increasingly centralized government, social security policy adapted to reflect the changing requirements of the economy. Initially, the vagrancy laws were concerned with preventing social unrest. Policy later responded to social and political threats, posed firstly by landless peasants and subsequently by the unwaged, unable at times to be accommodated by changing labour market conditions. Although this process of containment occasionally involved the use of force, it has generally (and especially since the growth of the labour movement) been achieved by combinations of social and economic policies, seeking for example to maintain differentials between wages and benefits. Regardless of the level of struggle between labour and capital, the abolition of poor relief altogether was never seriously considered. 'The ruling class were always aware of the usefulness of the Poor Law as an insurance against rebellion' (Townsend 1786).

State policies are legitimized by dominant ideological perspectives towards the poor (and towards women's place in the 'family'), classifying the poor into 'deserving' and 'undeserving', or into bread-winner and dependants. The process of classification, adapted in the light of changing circumstances, helps to reinforce political division within the working class. The growing number of ethnic minority claimants since the 1950s have, for example, been generally located within the 'undeserving' category (Gordon and Newnham 1985; NACAB 1991), as have, more recently, young people whose submissive labour market participation is required by the state (Craig 1991). This process is not without contradictions: the patriarchal family form has been challenged by recent demographic trends and increasing political activity among women. Conflicts between the competing ideologies of 'mother' and 'worker', resulting from the growth in lone parenthood, have created tensions in state policy (evidenced in debates about child support legislation).

Minimum subsistence incomes set by the state below the lowest wage contribute to the maintenance of a reserve army of labour. State social security is thus an essential element of capitalist economic relations, providing economic disincentives for workers to abandon work (ideologically defined as 'independence', debt and mortgages notwithstanding) in favour of 'social security' (represented in John Moore's colourful formulation as 'the sullen apathy of dependence'). As Dean (1991: 132) comments, modern poverty is created by the social security system, 'since it is through the distributive mechanisms of modern social security that the unproductive section of the population is marked off from the productive working class'. From this perspective, the aim of 'relief' has been not to prevent poverty or meet need but, as Townsend (1979) notes, to control individual behaviour. In the political conditions of the late 1980s, the government appeared, in the SF, to have dismissed the political necessity of incorporating the very poorest, effectively abandoning them to their poverty.

The main challenge to the state's ideological hegemony over social security might have come, in the early part of this century, from the developing labour movement, which had made significant economic and political gains. In fact, by a number of means, such as the construction of a national insurance (NI) scheme, it has been incorporated into an acceptance of the state's perspective. Winston Churchill, aware of the role of social reform in avoiding insurrection, spoke of substituting 'the pressures of the laws of insurance [for] the pressures of the force of nature . . . operating by chance on individuals . . . to deal with the awful jumbles of an obsolete Poor Law' (quoted in Golding and Middleton 1982: 36), which were threatening to undermine Britain's imperial economic role. NI was embraced by organized labour as part of the 'ransom which property will pay' to it, an approach that fitted well with the self-help approach of the friendly societies. However, state welfare has not been an unqualified social and economic gain for labour as a whole. As Adler and Asquith (1981: 27) note, 'the functional attribute of welfare [has been] that it serves to direct attention away from social, political and economic inequalities'. The price for labour has been the persistence of social, political and financial divisions within the working class, particularly continuing divisions between 'deserving' and 'undeserving' poor, between 'respectable' insured workers and those temporarily unemployed for structural reasons on the one hand, and those on assistance ('scroungers', 'malingerers', the residuum or underclass) on the other.

These divisions were enthusiastically espoused by the labour movement by the 1940s. The TUC response to the Beveridge Report was 'contemptuous of "dodgers" and [favouring] the withdrawal of public assistance from wives and children of workers who went on strike' (Harris 1975: 248). Similarly, the 1945 Labour government maintained the distinction between insurance and assistance schemes. That small element within the Labour Party which resisted that dominant ideology of social security at a local level (as in the 'Poplarist' councils of the 1920s (Branson 1979) and 'generous' Public Assistance Committees (PACs) of the early 1930s) had seen its powers abolished by the central state. At the same time, the ideological challenge of the National Unemployed Workers' Movement, with its attempts to build political bridges between employed and unemployed, was undermined by the failure of the TUC to support it. It is notable, in this context, that political lobbying on behalf of the poorest since the mid-1960s has fallen to the liberal pluralist poverty lobby (albeit in recent years with support from some trade unions and sections of local government) rather than to the formal organizations of the labour movement.

One-off payments schemes: a review

Record unemployment levels after the First World War meant that the insurance principle was not financially sustainable. *Ad hoc* schemes were introduced by successive governments to sidestep contribution rules. Simultaneously, the Poor Law principle, of the 'less eligible' position of the unemployed, had to be protected. 'Generous' boards of guardians were suspended, then abolished, to be replaced by the more centralized PACs. Some of these, offering public assistance to a level unacceptable to the government, were suspended in turn. Having failed to find a lasting solution to the threatened collapse of the insurance scheme, and in the light of the difficulties of controlling a locally administered scheme, the government strengthened its ideological and economic hold on social assistance by establishing a national, centrally controlled scheme of unemployment assistance.

The new organization, the Unemployment Assistance Board (UAB), had responsibility for relieving the many able-bodied unemployed workers not receiving insurance. Residual poor law organizations provided 'outdoor relief' for the elderly, sick and disabled. UAB benefits were set below insurance benefits, were applied on a discretionary basis and were means-tested. This model of social assistance 'continued to dominate the British system until the 1986 Social Security Act brought to an end many of the more elaborate features of means-testing which had characterised the original government response to the unrest about the initial form of the 1934 Act' (Hill 1990: 25). This unrest developed because UAB scale rates were lower than promised and, for many unemployed, below those offered even by the less generous PACs. The government attempted to 'take assistance out of politics' by creating the UAB as a separate agency not answerable directly to Parliament. The role of discretion was critical in its first years. Aneurin Bevan claimed that discretion was used to obscure the fact that 'the government are now engaged in carrying through the House Regulations which will brutally impoverish the conditions of all the distressed areas' (*Hansard* 17 December 1934: col. 886). The Solicitor-General of the time retorted that the allowances were 'only guides, and the over-riding provision makes it plain that the discretion remains to treat each particular case on its merits' (*Hansard* 17 December 1934: col. 1015). Although, as Deacon and Bradshaw (1983) note, most pressure on UAB officials was in the direction of economy, discretion thus offering the *appearance* but not the *substance* of generosity, this interchange reflects the use of discretion as a political mechanism, deflecting criticism of the failure of social assistance.

Political agitation persuaded the government to institute other means for incorporating dissent. Accordingly, Regulation VI allowed that 'a financial assessment may be increased to provide for needs of an exceptional character by such an amount as is reasonable', the first power to make one-off payments. The origin of these exceptional needs payments (ENPs) is attributed by Lynes to Violet Markham, who proposed that a head of household or single applicant, unemployed for at least six months, should be able to 'apply for a discretionary allowance (or credit) in respect of household or other personal replacements' (SBC 1977: 234). Markham said, reflecting concern about assistance levels, that although the UAB's scale purported to allow a weekly sum for clothes and, possibly, for household equipment, 'in practice, expenditure on these items could not be met by weekly payments but had to be met by a lump sum when the necessity arose' (SBC 1977: 234).

The role of discretionary one-off payments as a political safety valve (accommodating pressure arising from the failure of the weekly scale rates to provide against destitution) can be seen clearly. The payments also highlighted the problem of 'exceptionality': just *what* were the scale rates supposed to cover? Regulations did not refer specifically to replacement of clothing and equipment; nor was the power limited to long-term cases. But although local investigations revealed widespread needs not being met by the scale rates, the UAB drew tight boundaries around definitions of 'exceptionality'. 'Worn out clothing and household equipment was not regarded as an exceptional need because the Board's allowances were intended to provide a margin over the cost of food, rent and fuel to meet such needs' (SBC 1977: 236). There is no doubt that such essential needs *were* met on occasion by ENPs. What these debates illustrate is the potential for the state to manipulate the boundary between (and meanings of) 'essential' and 'exceptional' expenditure.

The UAB originally conceived of ENPs as a temporary but useful political device for dealing with difficulties arising from the establishment of a new scheme. However, they became part of the standard procedures of the UAB, although not enthusiastically encouraged from within the board. There is no doubt that few of those eligible even on the most restrictive criteria of 'deservingness' actually received ENPs. In the late 1930s, roughly 20,000 ENPs were paid annually. Yet one special investigation in areas of high unemployment generated 10,000 ENPs, one to each of 70 per cent of those visited.

The creation of appeal tribunals (adapted from NI Courts of Referees) within the UAB's structure was in part a political device to deflect demands by MPs for higher scale rates. Increased awareness of the UAB's powers and the NUWM's campaigning brought growing numbers of decisions contested by applicants. However, although this device appeared to offer gains to the formal labour movement through the positioning of 'workpeople's representatives' on tribunals, this distanced these representatives (often union officials) further from those whose claims for assistance they were to judge. The potential financial gains of the tribunal were, in any case, severely circumscribed by administrative means, and the power of the tribunal clerk was key in shifting the political balance against the claimant. In one case noted by Lynes, the Wrexham UAB manager requested his employment exchange colleague to prevent unemployed activists appearing as advocates for appellants by finding work for them, and instructed the clerk to stop one 'from making the same speech at every tribunal' (SBC 1977: 241).

Given the conditions under which the UAB was formed, and the interconnection of the poor law with charitable provision, it is not surprising that the respective roles and responsibilities of government, local government and charities should have been questioned. The UAB argued that it should not attempt to meet the needs of long-term unemployed if they could be met by voluntary organizations providing for the poor. At the same time, some local authorities attempted to oblige the UAB to assume responsibility for clothing children adequately in order that they could attend school. Glamorgan County Council identified 13,000 elementary school children needing footwear and 10,000 needing clothing. After careful sifting, removing the wage-stopped, for example, the list was finally reduced by the UAB to 1,700 children in 900 families, who each received six shillings (30p). Large numbers of potential claims were pared down to the small fraction defined as 'deserving'.

In 1940, the UAB took over poor law responsibility for supplementing old age pensions. Supplementary pensions had been introduced to head off demands for an increase in the rates of national insurance pensions. This meant, particularly in the light of low unemployment levels (a result of re-armament) and the increasing number of those made destitute by bombing, that the UAB was now not primarily concerned with the unemployed, and in 1941, it was renamed the Assistance Board. The response of pensioners, expected to be conditioned by continuing hostility to poor law stigma, to the supplementary pension scheme

> astonished everybody. The number of applications was eight times as great as had been expected, and it was up to twentyfour times as great in the more prosperous areas where the stigma of the Poor Law was strongest.... [The Board] began to see itself as the champion of pensioners' interests.
>
> (Deacon 1985: 3–4)

In 1942, of 478,000 home visits to pensioners, almost 75 per cent resulted in the award of a discretionary clothing grant. Pensioners, regarded as 'deserving' by the Board, presenting no threat to the work ethic, especially in a time of full employment, developed a benign attitude to the Board's officials. This attitude persisted for some years after the war, influencing early public perceptions of the National Assistance Board (NAB), formed in 1948.

The NAB arose from the Beveridge Report (Beveridge 1942). Beveridge's ideas had been shaped by experience in the Charity Organisation Society and at Toynbee Hall, with their emphasis on the remoralization of the poor.

> Three key ideas formed the tripod on which public understanding of poverty and welfare rested. These were efficiency, morality and pathology: efficiency of the labour market and the economy; morality of the work ethic and self-sufficiency; and the pathology of individual inadequacy as the cause of poverty.
>
> (Golding and Middleton 1982: 48)

Beveridge's corresponding perspective was that the contributory principle – emphasizing personal responsibility rather than dependency on the state – should continue as the cornerstone of welfare. Alongside the state-run system of contributory benefits, the NAB (structurally similar to the UAB) would be responsible for sick, disabled and the non-insured elderly and unemployed.

The transitional 'safety net' would be needed only for a very few. Beveridge stressed the 'less eligible' status of assistance:

> It must be felt to be something less desirable than insurance benefit . . . [subject] to any conditions as to behaviour which may seem likely to hasten restoration of earning capacity . . . [and penal] provision for a limited class of man or woman who through weakness or badness of character fail to comply.
>
> (Beveridge 1942: paras 369, 372)

He confidently expected that the need for assistance would diminish over time. In fact, assistance benefits have taken an increasingly central role in state provision, responsible at times for supporting up to 1 in 7 of the UK population, largely as a result of the failure of insurance benefits to be set at adequate levels and because of the impact of rising unemployment. By as early as 1952, Beveridge himself admitted that 'the picture of yesterday's hopeful collaboration in curing evils of want . . . looks like a dream today' (1952: 360–1).

Despite suggestions that the creation of a single ministry would remove residual stigma, the NAB was separated administratively, and in terms of the status of the service, from its insurance counterpart, the MPNI. This seems not to have reduced the stigma of the unemployed but to have revived the anxieties of the elderly about the opprobrium associated with claiming from the board. Its early emphasis was on the needs of the elderly, 66 per cent of those claiming assistance in 1948 being aged 60 or over, and it worked for most of its life in conditions of 'quiet obscurity' (Webb 1975: 467). The board occasionally expressed anxiety about demands from non-pensioners, those still regarded as 'poor law types'. As Deacon (1985: 9) remarks,

> the NAB could never have been accused of dealing *indiscriminately* with the pensioner and the vagabond. The concern for the welfare of some claimants co-existed with a pre-occupation with the dangers of fraud and abuse from others. If good was to be done for pensioners, it was to be done by stealth in case the less deserving character came to hear of it.

Demand by the unemployed was characterized in the press as 'abuse' by the 'workshy' once it began to get out of hand, a pattern that was to be repeated in the 1970s and 1980s.

Concern about the growth of weekly discretionary additions finally led to the abolition of the NAB in 1966. In relation to lump-sum grants, the NAB had surprisingly little to say publicly despite the fact that the increasing use of grants, initially by pensioners and later by others, must have been obvious. The number of ENPs – expressed as a proportion of those on weekly benefit – doubled from 1949 to 1965, with a quadrupling of expenditure. That demand for ENPs might pose problems for the control of expenditure was, however, privately known to the Board by the mid-1950s.

> The then under-secretary expressed some concern about women and children during a harsh winter. The scale rates were tight and there was some concern that their needs should not go uninvestigated. At the end of

the winter, the finance officer pointed out that we had spent £1/2M which hadn't been provided for, because of the upsurge in discretionary ENPs which had come about as a result of the lead given at that meeting. . . . That brought home to me how uncontrollable the system was and how difficult the task of budgeting for it.

(Stowe 1990)

This anecdote shows how the operation of discretion could be shaped by 'guidance' from above, as well as the flexibility of contemporary cash limits. These existed, in the sense of annual budgetary estimates, but they could accommodate varying levels of demand.

The role of discretion in classifying claimants was analysed by Hill, a former NAB official. He described the way in which discretion, used in relation to ENPs, could respond to demands on social assistance as decisions were 'influenced by the officer's assessment of the amount of pressure that might be put upon him if he made a decision unfavourable to the applicant' (Hill 1969: 78). Hill showed the capacity of a discretionary system to incorporate new groups (in this case the increasing numbers of black claimants) within refined assessments of desserts. Intersecting NAB officials' judgements of claimants' worth was the extent to which they were viewed as being able to 'work the system', an approach supported by a growing view of benefits as rights. Because ENPs were by then largely being paid to applicants with children, for clothing, and because in the view of many officers these were less 'deserving' cases than pensioners, the scope for variation in discriminatory decision-making was even more marked. 'Need' remained a highly subjective and ideologically constructed concept: protesting claimants could be 'bought off' by defining them as having 'unmet needs'.

Protests might be made by lodging an appeal, in itself often enough to shift an official. 'More appeals were withdrawn than ever went to the appeal tribunal largely because an appeal would provoke the revision of a harsh or hasty decision' (Hill 1969: 84). Although pressure was growing to see benefits as rights, the Franks Committee (Franks 1957), set up to look at the operation of tribunals, exempted National Assistance Tribunals from conditions of fairness and openness laid down for other tribunals. This reflected a perception of NATs as maintaining a discretion-based casework approach, able to revise decisions in the light of pressure put upon them but otherwise confirming the classification of claimants made by NAB officials, and reflecting the reluctance of the state to apply even the rules of a liberal legal system to the operation of assistance. To do so would have required confronting the practice of discretion and the ideological role of assistance.

Boundary problems with other organizations were of less significance for the NAB, which was content to leave the task of supervision of 'problem families' to charities: 'the Board do not think that the provision of a general service of moral rehabilitation is within their powers or duties' (NAB 1950: 18). However, tensions arose later as charities came to be seen not just as complementary partners in the task of classification but as a way to relieve pressure on the state's resources. The demands of post-war reconstruction masked political tensions between central and local government to some extent; the fact that local authorities then ran training and reception centres for the NAB suggests that relationships may have been less strained than they were to become from the 1970s onwards.

The NAB was replaced in 1966 by the Supplementary Benefits Commission (SBC) in a context shaped by the 'rediscovery of poverty' (Townsend 1957; Cole and Utting 1962; Abel-Smith and Townsend 1965). This revealed the large numbers living on incomes below assistance levels and the failure of many to take up means-tested benefits because of feelings of stigma. Labour's response was an attempt to honour its manifesto promise of an 'income guarantee' while containing expenditure and maintaining labour discipline, and, through the retention of distinctions between insurance and assistance, the classification of the poor. 'Deserving' pensioners received long-term additions to benefit as of right, from which long-term unemployed were always to be excluded. The major task of the SBC was to manage the allocation of discretionary ENPs which, at the time, were still not regarded by the state as a serious political problem. The state thus assumed greater control of expenditure while leaving the potentially contentious process of classification outside the direct ambit of Parliamentary responsibility.

The history of the SBC, particularly the period under Donnison's chairmanship (1975–80), has been well analysed and for reasons of space it is not proposed to discuss it in detail (see Bull 1980; Donnison 1982; Walker 1983). By the late 1980s, it was in a state of economic and administrative crisis, a result of the growing use of discretionary one-off payments, itself caused by rising unemployment during the 1970s, allied to the inadequacy of the scale rates. Criticism of the role of discretion had crystallized into demands for a rights-based one-off payment and appeal system to counter increasingly obvious discrimination and prejudice while the DHSS was concerned to contain or even reduce expenditure. The overall inadequacies of social assistance pushed demands on to local authorities. Increasingly politicized welfare rights workers within local authority social services departments were, however, using the tribunal system to good effect on behalf of claimants. By 1973, half the decisions revised by tribunals concerned ENPs, a reflection of growing political struggle over definitions of 'exceptionality'. 'Welfare rights campaigns tend to expose the inevitable inconsistencies in discretionary decision-making... When individuals press for their rights [and] if people start pressing collectively, the whole discretionary system could collapse' (Hill 1972: 71). By 1976, when the supplementary benefit review was announced, this prediction had almost come true.

By the late 1970s, with continuing blurring of the boundary between 'exceptional' and 'essential' needs reflected in rising ENP expenditure (growing annually by about 20 per cent), the ability of the discretionary one-off payments scheme to classify the poor and maintain labour discipline was under considerable strain. Donnison attempted to resolve competing demands for cuts in expenditure on the one hand and increasing numbers of ENP applications on the other by offering a package of regular 'bonus' lump sum payments, overall cash limits but better treatment for the unemployed.

The crisis was resolved, albeit temporarily, by the election of a Conservative government in 1979.

Within the perspective developed in this chapter, the single payments (SP) system of 1980 appears as an aberration. The mistake arose from the belief of the 1979 government that in adopting the guise (if not the philosophy) of a rights-based system, based on entitlement to a significantly reduced number of items, expenditure could be contained. The government, in effect, attempted to define the range of items to which claimants would *not* be entitled. In fact, despite the exclusion of clothing grants, and other manipulations of eligibility (Allbeson and Smith 1984), SP expenditure soon rose rapidly. In part this again reflected wider processes in the economy, particularly the rapid rise in unemployment consequent upon the 'war on inflation'. However, the entitlements – though limited – offered a visible series of targets to welfare rights workers. By 1986, although the 1983 government had announced its intention to replace SPs by the social fund, it was sufficiently alarmed at rising expenditure to introduce further reductions in the scope of entitlement. Despite claims that this was justified by real rises in scale rates (a further shift in the exceptional/essential boundary), it was clear that the real intention was to cut spending. By 1988 SP expenditure had fallen to half its 1986 level.

The removal of clothing grants was one way in which the government attempted to move the boundary between 'exceptional' and 'essential' expenditure. The impact of this, however, was felt by local authorities and charities, whose limited resources were put under increasing pressure, which added to criticism of state policy towards the poorest (Raphael and Roll 1984). The state justified its financial attacks on the poor (manipulation of eligibility conditions, cutting real benefit levels and increasingly shifting the emphasis within social security from contributory to means-tested benefits and from state to private provision) initially in economic terms but later with a growing ideological gloss. Social security cuts were to 'reduce apathy and dependency on the benefits culture'. An emphasis on the detection of fraud and abuse (Robinson and Wainwright 1981) rather than on attempts to increase take-up (Bradshaw 1985) also reflected the stress on ideological justifications for cuts.

The government appeared, by accepting the idea of entitlement, to give the classification of the poor a subsidiary role in favour of containing spending. It seems, however, that discretion had not been eliminated from one-off payments, merely driven underground. Berthoud (1984) noted that in the interpretation of regulations, staff asked claimants for different kinds of information and this had a significant impact on outcomes; Cooper (1985) observed the racist attitudes which informed many decisions towards black claimants' applications for help; and Howe (1985) reported that a managerial regime concerned with containing demand made extensive use of classification to deny help to 'undeserving' claimants. Berthoud also observed that the impact of various rationing devices, including hostile press coverage towards 'scroungers', feelings of stigma and the complexity of the system, resulted in significant under-claiming of SPs. Despite this DHSS-sponsored research finding, the government later suggested that rising SP spending was a clear example of 'abusive' claiming.

Because of the effectiveness of the poverty lobby (notwithstanding the impenetrability of the regulations) disputes continued over what was appropriate for SP expenditure and what was not, i.e. what should be met from weekly scale rates. The likelihood of claimants having a working knowledge of the SP regulations was so remote that 'they were very likely to fail to meet one of the conditions which would entitle them to advance a claim' (Andrews and Jacobs 1990: 202). This disadvantage was countered, to some degree, by the ability of advocates to fit claimants within the narrowing range of entitlements, often in bizarre circumstances. Struggles over the boundaries of 'exceptionality' continued after the 1986 regulations were introduced. These regulations had a wider significance. They 'selected a minority able to gain additional payments from the large mass of previously eligible claimants. This prefigures the social fund selection of a few claimants to be allowed community care grants neglecting the real needs of others' (Cohen and Davies 1988: 6). Because of the complex regulated nature of the scheme, appeals, though continuing to be a means by which some claimants might make limited gains in their social wage, had effectively pushed their needs to one side. The use of regulations binding on tribunals, however, acted to re-incorporate the appeal mechanism more fully within the ideology of assistance as a whole.

The Social Fund as a success story?

As noted, the SF was perceived as a significant departure from previous one-off payments schemes. However, I would argue, despite some apparent contradictions, that the fund continues the historic tasks of social assistance, of maintaining labour discipline and classifying the poor. Given the mass of research findings relating to the fund (e.g. Becker and Silburn 1990; Craig 1990; NACAB 1990; NAO 1991; SSRC 1991) I do not intend to review the performance of the fund in general here. I shall, however, demonstrate, through a discussion of the four features referred to above, the way in which the fund maintains the role that one-off payments have played since 1934.

First, the restoration of *discretionary* decision-making in the fund was a tacit admission by the government that its apparent abandonment in 1980 was a mistake, although this was obscured by claims of widespread abuse of SPs by social workers and claimants. Advantages claimed by the government for discretion, particularly that of 'flexibility', have now been discredited. Flexibility is associated, for individual claimants, with unpredictability and, for the fund as a whole, with the ability of the government to move the political goalposts, for example by defining cash limits as fixed or not in the light of changing pressure upon the fund. Given tight budgets, local officer discretion (more closely monitored by managers, through the microcomputer system, than ever before) is now a highly explicit tool for classifying claimants. This occurs (a) through the process of defining priority lists where, despite ministerial statements to the contrary, whole groups of claimants (such as sixteen and seventeen year olds) are effectively labelled as 'undeserving' and (b) by according separate roles to grants and loans (disguised under the rubrics of 'community care' and 'general budgetary help'), as Cohen and Davies (1988) predicted. Many 'deserving' claimants (notably the elderly and disabled) are refused loans and offered grants instead; unemployed applicants are rarely offered grants and, in many cases, are offered nothing (SSRC 1991). The facility to refuse help to certain claimants on the basis that they are too indebted takes this process of classification one step further: these claimants are effectively regarded as being economically and politically marginal.

Second, one contradiction that the state has had to manage in relation to one-off payments has been that low scale rates create extra demands on one-off payments for a range of 'essential' items, which are then met 'exceptionally'. This effect is particularly magnified during periods of high unemployment when benefit levels are under attack. In 1988, with the state enjoying an unprecedented level of power, at least within a recent historical context, the government experienced little political difficulty in shifting back this boundary, supporting its policies with a representation of the poor owing much to pre-Victorian imagery. 'Tis the men that won't work, not the men that can get no work, which makes the number of our poor' (Defoe 1704: 27). Demand is now contained both by limiting eligibility conditions (e.g. by having to be on IS for six months, limiting the scope of repeat applications, narrow interpretations of the meaning of community care and inflexible interpretations of the scope of goods and services for which awards may be made) and, most effectively, by the imposition of tight cash limits with the implicit requirement to prove 'deservingness'. Alongside cuts in spending represented by the failure of the scale rates adequately to compensate for poll/council tax and water rates (Craig and Glendinning 1990), the emphasis on repayable loans in the SF has moved the boundary between *exceptional* and *essential* expenditure to an unprecedented degree. The differences between the fund and previous schemes are that the cash limits, and the emphasis on loans, have enabled it to accommodate pressure without leading to large increases in spending (refusal rates simply rise), but also that the government has been able to disregard political criticism generated as a result. Most of those applying to the fund ('deserving' grants recipients aside) are now presented as the very few, the poorest, who have failed to conform to the dominant 'moral' imperative of managing household expenditure adequately, a view tacitly shared by many claimants, among whom the SF is deeply unpopular (Dean and Taylor-Gooby 1991).

Third, the scope of exceptional payments has been narrowed so much that further demand has spilled across *boundaries* into the local government and charitable arenas. Although the impact of this is smaller than initially feared, there is clear evidence that much unmet need is being driven underground, into individualized and private 'solutions' – loan sharks, help from family/friends, 'doing without'. Local government and charities have had neither the resources nor (at least in the latter case) the inclination to undermine the ideological role of social assistance by significantly subsidizing the benefits of the poorest and challenging their 'less eligible' status. In a period when the numbers of unemployed have rarely been below two million (even on the government's deflated counts), the state has been able to ensure, through spending limits and by political controls on local government, that threats to labour discipline can be contained. The bridging of the gap between wages and benefits for the unemployed implicit in the widespread use of one-off payments (as was close to happening in the late 1970s) has also been circumscribed. Local government may now offer alternative explanations for the growth of poverty and strategies for combating it (Balloch and Jones 1990) but it has become increasingly powerless to act. The state has not, therefore, had significantly to adjust the one-off payment scheme in order to absorb political protest. Despite increasing demand on the fund, and growing refusal rates, the government has maintained tight cash limits and the legal framework of the fund has, to date, accommodated challenges effectively.

The final illustrative feature of one-off payments schemes has been the mechanism of the *appeal* tribunal. In the turbulent 1930s, the state judged it necessary to use tribunals as a means of incorporating political dissent. In the changed economic and political circumstances of the 1980s, the need for this form of political incorporation diminished: the abolition of the right to appeal is a reflection of this political reality. Appeals were replaced by internal reviews, which merely serve to re-emphasize the role that discretion has within the scheme.

That the 1974 Labour government chose not to take up the option of abolishing appeals (a suggestion put to it by the DHSS) is of less political significance than that the option should have been raised at all. It was mooted as a possibility because the increasingly successful use of tribunals by ENP claimants of all kinds threatened to undermine the role of tribunals in confirming the classificatory function of social assistance. In 1978 the state judged that the time was not right to pursue the option of abolition without considerable political struggle, a judgement followed by the 1979 Conservative government. By 1985, the government had no such qualms: the abolition of appeals within the SF was a statement that political challenge from labour could be disregarded. Ironically, but appropriately, the only effective liberal protest at this move came from the House of Lords (a reflection of the influence of the poverty lobby), resulting in the establishment of a second-tier review body, the Social Fund Inspectorate. However, claimants using the review structure are not free to step outside the legal, financial and ideological framework of the fund: reviewing inspectors cannot challenge the basis on which SFOs determine priorities. Reviews thus mirror the function of the SF just as appeals formerly mirrored the function of one-off payments and social assistance as a whole. Because expenditure generated by reviews is set against local office budgets, reviews cannot offer even limited financial gains for the claimant against the state. Success for a claimant is now not a gain in the struggle for a better social wage, but failure for another claimant to make a similar gain. The review system thus contributes directly to the process of political division among the working class. The role of discretion, reflected in the review process, is more clearly to do with the task of classification and less to do with adjusting the one-off payment scheme to accommodate political pressure put upon it.

The fund thus appears, despite wide-ranging political criticism, as a more successful example of the state's attempts at 'managing the poorest', one that has clearly learnt from the mistakes of the past. Given the relative weakness of political opposition, a result of high unemployment levels, hostile trade union legislation and disarray in the Labour Party, the 1983 government was able to introduce a scheme that fitted well with its general policy emphases on social division, 'family responsibility' (i.e. cutting expenditure), 'individual enterprise' and a generally diminished role for the state in the provision of social services. The 1987 government contributed an explicit ideological overlay to these perspectives.

The reversion to local officer discretion, and the division of responsibility between the DSS (which retains strategic and overall financial responsibility for benefits policy) and the Benefits Agency (which delivers the benefits), strikingly similar to the division of 1934, refocuses opposition away from ministers and towards the practice of non-accountable administrators or individual SFOs. At the same time, the potential for SFOs to exercise that discretion generously (highlighted in the summer of 1990 when maverick offices almost ran out of money) is severely constrained by tight management. The review process is no longer a means for generating increased expenditure and offers small scope for challenging the fund's ideology.

Just as the state continues to place the needs of capitalist economic organization before the social and economic well-being of individuals, so social assistance will continue to be one means by which it controls the potential political challenge posed by the poorest, and at minimal economic cost. The retention of a one-off payments scheme at all in 1988 in the form of the social fund, despite the parliamentary superiority of the Conservatives, was a recognition by the state of the continuing need for political safety valves within the ambit of assistance, although in the fund the scope of that safety valve has been more limited than hitherto. Ironically, the degree of attention given to the fund has deflected interest away from the fundamental issue of the level of the scale rates. In this sense, the one-off payment scheme has proved yet again to be an effective smokescreen for the wider failings of social assistance. Both Labour and Conservative Parties have committed themselves to maintaining a one-off payments scheme in future social assistance schemes. Either may, albeit to differing degrees, soften the more punitive aspects of the fund in order to diffuse the explicit ideological emphasis of the 1987 government. Whether the poverty lobby can exploit a backlash to the most outrageous aspects of the fund remains an open question. Whichever party is in government, the ideological, political and economic usefulness of one-off payments in managing the poorest cannot fail to have been impressed on them.

Acknowledgements

Thanks are due to Hartley Dean, Alan Deacon and Roy Sainsbury for helpful comments on an earlier draft of this chapter.

References

Abel-Smith, B. and Townsend, P. (1965) *The Poor and the Poorest*, London: Bell and Hyman.
Adler, M. and Asquith, S. (1981) *The Politics of Discretion*, London: Heinemann.

Allbeson, J. and Smith, R. (1984) *We Don't Give Clothing Grants Any More*, Poverty Pamphlet no. 62, London: CPAG.
Andrews, K. and Jacobs, J. (1990) *Punishing the Poor*, London: Macmillan.
Balloch, S. and Jones, B. (1990) *Poverty and Anti-Poverty Strategy*, London: Association of Metropolitan Authorities.
Becker, S. and Silburn, R. (1990) *The New Poor Clients*, Nottingham: Nottingham University/Community Care.
Berthoud, R. (1984) *The Reform of Supplementary Benefit*, London: Policy Studies Institute.
Beveridge, W. H. (1942) *Social Insurance and Allied Services*, Cmd 6404, London: HMSO.
Beveridge, W. H. (1952) *Power and Influence*, London: Hodder and Stoughton.
Bradshaw, J. R. (1985) 'Tried and found wanting', in S. Ward (ed.) *DHSS in Crisis*, Poverty Pamphlet no. 66, London: CPAG.
Branson, N. (1979) *Poplarism, 1919–25*, London: Lawrence and Wishart.
Bull, D. (1980) 'Open government and the review of supplementary benefit', in M. Brown and S. Baldwin (eds) *Yearbook of Social Policy, 1978*, London: Routledge and Kegan Paul.
Cohen, R. and Davies, C. (1988) 'The background', in R. Cohen and M. Tarpey (eds) *Single Payments – the Disappearing Safety Net*, Poverty Pamphlet no. 74, London: CPAG.
Cole, D. and Utting, J. (1962) *The Economic Circumstances of Old People*, London: Codicote.
Cooper, S. (1985) *Observations in Supplementary Benefit Offices*, London: Policy Studies Institute.
Craig, G. (1990) 'Watching the Fund', in N. Manning and C. Ungerson (eds) *Social Policy Review, 1989–90*, Harlow: Longman.
Craig, G. (1991) *Fit for Nothing?* London: Children's Society.
Craig, G. and Glendinning, C. (1990) 'Parenting in poverty', *Community Care* 15 March: 24–7.
Deacon, A. (1985) *Assistance and Welfare: the Experience of the '40s*, Mimeo, University of York.
Deacon, A. and Bradshaw, J. R. (1983) *Reserved for the Poor*, Oxford: Basil Blackwell and Martin Robertson.
Dean, H. (1991) *Social Security and Social Control*, London: Routledge.
Dean, H. and Taylor-Gooby, P. (1991) *Dependency Culture: the Explosion of a Myth*, Brighton: Harvester Wheatsheaf.
Defoe, D. (1704) *Giving Alms no Charity and Employing the Poor a Grievance to the Nation*, Booksellers of London and West (Reprinted by S. R. Publishers, Yorkshire, 1975).
Donnison, D. (1982) *The Politics of Poverty*, Oxford: Martin Robertson.
Franks, O. (1957) *Report of the Committee on Administrative Tribunals and Enquiries*, Cmnd 218, London: HMSO.
Golding, P. and Middleton, S. (1982) *Images of Welfare*, Oxford: Basil Blackwell and Martin Robertson.
Gordon, P. and Newnham, A. (1985) *Passport to Benefits*, Poverty Pamphlet no. 67, London: CPAG.
Harris, J. (1975) 'Social planning in war-time: some aspects of the Beveridge Report', in J. Winter (ed.) *War and Economic Development*, Cambridge: Cambridge University Press.
Hill, M. (1969) 'The exercise of discretion in the National Assistance Board', *Public Administration* Spring: 75–90.
Hill, M. (1972) *The Sociology of Public Administration*, London: Weidenfeld and Nicolson.

Hill, M. (1990) *Social Security Policy in Britain*, Aldershot: Edward Elgar.
HMSO (1985) *Reform of Social Security: Programme for Change*, Cmnds 9517–19, London: HMSO.
Howe, L.E.A. (1985) 'The "deserving" and the "undeserving": practice in an urban local social security office', *Journal of Social Policy* 14, 1: 49–72.
Jordan, B. (1985) 'Sorry – no cash for you', *Social Work Today* 29 July: 15–17.
Meacher, M. (1985) *The Proposed Social Fund*, Birmingham: British Association of Social Workers.
NAB (1950) *Annual Report of the National Assistance Board 1949*, Cmd 8030, London: HMSO.
NACAB (1990) *Hard Times for Social Fund Applicants*, London: NACAB.
NACAB (1991) *Barriers to Benefit*, London: NACAB.
NAO (1991) *The Social Fund*, London: National Audit Office.
Novak, T. (1978) 'Poverty and the state', unpublished PhD thesis, University of Durham.
Raphael, T. and Roll, J. (1984) *Carrying the Can*, Poverty Pamphlet no. 63, London: CPAG/Family Welfare Association.
Robinson, A. and Wainwright, S. (1981) 'Specialist claims control: a local experience', *Poverty* 49: 8–14.
SBC (1977) *Annual Report of the Supplementary Benefits Commission, 1976*, Cmnd 6910, London: HMSO.
SSRC (1991) *Cash Limited – Limited Cash*, London: Association of Metropolitan Authorities/SSRC.
Stowe, K. (1990) Interview with Author, London, 13 November.
Townsend, J. (1786) 'A dissertation on the poor laws', quoted in J. R. Poynter (1969) *Society and Pauperism*, London: Routledge.
Townsend, P. (1957) *The Family Life of Old People*, London: Routledge and Kegan Paul.
Townsend, P. (1979) *Poverty in the United Kingdom*, Harmondsworth: Penguin.
Walker, C. (1983) *Changing Social Policy*, London: Bedford Square Press.
Webb, A. (1975) 'The abolition of National Assistance', in P. Hall *et al.* (eds) *Change, Choice and Conflict in Social Policy*, London: Heinemann.

7
Housing issues in social work

Gill Stewart and John Stewart

Among all areas of social policy, it was housing that bore the main brunt of Thatcherism during the 1980s. Public expenditure on rented housing was cut by 75 per cent within the first four years, and new building declined correspondingly – down to only 13,000 completions for the whole of England in 1990. A policy that regarded council housing as a social problem, and aimed ultimately to abolish it by privatization, reduced the public sector from 25 per cent of all dwellings at the beginning of the decade to 21 per cent at the end; meanwhile tax subsidies to owner occupation escalated. Against this background, officially recorded homelessness nearly tripled to include 145,800 households, mainly families, by 1990 (all figures are from various Department of the Environment statistical sources).

Decent housing is something which we all need, but there are political and structural determinants of its availability to those whose need is greatest. An issue of the *Social Work and Social Welfare Yearbook* included a critique of the 'Thatcher revolution' in housing policy by Peter Malpass (1990). In this chapter we concentrate specifically on housing issues that recur in *social work* policy and practice, because restricted housing opportunity is one of the main constraints in clients' experience and consequently on social workers', including probation officers', ability to help.

In a society where housing is regarded as property and even 'social' rented housing has been 'commodified' as appropriate for sale, the main issues around what remains of a public sector housing policy can be summarized as follows. There is no right to housing, even though it is a basic essential. Dwelling ownership is treated as a capital asset and the national housing stock is conventionally divided into public, voluntary, owner-occupied and private rented sectors, according to who owns it. Of course there are specific rights to do with housing but these apply to selected groups of people in particular circumstances, which often reinforce rather than remedy inequalities. So, for example, existing council tenants have the right to buy their home – but not to rent it in the first place.

In the absence of a general right, the concept of housing need has become ever more selectively applied to 'special' groups, to the extent that a 'special needs' approach has become the norm, reflecting priorities in resource allocation from central government, and consideration of general housing needs is a luxury of the past. In many inner-city authorities, the usual way into a council tenancy is through the statutory homelessness process. The resulting housing problems that are presented to helping agencies can be understood in terms of quantity, quality and access: there is an insufficient supply of housing in adequate condition, and rationing processes often discriminate against those who are already most disadvantaged.

While that is a summary of the housing situation that welfare state workers can observe around them, social workers and probation officers are professionally concerned with clients' housing problems only in so far as these affect their primary social work activity. Turning now to social work policy, we can see the priorities for the 1990s prescribed in new legislation as 'child protection', 'punishment in the community' and 'community care'. Together, those policy directions affect work with all the main client groups of social work agencies. Taking each area in turn, for the rest of this chapter we shall consider the housing issues that commonly arise in practice and the extent to which they are confronted in policy.

Child protection

Procedures to protect children from harm by their parents are the main focus of the Children Act 1989 and by comparison preventive social work aimed at family support receives less attention and fewer resources. In this respect the new legislation both reflects and perpetuates the tensions that had developed over preceding decades between policy and practice in child care (highlighted by Hardiker *et al.* 1991). While children may be victims of abuse by adults, their parents are often subject to environmental pressures and at the mercy of housing policies whose effect can be to undermine the self-reliance that they purport to uphold. The possibilities in social work with families are substantially limited by the environment in which they live; we shall examine the nature of these limitations in work on 'difficult estates' and with homeless families in temporary accommodation.

'Difficult estates' is a shorthand term for council estates that are difficult to let from the housing department's point of view and difficult to live in for tenants. Residualization of the public sector through the policy of sales and reduced expenditure on repairs has left the remaining mass housing estates in a worsening condition and given few prospective tenants any choice in allocation. 'Difficult' is a less perjorative alternative to the old description 'problem estates', which were traditionally thought to be inhabited by 'problem families': those who would now be labelled, equally unsatisfactorily, as an 'underclass'. Every town and city has at least one such estate, where no one wants to live and social workers and probation officers are regular visitors.

Child care referrals, in particular, tend to be concentrated in the worst housing: this was a finding of research in SSDs during the 1980s. They are likely to be 'volunteers', rather than 'victims' or 'villains', by Packman et al.'s (1986) classification; but another study found that those parents of children whom social workers regarded as being seriously 'at risk' tended to be more dissatisfied with their housing than other families referred from the same neighbourhood (Gibbons et al. 1990).

Trying to establish linkages between housing conditions, or any other manifestations of poverty, and child abuse is a problematic business, fraught with empirical and ideological pitfalls, some of which are discussed by Parton in Violence Against Children Study Group (1990). Obviously most parents who are badly housed do not harm their children; but equally, the constraints imposed by housing conditions, and the structural context of housing deprivation, form the backdrop to so much child protection work that they cannot be discounted. Certain factors recur in research reports: sleep loss and intolerance of babies crying in crowded buildings with poor sound insulation was highlighted by Thoburn (1980). Difficulties in disciplining children and harsh restraint of unsafe play were associated with overcrowded housing and lack of private space by Wilson and Herbert (1978); the researchers and parents alike attributed unsatisfactory child-rearing practices to the environmental constraints under which the families were living. Similarly, Home Office researchers linked early onset of delinquency with parents' inability to supervise play in and near crowded homes without neighbourhood facilities (Riley and Shaw 1985).

The connections are evident between housing circumstances and difficulties in bringing up children, but any search for causal relationships with abuse is misguided because it would isolate one factor, albeit an important one, in a family's experience at the expense of ignoring others of possibly greater importance. The oppressive influence of patriarchy on family relationships is one such overriding factor; another is the great expectations that are made of parents' ability to cope under almost any material adversity. The concept of 'reasonable parenting', which permeates the Children Act 1989, seems to set a variable standard of care, adjustable according to the family's living conditions. Objection could be sustained on grounds of social justice because the existence of acceptable levels of deprivation appears to be taken for granted, but one might at least expect that allowances would consequently be made. The Department of Health's guide to assessment acknowledges that 'poor housing can place considerable strains on families', but then stresses that nevertheless 'parents have a responsibility to provide adequate shelter . . . for their children', despite any 'environmental factors beyond their control', which they are evidently expected to overcome (Social Services Inspectorate 1988: 63). The conclusion must be that poor and badly housed parents have to try harder.

Housing problems are a recurrent theme running through most (perhaps all) of the child abuse inquiry reports about deaths that have occurred during the

1980s and early 1990s; however, this is nowhere acknowledged and, as a DoH-commissioned review of reports recognizes, 'the effects of environmental disadvantage are not generally analysed' (Noyes 1991: 109). In fact the details in some of these reports read like the Department of the Environment's catalogue of the nationally most 'difficult-to-let' estates: the Ferrier Estate in Greenwich, Aylesbury Estate in Southwark, Sholver Estate in the Pennines outside Oldham.

The report on the death of Doreen Mason gave a profile of the 2,000 flatted Aylesbury Estate, where 'normal conditions included high unemployment, high density population, poor housing conditions, a high and rising crime rate, drug abuse, poor take-up of health services, a high level of single parenthood, and high levels of child abuse. Primary prevention . . . was difficult to achieve' (Southwark Area Review Committee 1989). The Ferrier Estate, where Kimberley Carlile died, was described in similar terms and the Commission of Inquiry commented 'we heard hardly a good word about the place', where 7,000 people lived in 1,900 homes. 'We were told that "those who can, move off the Estate" and that "the overwhelming majority of people who live on the Estate would rather live somewhere else".' However, 'many worse estates are to be found across the country, so that the "survivors" in Ferrier are not even awarded the kudos that goes with bringing up a family successfully in, say, the East End of London' (Blom Cooper 1987).

Greenwich Council was credited with 'many attempts . . . to make the Ferrier Estate a decent place in which to live', whereas the housing policies of Wandsworth Council were specifically said to have contributed to the death of Stephanie Fox. Privatization of more desirable estates in the borough had left the council with only 28,000 tenancies, mainly contained in 180 high rise blocks, and responsibility for housing 1,000 homeless families a year. This meant that families with young children were necessarily being allocated flats high above the ground – on the nineteenth floor in the Fox case, despite social work attempts to get a 'more appropriate' offer. The panel commented:

> We were surprised that such a young and vulnerable family were housed so high. . . . Apart from all other considerations, it was not possible to get a triple buggy into the lift. . . . The diminishing housing stock has clearly affected Council housing policy and we believe that the increased pressure on the family created by such accommodation played its part in increasing the risk to Stephanie.
> (Wandsworth Area Child Protection Committee 1990)

Both the Fox and Carlile families had recently moved to difficult estates after spending extended periods in temporary accommodation. Families who become homeless are commonly put through a process that is partly dictated by the shortage of housing supply but is also intended as a deterrent. If they pass the various tests administered by housing officers, investigating 'priority need', 'intentionality' and 'local connection', the family face a prolonged stay in a bed and breakfast hotel or a crowded hostel awaiting their one offer of a permanent tenancy, which is likely to be on a difficult estate. The homelessness process can be quite destructive, as a senior social worker explained in an interview:

> Once a housing department gets its hands on a family and puts it into temporary accommodation, that family is immediately put into a system which is essentially disruptive to family life. So if you've got a functioning family who does just need a roof over its head, they spend six months in the system and come out of that system at the end of it as a non-functioning, non-viable family unit, to use jargon.

Homelessness legislation requires social services co-operation with housing to prevent homelessness, but different interpretations of prevention tend to produce conflict rather than collaboration between the two groups of practitioners. Social workers' idea of prevention means trying to get families accepted as statutorily homeless so that they remain safely together and do not become literally roofless, without anywhere to stay. Housing workers see prevention in terms of minimizing the number of successful applications. This can amount to denial and using all manner of delaying tactics in the hope that applicants will 'disappear', as Department of the Environment researchers found (Niner 1989).

Social workers' involvement with homeless families is largely concentrated during their stay in temporary accommodation, where there has been much concern about the possibility of child abuse. In fact there appears to be more professional anxiety than actual risk of serious abuse in temporary accommodation, where absence of men and being overheard are probably the main reasons for the relative lack of violence. Commenting that 'The incidence of child abuse occurring while families are in temporary accommodation is negligible, despite the stress which parents are under', a social work team leader explained: 'A more common problem is child neglect. The hotel staff, health visitor and other residents are concerned about parents who do not feed their children, leave them in wet and soiled clothes, do not supervise them adequately and leave them alone for hours.' (The quotations are from original research that is described more fully in Stewart and Stewart (1992).)

Although there has been no child abuse fatality resulting in an inquiry report while a family was actually living in temporary accommodation, at least six deaths in recent years have been the children of formerly homeless families. Tyra Henry's mother was considered to be 'intentionally' homeless, having abandoned a flat and returned to her mother's overcrowded home. Stephanie Fox's parents were placed in a residential family centre before being rehoused under homelessness procedures. The mothers of Sukina Hammond and Liam Johnson took refuge in temporary accommodation from their partners' violence but returned because there seemed to be no alternative. The mothers of Kimberley Carlile and Doreen Mason met and moved in with violent partners while they were homeless (Sedley 1987; Blom Cooper 1987; Avon Social Services Department 1989; Islington Social Services Department 1989; Southwark Area Review Committee 1989; Wandsworth Area Child Protection Committee 1990). It seems that homeless women and their children are especially vulnerable to violent men, and that the destructive experience of homelessness can leave its mark on families long after they have been rehoused.

Punishment in the community

The direction of criminal justice policy for the 1990s is towards 'punishment in the community' as the alternative to custody for all but the most serious young offenders, and the probation service is to be responsible (discussed by Allan 1990). The close supervision that it is intended that probation officers will exercise over offenders (who are not to be called clients) requires that they take an interest in housing because it would be difficult to maintain surveillance over someone who is homeless (acknowledged by the Home Office 1988: para. 3.18). In practice probation officers have, for a long time, been generally more responsive to their clients' housing problems than have local authority social workers. But they are not altogether supported in this good practice by area management, which is likely to be led by Home Office policy.

Homelessness has been traditionally associated with voluntary after-care and as such was marginalized from the mainstream of probation work. 'NFA', meaning a person of no fixed abode, represents a powerful negative stereotype for probation officers (as Rojek *et al.* 1988 argue). Home Office research (e.g. by Fairhead 1981) confirmed that homelessness was commonplace among those older single men who were likely to become voluntary after-care clients after serving short prison sentences, but the characterization of this group as 'persistent petty offenders' did nothing to encourage positive attitudes towards working with them. Instead, any attempt at resettling 'NFAs' was commonly left to unqualified and lower paid ancillary workers, whose failure would serve to reinforce the stereotype of an unhelpable client group (as in a project researched by Corden and Clifton 1985).

In the mid-1980s there were signs of a wider awareness within the probation service of the varied nature of clients' housing problems, including a willingness to think in terms of housing as applicable to everyone, rather than 'accommodation', which was something different, provided only for clients. The National Association of Probation Officers (NAPO) issued a resource pack on probation and housing to its members. Nearly all the after-care units changed their names to, for example, probation housing units and broadened their clientele accordingly. The Home Office instructed areas to develop area accommodation strategies that would cater for a range of local needs. Practitioners in many areas became involved in community development initiatives on local difficult housing estates and were encouraged in this by the Home Office's *Statement of National Objectives and Priorities* (Home Office 1984: para. 3; Henderson 1986; Hope and Shaw 1988).

That new enlightenment may have been short-lived. Area accommodation strategies were duly submitted to the Home Office but nothing further was heard on the subject. The White and Green Papers that set the agenda for the 1990s envisaged that the resettlement aspects of after-care and anything to do with housing would be removed from probation officers' sphere of work and contracted out to the voluntary and private sectors, on the grounds that:

'Arranging for, and actually providing, accommodation for offenders are both functions which require expertise distinct from professional probation skills.' This policy change was supported by political arguments, familiar from social services community care policy, that promote the 'independent' sector for its own sake and in pursuit of that elusive goal, 'value for money', which is assumed to be attainable only through 'the disciplines of the market' (Home Office 1990: paras 9.13, 10.5, 10.9, 10.16).

It was also accompanied by rhetoric presenting 'offending behaviour' as a matter of personal choice, where material disadvantage is not recognized as a relevant constraint: offenders were described as, 'wayward, muddled and destructive' (Home Office 1990: para. 9.15). The Home Affairs minister said 'people commit crime because they are bad' (Patten 1988). Meanwhile the application of similar attitudes to social security policies, resulting in widespread benefit cuts for clients, prompted one probation housing team to question whether resettling homeless offenders was any longer feasible (Nottingham Probation Housing Team 1989).

Most probation clients under statutory supervision are young, as annual statistics from the Home Office show: over a third come into the narrow 'young offenders' age bracket of seventeen to twenty years. This makes social policies that affect young people leaving home especially relevant to probation work. Among the entire population, single young people are the group least likely to qualify for council housing; in fact they tend to be bottom of every agency's priorities, as we have argued elsewhere (Stewart and Stewart 1988). Those under twenty-five years comprise more than a third of the registered unemployed and a series of policies during the latter half of the 1980s contrived to make the position of young people generally much worse.

First they were subject to special regulations that required them to move on from lodgings after a short period or take a drastic cut in benefit. Then the abolition of board and lodging regulations closed that housing option altogether. People under twenty-one years were removed from the protection of Wages Councils on the grounds that they had priced themselves out of work. People under twenty-five years were allowed an age-related benefit rate 22 per cent below that of their elders because, it was argued, they were not fully independent and should be living with their parents. Then people under eighteen years were disqualified from benefit altogether as the only permitted alternative to going on the Youth Training Scheme, thereby fulfilling a Conservative Party election manifesto pledge that youth unemployment would become 'a thing of the past'.

All these measures have severely undermined young people's ability to become self-reliant. While temporary exemption from benefit disqualification is possible on grounds of 'severe hardship', usually requiring validation by a probation officer or another authority figure, the money allowed (£15 a week for under eighteens) is insufficient to pay for even the lowest standard accommodation. Survey evidence indicates that probation clients are much more likely than those of other agencies to be without independent housing and therefore dependent on formally provided services or informal support from relatives (Stewart and Stewart 1991: 17–18). Another finding, which may help to explain this situation, is that half have spent at least part of their childhood in care, and so cannot necessarily rely on the family back-up which most young people leaving home would expect (evidence cited in Stewart and Stewart 1989: para. 5.22). It appears that for young offenders, problems with access to housing and lack of money are closely interrelated and both are commonly associated with conflict in the family or release from custody.

The position of homeless youth has been publicized in recent years by organizations that are primarily concerned with young people leaving care. The big national children's charities, such as Barnardo's, being in search of an issue after running down their residential provision, were able to attract publicity and the attention of ministers in an area where others had failed. Partly in response to this pressure, the Children Act 1989 puts an obligation on social services departments to accommodate care leavers and young people who are otherwise at risk; but up to the time of implementation no detailed guidance has been issued, nor firm plans announced, to clarify whether new services will actually become available. A duty in the Act for housing departments to co-operate with social services is qualified by what has been called a 'designer loophole', applying only if it 'does not unduly prejudice the discharge of any of their functions' (S.27).

Community care

The status and enforceability of housing department duties continues as an issue when we turn to policies for community care. The importance of adequate housing has frequently been stressed in policy documents, for example in the White Paper that preceded the NHS and Community Care Act 1990. 'The Government believes that housing is a vital component of community care and it is often the key to independent living' (Department of Health 1989: para. 3.5.1). However, the Act and its voluminous accompanying guidance convey mixed messages about practical implementation.

Social services departments must consult housing departments (and housing associations) when making their community care plans, with the objective of providing a 'seamless service for users'. But both departments are told to 'determine their objectives and priorities within the resources available' and warned that 'care management systems will have to operate in the context of these decisions' (Department of Health 1990: paras 1.2, 3.6). Separate draft guidance to housing authorities makes it clear that they will receive no extra funding and that they are not, in practice, expected to do anything more. 'There is no change in longstanding policy . . . the impact should be gradual. These developments in community care policy do not fundamentally alter the role of local housing authorities, or the priorities to be observed in catering for their various types of clients' (Department of the Environment 1991: para. 4).

The confusion continues in sections of the guidance that are addressed to practitioners, rather than planners. They are informed that: 'Care management is based on a needs-led approach [to] assessment of the user's circumstances in the round', which appears to be positive support for good practice, although it is recognized that 'assessment does not take place in a vacuum', but tends to reflect the availability of services. There is a requirement to 'bring apparent housing ... needs to the attention of the appropriate authority and invite them to assist in the assessment', but no consequent duty to provide housing or even, apparently, to respond at all in individual cases. Unmet needs have to be fed back into the planning process, where they can compete in the setting of future priorities (Department of Health 1990: 23–9).

Past experience of collaboration between housing and social services over what could be described as community care has varied according to the tier of government and other characteristics of the authorities concerned, and especially with the client group. For older people and others with physical disabilities, it was usually a matter of improving or adapting existing housing in order to keep the person living independently in his or her own home and to accommodate any carer – in support of the government's policy for 'care *by* the community.' Negotiations were generally concerned with the allocation of sheltered housing if care needs could be met only through a move. A survey of ten local authorities in the early 1980s suggested that co-operation in this area was reasonably good, although dependent on local goodwill in the absence of standardized procedures (Hearnden 1984).

The picture is different when we consider the position of people with learning difficulties and particularly those who have been diagnosed as mentally ill. At issue is the provision of 'care *in* the community', in the form of housing and support services, for people leaving mental hospitals; the needs of the majority who are already outside institutions have scarcely been considered. Department of Health statistics showed a 28 per cent decline in both in-patient populations over a decade, and that two and a quarter times more alternative residential places were provided for former mental handicap hospital patients, although the number of psychiatric hospital beds closed was nearly double. People who have been hospitalized for mental illness are unlikely to receive continuing 'care in the community' and it seems that in most cases no one knows what happens to them (as shown in local surveys, e.g. Kay and Legg 1986).

Research into the attitudes and practices of housing workers identifies 'care in the community' as a recurring area of conflict with social workers. The Audit Commission (1989: para. 84) reported that: 'Every housing department visited had experienced difficulties over referrals from social services and health authorities, particularly over the discharge of ex-psychiatric patients under care in the community policies.' Such applicants were often considered to be '"unrehouseable" – that is, unable to sustain an orthodox council tenancy without guaranteed social work support. . . . Because they have a duty to help the most vulnerable [housing staff] are being forced into an area where their skills and resources are inappropriate' (Niner 1989: 78).

One solution would be for homeless persons units to reject applications from the 'vulnerable' groups: thus Department of the Environment statistics show that only 3 per cent of acceptances for rehousing during 1990 were on grounds of mental illness. Another common reaction is to expect social workers to undertake assessments in 'problematic' areas, which half of all housing authorities did 'as a matter of course in the case of mental illness or handicap', leaving their staff feeling 'generally relieved' (Evans and Duncan 1988: 29; Niner 1989: 32). Perhaps in recognition of these attitudes, and as a trade-off inviting housing departments to co-operate under the new legislation, the Department of Health guidance advises social services departments that they, 'should recognise that the assessment process they originate may be used by other agencies to assist them in fulfilling their statutory responsibilities, for example by local housing authorities in assessing homelessness applications' (Department of Health 1990: para. 3.3).

There is no indication of whether SSDs can charge housing departments for this service, but the emphasis throughout the 1990 Act is on local authorities as purchasers rather than providers of community care. They have an obligation to promote the 'independent' sector, comprising private and voluntary organizations. The relevant national charities are ambivalent about the future prospects for local authority housing while keen to promote their own role (Wertheimer 1988, 1989). Central government subsidies for 'special needs' housing provided by voluntary housing associations has already increased the possibilities for some of the people discharged from mental hospitals, but as the House of Commons Social Services Committee (1985: para. 136) said, 'investing in special schemes is no substitute for adequate general housing policies' (supported by Clapham and Smith 1990).

Accommodating discharged mental hospital patients may be the only subject on which the Department of Health guidance makes an apparently categorical statement: 'Patients who have lost their homes should not be expected to leave hospital until suitable accommodation has been arranged', to avoid placing 'even greater burdens on particular services . . . where a person becomes homeless as a result of leaving inappropriate accommodation which has been provided following discharge from hospital' (Department of Health 1990: paras 3.25, 3.44). How this can be achieved with no projected expansion in housing provision is likely to remain a mystery until after the Act's implementation in 1993.

Conclusion

The subject of housing issues in social work has generally been neglected by researchers on both sides (as Hudson 1986 has pointed out). In this chapter, we have identified more problems than solutions for social workers and their clients: the destructive influence of homelessness procedures, which forms a backdrop to child protection work; discouragement for probation officers who engage with young offenders' housing difficulties; poor inter-agency relations and confusion over policies for community care.

We have argued elsewhere for a 'rights approach' to social work, by which we mean the integration within practice of all the material circumstances of clients with the assessment of personal and social difficulties (Stewart 1989: ch. 1). One place to make such changes is on social work training courses. Being armed with knowledge and understanding about the policy and rights contexts of clients' material circumstances should aid social workers in negotiating for improvement. Generally social workers will be negotiating with other agencies for housing and associated services or benefits because of the decreasing likelihood that either social services or probation will be able to provide them directly. However, one must admit that the attitudes of policy-makers to involvement with the housing problems of clients are both confusing and negative: engage with housing over care in the community, withdraw from housing over punishment in the community – but in neither case will there be extra resources. Despite the decline in public housing, the former Central Policy Review Staff's observation still holds true: housing has priority and hence other local authority departments and allied services are expected to adapt to its policies, priorities and resource restraints (Central Policy Review Staff 1978: para. 28.1). But people's immediate living environment remains perhaps the most important single influence on their well-being, and lack of adequate housing is a major constraint. Social policies that restrict clients' housing opportunities are therefore a hindrance to social work agencies.

References

Allan, R. (1990) 'Punishment in the community', in P. Carter, T. Jeffs and M. K. Smith (eds) *Social Work and Social Welfare Yearbook 2*, Milton Keynes: Open University Press.
Audit Commission (1989) *Housing the Homeless: the Local Authority Role*, London: HMSO.
Avon Social Services Department (1989) *Management Review of the Case of Sukina Hammond*, Bristol: Avon SSD.
Blom Cooper, L. (chair) (1987) *A Child in Mind: Protection of Children in a Responsible Society*, Greenwich: London Borough of Greenwich Social Services Department.
Central Policy Review Staff (1978) *Housing and Social Policies: Some Interactions*, London: HMSO.
Clapham, D. and Smith, S. J. (1990) 'Housing policy and special needs', *Policy and Politics* 18, 3: 193–205.
Corden, J. and Clifton, M. (1985) 'Helping socially isolated prisoners', *British Journal of Social Work* 15: 331–50.
Department of the Environment (1991) *Community Care – Draft Circular to Housing Authorities*, London: HMSO.
Department of Health (1989) *Caring for People*, Cmd 849, London: HMSO.
Department of Health (1990) *Community Care in the Next Decade and Beyond: Policy Guidance*, London: HMSO.
Evans, A. and Duncan, S. (1988) *Responding to Homelessness: Local Authority Policy and Practice*, London: HMSO.
Fairhead, S. (1981) *Persistent Petty Offenders*, Home Office Research Study no. 66, London: HMSO.
Gibbons, J., Thorpe, S. and Wilkinson, P. (1990) *Family Support and Prevention: Studies in Local Areas*, London: HMSO.
Hardiker, P., Exton, K. and Barker, M. (1991) 'Analysing policy-practice links in preventive child care', in P. Carter, T. Jeffs and M. K. Smith (eds) *Social Work and Social Welfare Yearbook 3*, Milton Keynes: Open University Press.
Hearnden, D. (1984) *Co-ordinating Housing and Social Services: from Good Intentions to Good Practice*, London: Centre for Policy on Ageing.
Henderson, P. (1986) *Community Work and the Probation Service*, London: National Institute for Social Work.
Home Office (1984) *Statement of National Objectives and Priorities*, London: HMSO.

Home Office (1988) *Punishment, Custody and the Community*, Cmd 424, London: HMSO.
Home Office (1990) *Supervision and Punishment in the Community*, Cmd 966, London: HMSO.
Hope, T. and Shaw, M. (eds) (1988) *Communities and Crime Reduction*, London: HMSO.
House of Commons Social Services Committee (1985) *Community Care*, HCP 13–1, session 1984–5, London: HMSO.
Hudson, B. (1986) 'In pursuit of coordination: housing and the personal social services', *Local Government Studies* March/April: 53–66.
Islington Social Services Department (1989) *Liam Johnson Review: Report of Panel of Inquiry*, Islington: London Borough of Islington.
Kay, A. and Legg, C. (1986) *Discharged to the Community: a Review of Housing and Support in London for People Leaving Psychiatric Care*, London: Housing Research Group, City University.
Malpass, P. (1990) 'Housing policy and the Thatcher revolution', in P. Carter, T. Jeffs and M. K. Smith (eds) *Social Work and Social Welfare Yearbook 2*, Milton Keynes: Open University Press.
Niner, P. (1989) *Homelessness in Nine Local Authorities: Case Studies of Policy and Practice*, London: HMSO.
Nottingham Probation Housing Team (1989) 'Poverty and accommodation: is "resettlement" feasible any longer?', *Probation Journal* 36, 4: 171–6.
Noyes, P. (1991) *Child Abuse: a Study of Inquiry Reports 1980–1989*, London: HMSO.
Packman, J., Randall, J. and Jaques, N. (1986) *Who Needs Care?* Oxford: Basil Blackwell.
Patten, J. (1988) 'A new world of punishment', *Probation Journal* 35, 3: 81–4.
Riley, D. and Shaw, M. (1985) *Parental Supervision and Juvenile Delinquency*, Home Office Research Study 83, London: HMSO.
Rojek, C., Peacock, G. and Collins, S. (1988) *Social Work and Received Ideas*, London: Routledge.
Sedley, S. (chair) (1987) *Whose Child? Report of the Public Inquiry into the Death of Tyra Henry*, Lambeth: London Borough of Lambeth.
Social Services Inspectorate, Department of Health (1988) *Protecting Children: a Guide for Social Workers Undertaking a Comprehensive Assessment*, London: HMSO.
Southwark Area Review Committee (1989) *The Doreen Aston Report*, Lewisham: London Borough of Lewisham Social Services Department.
Stewart, G. and Stewart, J. (1988) 'Targeting youth, or how the state obstructs young people's independence', *Youth and Policy* 25: 19–24.
Stewart, G. and Stewart, J. (1989) *Surviving Poverty: Probation Work and Benefits Policy*, Wakefield: Association of Chief Officers of Probation.
Stewart, G. and Stewart, J. (1991) *Relieving Poverty? Use of the Social Fund by Social Work Clients and Other Agencies*, London: Association of Metropolitan Authorities.
Stewart, G. and Stewart, J. (1992) *Social Work and Housing*, Basingstoke: Macmillan.
Stewart, J. (ed.) (1989) *Welfare Rights in Social Work Education: Report by a Curriculum Development Group*, Paper 28.1, London: Central Council for Education and Training in Social Work.
Thoburn, J. (1980) *Captive Clients: Social Work with Families of Children Home on Trial*, London: Routledge.
Violence Against Children Study Group (1990) *Taking Child Abuse Seriously*, London: Unwin Hyman.
Wandsworth Area Child Protection Committee (1990) *The Report of the Stephanie*

Fox Practice Review, Wandsworth: London Borough of Wandsworth Social Services Department.

Wertheimer, A. (1988) *Housing Consortia for Community Care*, London: National Federation of Housing Associations and National Council for Voluntary Organisations.

Wertheimer, A. (1989) *Housing: the Foundation of Community Care*, 2nd edn, London: National Federation of Housing Associations and Mind.

Wilson, H. and Herbert G. W. (1978) *Parents and Children in the Inner City*, London: Routledge.

8
Social welfare developments in Eastern Europe and the future for socialist welfare

Bob Deacon

The collapse of the 'communist' regimes across Eastern Europe in 1989 and the continuing unfolding of *perestroika* in the Soviet Union have posed a number of questions for critical social welfare analysts. These questions extend from the simple puzzle about how the new governments of Eastern Europe will actually deconstruct the bureaucratic state collectivist welfare system to the meaning of these developments for those of us who might still want to argue that there is a socialist future for welfare.

This chapter, which addresses these and related questions, is divided into three parts. First it will briefly restate the achievements and limitations of 'state socialist' social policy as it existed across Eastern Europe before the collapse of 'communism' in 1989. Second, it will describe the diverse developments in social policy that have been taking place since then. Within this section the chapter will examine the impact of the marketization of the economies on social problems. A focus of analysis will be whether anything new is emerging in terms of social policy strategies or whether the East is now merely copying the West and creating one or other variant of welfare capitalism. Finally the chapter concludes with a discussion of what, if anything, can now remain of the socialist welfare project that many critical social policy-thinkers, including myself, were identified with in the 1970s and 1980s.

Social policy before the collapse of 'communism': a balance sheet

Had we been present in 1989 and able to stop the clock of Soviet *perestroika* or the revolutions of Eastern Europe what, as critical analysts of capitalist welfare states, would we have wished to preserve? For some internal critics of the old regime the answer was simple: very little. Julia Szalai stated in 1989 before the end of 'communism' in Hungary that

> What social policy today gives its subjects are the many irritating, humiliating and painful experiences of unfairness, defencelessness and chronic shortage. Social policy has come to be associated with widely unsatisfied needs, of unacceptable bureaucratic regulations, of haphazard provision of services at more and more unacceptable levels.
>
> (Deacon and Szalai 1990: 92)

On the other hand, Western social policy analysts (Feher and Arato 1989) have drawn attention to the ways in which the heavily subsidized foods and rents, full employment, the relatively high (as a percentage of average) wages of workers, the provision of free or cheap health, education and culture services represented a type of welfare contract between the party–state apparatus and the people, which was marred only by its inefficiency and the hidden privileges of the *nomenklatura*. Is it not possible to draw up a balance sheet of positive and negative features of the pre- 1989 system? Table 8.1 attempts such a balance sheet. This balance sheet appears to balance. It does not. On the left the apparent advantages for some workers were offered for productivist, demographic and political stabilization reasons rather than out of a commitment to welfare. On the other hand, these societies outlawed organizations for the defence of the poor, built houses for gypsies without running water, sanitation or heating, and effectively denied the elementary rights of citizenship to their own population.

Table 8.1 A system of welfare across Eastern Europe and the Soviet Union

Advantages	Disadvantages
Job security for many	Inadequate or absent unemployment pay
Workers' wages high percentage of average wages	Hidden privileges of party–state bureaucrats
Free health services (but oiled with bribes and gifts)	Underdevelopment of preventative approach to health; high mortality and morbidity rates
Three-year child-care grants to working women and the right to return to work (especially in the GDR and Hungary)	Obligation upon women to work and care; sexist division of labour
Highly subsidized flats	Maldistributed flats so better off live in most heavily subsidized
State-organized social security, pension and sick pay system	No index-linking of benefits and heavily work record regulated; totally inadequate back up social aid
State party/workplace paternalism	Total absence of rights to autonomously articulate social needs from below

We arrive at the paradox that if they existed in the context of the democratic pluralist politics of the capitalist economies of Western Europe, some of the social policies of the old Eastern Europe (child-care grants and the guarantee of work for mothers and fathers, liberal abortion legislation, subsidized housing, benefits levels set at a high percentage of average earnings) would be heralded by many as the progressive achievements of the social democratic regulation of market capitalism. However, within Eastern Europe they are perceived as part and parcel of the totalitarian state project of forcing work out of reluctant citizens for purposes which seem to benefit only the privileged party state apparatus.

We are also faced with the conclusion that the positive (from the Western critic's standpoint) features of Eastern European social policy – its egalitarianism, for example – sit side by side with an underdeveloped and inefficient economy. The Eastern European experience does underline the point that a balance of advantages has to be struck between economic efficiency and distributive justice. We are reminded of Kornai's conclusion that

> It is impossible to create a closed and consistent social-economic normative theory which would assert, without contradiction, a political-ethical value system and would at the same time provide for the efficiency of the economy. . . . What compromises are brought about between the different normative principles by the social forces of different social systems [is a scientific question].
>
> (Kornai 1986: 124)

The balance that has been struck historically in Eastern Europe and the Soviet Union has favoured an egalitarianism of underdevelopment. This understanding prompted Gorbachev, in the very early days of *perestroika*, to pronounce against crude egalitarianism and social levelling.

> Equalising attitudes crop up from time to time even today. Some citizens understood the call for social justice as 'equalising everyone'. . . . On this point we want to be perfectly clear: socialism has nothing to do with equalising. Socialism has a different criterion for distributing social benefits: 'From each according to his ability, to each according to his work'.
>
> (Gorbachev 1987: 100)

I shall now turn to the new post-1989 developments in social policy and ask whether, in the attempt to construct efficient economies that reward real work, the concerns of justice and security have been forgotten.

Diverse developments in social policy since 1989

In response to the legacy of social problems of the past, and in recognition of the need to develop social policies that facilitate the move to marketization but compensate those who are paying the highest price for this, all of the governments of Eastern Europe are developing initial policy responses that are broadly similar. These measures and their immediate consequences include.

- adhocism in development of services for the new unemployed and in terms of compensating social security recipients and employees for rapid inflation;
- appeals to philanthropy and voluntary effort to fill gaps left by withdrawal of state services;
- rapid removal of subsidies on many goods and services, including housing, with limited anticipation of social consequences;
- limited privatization of some health and social care services (although this may speed up);
- flourishing of independent social initiatives in the sphere of social care but with evident differential capacity of citizens to participate in these;
- desecularization of education and pluralization of control over schools and colleges;
- erosion of women's rights to some child-care benefits and services and free legal abortions (again the final outcome is not clear);
- deconstruction of the state social security system in favour of fully funded social insurance funds, often differentiated by categories of worker;
- abolition of many health and recreational facilities provided by firms for their employees and/or their conversion into local community or private facilities;
- ending of privileged access, by virtue of *nomenklatura* status of the old state–party apparatus, to special clinics and services;
- increase of local community control over local social provision, but in an impoverished context;
- tension between limitation of social citizenship rights for certain ethnic minorities (gypsies everywhere, Turks in Bulgaria, Hungarians in Romania) on one hand and increased autonomous articulation of ethnic minority needs on the other;
- a shift in the nature of social inequalities in the use of and access to social provision, from those based on bureaucratic/political privilege to those based on market relations.

There are, however, some obvious differences between countries even in the initial responses.

Commitment to socialist values and the juggling of egalitarianism versus efficiency, and social guarantees versus autonomy, *still* seems to apply in the USSR, Romania and Bulgaria but *not* in the rest of Eastern Europe, where the old ideology has been abandoned in favour of accepting the inequalities and efficiency of capitalism. The new civil society and democratic politics appear to hold sway in Czechoslovakia and Hungary, whereas authoritarian populism is a much greater tendency in Poland. The Catholic Church influences abortion policy and contributes to voluntary provision in Poland, whereas the Orthodox Church in Bulgaria has little to say or do in these areas. The old social democratic infrastructure appears to be being put to use in Czechoslovakia whereas this did not exist elsewhere. The rapid absorption of East Germany has led to a different pace of change.

Although it is too early to draw any firm conclusions about the longer term direction that social policy will take in each of the countries, some initial speculation might provide a framework for thinking about and analysing events as they unfold. It is evident that Hungary, Poland, Czechoslovakia, what was the GDR and parts of Yugoslavia, e.g. Slovenia, are likely to develop into one or other variant of Western welfare states.

Western welfare states *are* varied. They range (Esping-Anderson 1990) from those that provide for a minimal state entitlement and act on the subsidiarity principle (liberal welfare states like the USA), through those that conserve and reflect the inequalities of capitalism within their welfare policy by, for example, providing differentiated benefits according to status (conservature corporatist welfare states like Germany), to social democratic welfare states that are concerned to redistribute from richer to poorer and extend the full range of services to all social classes (such as Sweden). A first guess would be that Czechoslovakia, or certainly the Czech part, will eventually develop social democratic policies, reflective of its inter-war social democratic traditions. Hungary will probably emerge as a liberal welfare regime. The effect of the impact of the Catholic Church in Poland and Slovenia is hard to judge but something more approaching a conservative corporatist welfare regime may develop.

The countries of the Balkans – Romania, Bulgaria, Albania, Serbia and large parts of the Soviet Union – appear, at this stage, to be developing a new historical variant. There is a less than wholehearted rush to unfettered markets, property changes are taking place more slowly, the influence of the communist ideology of equality and protection for workers is higher, the trade unions appear still to be playing a role and many of the old *nomenklatura* wish to retain something of the past. A post-communist corporatism may be developing that strikes a new trade off between efficiency and justice. Deals are being struck whereby price rises are being partially or even wholly compensated for with agreed wage rises at the clear cost of less efficiency. It might, however, be that this is a temporary phase before these countries join the market leaders of Hungary and Poland. Some republics of the USSR would wish to move more quickly in this direction. The failed Soviet coup of August 1991 will probably have the effect of shortening the life of this post-communist corporatist phase.

I shall now describe in outline particular social policy measures taken in each field by each country, where this information is available to me.

The basic information available is summarized in Table 8.2. It has to be appreciated, however, that by the time you read this table much of it may be out of date. Policy and provision is changing, often by the month in some countries, in this period of transition. Table 8.2 is a snapshot of a moving picture.

In the related fields of unemployment benefit, retraining provision and compensation for price rises consequent upon the move to marketization there are several points to note. There is diversity between countries, ranging from those like the USSR where measures to compensate the unemployed have hardly begun to those like Poland where detailed schemes are now in operation. Even here it must be noted that the provision, for example, for labour exchanges and retraining is often only formal as the network of offices is only just being set up and provision is patchy and underfunded. There is also a broad distinction to be drawn between countries like the USSR, Bulgaria and Romania (not shown on Table 8.2), where prices rises are being systematically compensated for in the case of both workers and welfare beneficiaries by agreements struck or regulations about wages and prices promulgated at a national level, and countries like Poland where no such all-embracing wage compensation exists. For those dependent on state benefits (pensioners, the ill, children) the compensation situation is patchy and variable. Compensation tied to wage levels as in Poland means these categories share in the falling living standards. In Czechoslovakia compensation or valorization seems to be tied to price rises, which is better.

Housing policy, where it is becoming clear, seems to be taking the same direction in all of the countries, but with the USSR, Bulgaria and Romania adopting their distinctive pace. The goal, certainly in Poland and Hungary and to a large extent in Czechoslovakia, is the removal of state subsidy on rent and mortgages over a three-year period and their replacement by specific targeted housing or equivalent benefits for those who cannot afford to pay. There are differences between countries on what is regarded as a reasonable percentage of family income to be spent on housing costs. Poland thinks 8 per cent (including heating and lighting), Hungary prefers 20 per cent. In Czechoslovakia and Hungary whole categories of persons, such as pensioners, are excluded from rent rises. The other arm of the policy is to privatize building and construction and to sell off to sitting tenants the rented state sector. The development of the second of these policies would seem to depend on the capacity of the tenant to purchase.

In medical care and education policy there is, not surprisingly, a much greater intention, at least in the short term, to retain a large state stake in policy and provision. There are moves towards cost accounting, which is leading to closures, and towards allowing private health and educational facilities to be developed alongside the state sector. Religious organizations are being allowed an increased influence over both medical care and educational institutions and policy. Religious education is returning, both as a separate provision and as a part of the curriculum in all schools. Catholic influence to change the previously freely available abortion provision is beginning to be felt. The salaries of doctors and teachers are being raised everywhere.

There are important features of policy that do not show up in Table 8.2. There is pressure to increase the pension age in Hungary and Bulgaria. In both it stands at 55 for women and 60 for men. The cost is regarded as too high. On the other hand increasing unemployment may lead to a countervailing pressure.

The existing often generous provisions of child-care grants and allowances for women are under discussion. It is too early to say whether these will be eroded or whether again the countervailing pressures of reducing the unemployment total by removing women from the figures of the unemployed will work in the opposite direction. Certainly in Poland, when women registered for the new unemployment benefit the law was rapidly changed to

100 Changing social work and welfare

Table 8.2 Recent social policy measures

	Unemployment benefit	Retraining measures	Price rise compensation measures
Bulgaria	Benefit introduced at 80% of previous earnings. Years of work and age generate length of entitlement.	Being given priority.	Wages raised by 70% of inflation every six months and monthly if inflation exceeds 10%. Benefits similarly protected.
Czechoslovakia	Benefit at 50 or 60% of past earnings for one year. Small earnings allowed in addition. Means tested after one year. Benefit appears to be conditional on accepting retraining.	Benefits during retraining. Enterprise start-up allowances available.	Minimum wages according to ILO criteria. Benefit levels tied to price rises every quarter. Pensions stabilized at 79% average real wage.
Hungary	Benefit level 70% of previous unindexed earnings for first half of entitlement falling to 50% for second. Period of benefit related to contribution. One year earns 180 days. Four years earns maximum 2 years.	Retraining schemes being developed. Enterprise lump sum worth 2 years benefit available.	No systematic policy for wages. Benefit levels inflation related. Independent social security fund being established.
Poland	Benefit levels are 70% past earnings for 3 months, 50% for next 6, 40% subsequently. Maximum benefit is average public sector wage. Minimum benefit is minimum wage. Registration for work obligatory. Disqualified if refuse two jobs or retraining or public works programme.	Six or twelve months training at 80% previous earnings, 100% if redundant. Training allowance 125% minimum wage if not previously worked. Business start-up loans.	Measures emphasize the prevention of meeting compensatory wage claims. Pensions and benefit levels tied to falling real wage levels. SOS voluntary fund established.
USSR	Not yet officially acknowledged. Minimal short-term benefits for those between jobs (this will change after the collapsed coup).	At present 'all redundant workers being found new employment or retrained on full wages'.	In 1991, 60% price rise compensated at 85% level for pensioners, students, low-wage families. Pensions set at minimum wage level. Wage claims that over-compensate are still being met.

Housing policy	Medical care policy	Education policy
–	Retention of state service. Encouragement to private provision. Drs. salaries raised.	–
Subsidy reduction in stages. Marketization of new houses. New supplementary benefit for those unable to meet higher housing costs.	Retention of state service but cost accounting. Private initiatives and church provision allowed 'under local government control'. Shift to insurance funding by 1993?	Retention of state schooling but private and religious schools now allowed.
Staged reduction of rent and mortgage subsidy. Mortgage payments raised by 100% or 50% depending on whether more than 10 year old loan. Rents cannot exceed 20% family income. Pensioners excluded from rent rises. Sale of state flats to tenants.	Retention of state service. Insurance funding planned. Private facilities encouraged.	Diversification of forms of state schooling. Religious schools allowed.
Staged reduction of rent subsidy. Tenants to real housing costs by 1993. Benefits available for families where rent exceeds 8% of family budget. Privatization of house building.	Initial retention of state services but cost accounting closed some services. New charges for some services and drugs. Private sector envisaged eventually.	Retention of state schooling but private schools now allowed. Introduction of religious education (optional) by priests into schools being contested.
Rents, presently 3% household costs not yet raised despite cost accounting decrees. Tenants right to buy (in Moscow) not being implemented.	Some cost accounting in some authorities. Major anti-alcohol campaign.	Attempts to shift from too much academic education to more vocational training.

disqualify from receipt of benefit those who had not worked for at least six weeks in the previous twelve months. The likely outcome is the continuation of grants and allowances for the early years of motherhood, but the removal of the right to return to work without loss of status and salary.

New services for the care of dependants, for the alleviation of new poverty and for coping with the increasing homelessness and destitution are being developed within local areas in many of the countries. Often these are new voluntary initiatives. However, they exist within or alongside presently underfunded, ill-organized local social welfare or social aid services. A large part of the social costs of transition appears to be being placed at the doors of local agencies, who themselves are impoverished because of the new rigours of cost accounting. It is evident that in the short term they are often not coping.

Time will tell whether the period of transition to market economies will be tunnelled through by the new governments and whether the populations will allow this to happen when they are only partially compensated for their impoverishment and unemployment, as they are at present by the very patchy welfare measures. In some countries the process may become frozen into a new type of post-communist regime that is only partially marketized, perhaps less efficient, but with many of its old statist welfare policies and provisions in place. In other countries variations on the theme of developed welfare capitalism will emerge within the next five years. Readers wishing to develop further their knowledge of this subject matter should consult Deacon and Szalai (1990) and Deacon (1992).

What future for socialist welfare?

In the immediate and foreseeable future there is little that is going to develop within Eastern Europe that socialist critics of welfare capitalism will be able to point to and say 'There, that's the socialist future for welfare'. Equally we already knew that there was little about the social policy of the earlier bureaucratic state collectivist regimes that could be defended as socialist. What then of a future for socialist social policy as a guiding idea and a realizable practice? It is necessary to take stock, throw out the ideas and politics whose sell-by date has gone, and continue to preserve those with shelf life left in them.

An earlier (Deacon 1983) attempt I made to paint a picture of an ideal socialist social policy still has something of value but was flawed in a number of ways. Events in Eastern Europe have merely served to underline these flaws. The questions posed in that text, which I argued that socialist welfare analysts, indeed any welfare analysts, would need to have answered in order to establish the character of a country's social policy, remain of value. These concerned the priority afforded to welfare spending, the form of control over institutions of welfare, the agency of provision, the type of relationship between provider and user, the distribution and rationing principles, and the impact on the sexual division of caring. Now, in the light of Williams (1989), we can add a seventh concerning the racist dimension of policy. As socialists, I argued then and would argue now that we would applaud those countries that: spent more rather than less on welfare; provided for democratic forms of control of welfare institutions; utilized the state as an agency of provision but not exclusively (I shall return to this point shortly); facilitated social relations of welfare that were reciprocally co-operative; emphasized egalitarian principles of distribution (again a point to be returned to shortly); and facilitated non-gendered forms of care. We would also prefer policy that reflected ethnic diversity and was not based on racially exclusive citizenship rights. Lee and Raban (1988: 149) have pointed to the tension that exists in attempting to realize all of these socialist goals simultaneously. They argued, correctly in my view, that democratic and egalitarian measures may work against each other. The extent to which trade-offs might be required between local democracy and egalitarianism, or between egalitarianism and quantity (efficiency) in any feasible socialist future is an important point, which I alluded to in the first section of this chapter and will return to later. Certainly these considerations were missing from this earlier attempt to paint a picture of socialist social policy.

To these critical points must be added the implications of the experience of Eastern Europe and the collapse of 'communism'. I do not hold to the view that Eastern Europe and the Soviet Union have nothing to do with socialism, either as an idea or as a political practice. Of course Lenin's historic 'mistake' was to attempt to build socialism in conditions of underdevelopment where the working class were a decimated minority of the population (Feher et al. 1983). Of course, the Stalinist atrocity of substituting the party for the class and the general secretary for the party and then imposing that across Eastern Europe has nothing to do with the dream of communist democracy. It is not possible, however, for socialists to wipe their hands of the negative experiences that have been suffered under the name of socialism since Lenin's mistake. The idea that a party can know better what the people want and, should the people not choose it, impose the idea because it knows better contains the seeds of totalitarianism. The notion that the state can plan for the needs of people without also utilizing any of the available methods to find out what those needs are — both democratic choices and market places — must surely now be abandoned. To be fair to myself, I did write in 1983:

> There is thus considerable dispute among Marxists as to whether some form of market mechanism will play a part under socialism and communism. How far a democratic pluralist political process could be constructed that permitted full expression of the continuing diversity of, and disagreement about, need under socialism that excludes any form of market as a mechanism of registering preferences is far from having been worked out in detail. Equally, it has not yet been shown how a socialist system that permitted that expression of consumer preference through a market mechanism could avoid generalised commodity production and the restoration of capitalism.
>
> (Deacon 1983: 29)

The negative lessons that must be learned from the Soviet and Eastern European experience combine with the Western critical writings on Marxism in recent years to suggest a less certain picture of socialism and a less sure political strategy for its realization.

Where once, in the Western Marxist literature, it was presumed that the politics of a post-revolutionary society would be an unproblematic matter as all interests expressed through workers' councils would be the same, now no such certainty can be expressed (Polan 1984). A political process for a socialistic future has still to be fashioned. Where once, in the Western Marxist literature, it was presumed that markets would play no part in the decommodified economy, no such certainty can now be expressed (Nove 1983). While markets as social forces and as criteria of evaluation might still be suspect, markets as mechanisms for affording democratic choice and for facilitating efficiency are to be valued. To an extent markets *are* facilitators of the autonomous expression of need. Where once, in the Western Marxist literature, it was presumed that the morality of the socialist future was something that could safely be left to the future to create in new material circumstances, now no such amoral position can be afforded. Marxists are enjoined to make moral choices on matters social and political (Geras 1985; Lukes 1985). Where once, in the Western Marxist literature, it was presumed that human needs of a certain radical kind would flourish in the new society, now no such faith can be expressed. A genuine politics of needs is all that can and must be aspired to (Soper 1981).

The negative lessons of actually existing socialism coalesce, then, with self-critical analysis of Western Marxism to suggest a socialist future that embodies a political pluralism, involves contended moral choices, and envisages a role for markets and a political debate over needs. This does not mean, in my view, the abandoning of the Marxist analysis of the dynamics of capitalist society. Class struggle exists and will continue to exist as long as capitalism continues to exist, which will be for a long time. The dimensions of gender and race and the struggles that arise out of them must, of course, be integrated with this class analysis. What, therefore, do the foregoing considerations lead us to say now about a socialist future for welfare? Four main things follow, I think.

First, we must abandon for all practical purposes the form of politics that is guided solely by the idea that nothing can be achieved until capitalism collapses and therefore everything is measured by whether it hastens its downfall. While we may retain (if it helps) as a final vision a social transformation to a classless society, this possibility is so unlikely, and perhaps impossible to realize, that it is irrelevant to any socialist welfare politics of the present.

Second, we must defend and argue for the ideals of socialist social policy (for example the seven questions and preferred answers suggested earlier) as goals and as principles to be struggled for now, at the level of ideas and with those class and other forces in whose interests they are fashioned. With these values backed up by this democratic class struggle we can realize them by degree within capitalism. Capitalism East and West can be mended by the struggle of socialists.

Third, and perhaps this is a point that flows most directly from the experience of Eastern European welfare and the struggle now to fashion a new future for welfare capitalism in its place, we must acknowledge the trade-off between efficiency and equality, and between state guarantees and personal and group autonomy. The balance that will exist between these and other trade-offs will vary between societies and will depend on the diverse forms of struggle of diverse interests within them. Nothing more can be said on this point.

Fourth, and this is probably the point with the most exciting potential for the future, those who wish to establish within capitalism a socialist social policy need to broaden their canvas to a global level. Capitalism cannot, in the long run, be mended with socialist values backed up by struggle in one region of the globe if it is to be undermined by an unmended cut-throat capitalism existing elsewhere. The level playing field of the European Social Charter has eventually to encompass the globe, and when it does it can be raised even higher. It will not matter then that egalitarianism is being traded for efficiency because there will be nowhere more efficient (because less equal) to undermine the existing welfare achievements (discounting interplanetary capitalist competition!). The collapse of the false East–West ideological political and systems posturing of the past decades liberates this potential for a global reformist politics and gives it a real chance of success.

In the early days after the collapse of the 'communist' regimes of Eastern Europe I wrote the following passage about the future for socialist welfare. Nothing has happened subsequently to encourage me to rethink this.

> We may still be allowed to paint a picture of a welfare future that is more egalitarian, whose provisions are not so closely tied to a work ethic, that facilitate forms of care that are not sexist or racist, that is less structured by nationally bound citizenship rights, that allows for variety and difference in the social needs that are articulated and in the ways in which they are met, that is more reciprocal and less paternalistic, more enabling and less dependency creating, more empowering and less stigmatising. We may still be allowed to argue that the democratic state has a duty to guarantee some territorial justice and that international authority has a duty to guarantee some global justice. We may still be allowed to argue that markets between competing collective properties must operate within a regulating framework that tries to ensure they help achieve democratically agreed ends. What we are not able to do is to place our faith in the mysterious mechanisms whereby the universal interest in all of this is carried for us all by the working class. We require instead a re-doubling of commitment and argument at the level of social values as a necessary part of the process of realising this welfare future.
>
> (Deacon and Szalai 1990: 24)

It is important, and reassuring, to note that I am not alone in this! Those who have stepped outside the twin traps of either defending the past in Eastern Europe as socialist or claiming that its terrible legacy has had nothing to do with socialism seem to agree about what is now to be done. Stephen Lukes (1990), reviewing the lessons of Eastern Europe, argues that from now on the left must be guided by both the republican principle that tries to ensure equal social citizenship and the rectification principle that rectifies inequalities where they exist and makes real existing paper equalities. He adds: 'From which I think we must conclude that the future of socialism, if it has one, can only lie within capitalism, and it can only consist of one or other version of social democracy' (Lukes 1990: 544). Anthony Giddens in similar vein has argued that

> The left at this point has finally and absolutely to relinquish the conceptual security once offered by panoramas of historical inevitability, or by the theme that the working class is a privileged historical agent. . . . There are no guarantees for the future . . . yet the reconstructive tasks which a left political programme might develop thereby actually become all the more urgent.
>
> (Giddens 1990: 22)

This, and it is important to clarify the point, is not the conclusion that in the struggle between capitalism and socialism capitalism won, or in the struggle between capitalist welfare and socialist welfare capitalist welfare won. It is the conclusion that socialist values and socialist welfare objectives can only be won within any foreseeable future in the struggle within capitalism to mend it in the interests of human needs. It is also the conclusion that this struggle now has as an urgent priority a transnational and global dimension in the interests of socialist welfare objectives East and West, North and South. The time of radical global reformism has arrived, inspired by socialist values, struggled for with the tools of class struggle and guided by an analysis of the global economy that continues to utilize the insights of Marxism.

References

Deacon, B. (1983) *Social Policy and Socialism*, London: Pluto Press.
Deacon, B. (1992) *Eastern Europe in the 1990s: Past Developments and Future Prospects for Social Policy*, London: Sage.
Deacon, B. (1992) *Social Policy, Social Justice and Citizenship in Eastern Europe*, Aldershot: Avebury.
Deacon, B. and Szalai, J. (1990) *Social Policy in the New Eastern Europe*, Aldershot: Avebury.
Esping-Anderson, G. (1990) *The Three Worlds of Welfare Capitalism*, Cambridge: Polity Press.
Feher, F. and Arato, A. (1989) *Gorbachev: the Debate*, Cambridge: Polity Press.
Feher, F., Markus, G. and Heller, A. (1983) *Dictatorship over Needs*, Oxford: Basil Blackwell.
Geras, N. (1985) 'On Marx and justice', *New Left Review* 156: 47–85.
Giddens, A. (1990) 'Modernity and utopia', *New Statesman* 2 November: 20–2.
Gorbachev, M. (1987) *Perestroika*, London: Fontana.
Kornai, J. (1986) *Contradictions and Dilemmas*, Cambridge MA: MIT Press.
Lee, P. and Raban, C. (1988) *Welfare Theory and Social Policy*, London: Sage.
Lukes, S. (1985) *Marxism and Morality*, Oxford: Oxford University Press.
Lukes, S. (1990) 'Comment on Goldfarb, J.: Post totalitarian politics – ideology ends again', *Social Research* 57, 3: 544.

Nove, A. (1983) *The Economics of Feasible Socialism*, London: George Allen and Unwin.
Polan, A. J. (1984) *Lenin and the End of Politics*, London: Methuen.
Soper, K. (1981) *On Human Needs*, Brighton: Harvester.
Williams, F. (1989) *Social Policy: a Critical Introduction*, Cambridge: Polity Press.

9
Countdown to 1992: preparing social work for the single market

Hugh Barr

The date 31 December 1992 is the deadline set to achieve the objectives of the Single European Act 1986. Those objectives call for the free movement of goods, persons, capital and services between the twelve member states of the European Community (EC) to create an internal market without frontiers.

Implications for social work are becoming clearer as a result of painstaking work within and between the member states, stimulated by an EC Directive (European Commission 1989). This chapter assesses its implications for social work, and reviews the course of discussions which it has stimulated among bodies responsible for social work in the United Kingdom, and between member states. It then draws attention to other European developments as they affect social work. Finally, it makes a case for putting Europe into the social work curriculum, suggesting some starting points and raising questions about the availability of source material.

Facilitating the mobility of professionals

The Directive lays down ground rules regarding the currency of professional awards when a worker qualified in one member state wants to practise in another. It applies to professions that satisfy three conditions: that their qualifying training is in higher education; that it lasts not less than three years; and that practice is regulated.

A profession may be covered by this Directive in one member state, but not in another. Workers whose profession is covered in their home member state are entitled to practise in other member states where that profession is also covered on the same terms as apply to nationals. In specified circumstances, they may be required to complete adaptation periods or take aptitude tests, but limits are set upon conditions that a host member state may impose. However, workers whose profession is covered in their home member state and want to practise in one where that profession is not covered cannot claim the Directive's protection. Workers whose professions fail to meet the Directive's requirements in their home member state cannot claim its protection when seeking to practise in a member state which is covered. Where that profession is covered in neither member state the Directive is clearly not applicable.

In all circumstances, the host member state must comply with the Treaty of Rome. In other words, it must not discriminate on grounds of nationality in matters relating to employment, remuneration and other conditions of service. The European Community has published a guide (Seche 1988) to help workers, their representatives and employers to understand the implications of the Treaty and related court judgments for the mobility of labour, but unfortunately this has yet to be updated to take account of the Directive.

So the degree to which a professional, unable to invoke the Directive, is disadvantaged is unclear and, as yet, largely untested in practice or by recourse to the European courts. The Directive only took effect from 4 January 1991.

Two reactions

The Directive has prompted two quite different reactions among opinion leaders in social work. Some have wrestled with the complexities of Eurospeak, debating endlessly the precise interpretation (and sometimes translation) of convoluted clauses. For them, the minutiae have proved absorbing. Who would be affected and how in moving between member states? What would constitute an effective aptitude test? Can competence in a second language be taken into account? How would an adaptation period be supervised? Is social work one profession or several? Might parts of it be covered, but not others? How can account be taken of different functions carried by social workers in different member states? And so on. They have searched for ways to reconcile the rights of workers to move freely within the Community with the protection of consumers. In a culture-bound field like social work systematic re-orientation seems essential when workers from one member state move to another. Can they be relied upon to do that for themselves or should it be provided, or even required? Making it a requirement may contravene EC law, including the Directive.

Others have been more exercised about the Directive's broad political implications. For them, it is the invidious comparisons between professions included and excluded from the Directive that gives rise to concern – comparisons between social work in one member state and another, and with other professions in the same member state.

Implications for social work in the United Kingdom

First indications suggested that social work in the United Kingdom would fail to satisfy the Directive on two counts: qualifying courses were not required to last three years and typically lasted only two, and practice was not normally regulated. Was this to be yet another blow to a punch-drunk profession –

already reeling from cuts in public expenditure, taking stick from the media, the public and politicians, and feeling scapegoated along with its clients? Morale was low and still falling.

Government had rejected the case made by the Central Council for Education and Training in Social Work (CCETSW) for a three-year course leading to its proposed Qualifying Diploma in Social Work (QDSW). CCETSW had settled, reluctantly, for two years leading to its Diploma in Social Work (DipSW). It now dawned that UK social workers would, as a result of the Directive, be disadvantaged compared with all or some of their continental colleagues. CCETSW therefore called upon government to reverse its decision, but ministers were unimpressed.

Once CCETSW had given the Directive such high visibility, implications for the status of social work in the UK could no longer be hidden. Letters in journals protested that qualifying courses in the UK were better than those in other parts of Europe, albeit shorter. Anxiety was reinforced. Less emphasized, but no less worrying, was news that other professions in the UK, alongside whom social workers practised, would be covered by the Directive. These seemed likely to include occupational therapists, physiotherapists and psychologists, as well as doctors and nurses who were already covered by their own 'sectoral' directives.

Frustrated by the Department of Health's (DoH) response, CCETSW turned its attention to the Department of Trade and Industry (DTI). In place of arguments about the serious consequences for social work in the UK because it fell short of the Directive's requirements, CCETSW now saw a chance to argue that social work in the UK did, indeed, satisfy the Directive's conditions. Grounds for this belated optimism were fuelled by the comments of a DTI official addressing a CCETSW workshop (CCETSW 1988). He speculated that the three years might be deemed to be met on the strength of 'the dominant route' to qualification, even though courses were shorter for some students. CCETSW therefore based its case to the DTI on data which demonstrated that some 75 per cent of Certificate of Qualification in Social Work (CQSW) students satisfied the three year requirement (most by virtue of their total period in higher education). It went on to list the circumstances in which social work practice in the UK was regulated. DTI was not persuaded. Three years and an overall system for regulation would both be required.

Throughout these negotiations, it was becoming increasingly apparent that DTI officials were struggling to interpret the Directive and to apply it across disparate professions, in a manner consistent with discussions in other member states, as monitored by Brussels. Informal comments at one stage did not always seem to tally with considered judgements at another. Social work in the UK might, said the DTI, come under another directive (European Community 1988). This would cover professions whose training was less than three years, provided that they were regulated. Far from proving reassuring, this prospect promised only to confirm fears of invidious comparisons at home and abroad.

The introduction of this draft directive into the debate may prove to have been a red herring. If one of the grounds on which social work in the UK failed to satisfy the first Directive was lack of adequate regulation, how could it be covered by another which included essentially the same requirement? Much depends upon the outcome of continuing debate about the case for a General Social Services Council (Parker 1990). If and when it is set up, social work, and perhaps other social services professions, will be regulated within the meaning of both these directives.

At one stage, it seemed likely that the UK would be the only member state where social work was not covered by the (first) Directive. However, reports began to arrive that negotiations were not always running smoothly in other member states. Problems were reported in Denmark, France and Germany. At the time of writing (July 1991), the DTI had no information about the designation of 'competent authorities' to administer the Directive for social work in other member states, with the solitary exception of the Department of Health in the Republic of Ireland. Indeed, only two member states, Ireland and the United Kingdom, had formally adopted the Directive, although it may be unwise to read too much into that, given the speed at which such developments move. It does, however, suggest that it will be some considerable time before we know in which member states social work is to be covered.

It may be tempting to lay the blame wholly on government for the predicament in which social work in the UK finds itself, but the profession itself also bears some responsibility. During the past twenty or so years, professional associations, including the British Association of Social Workers (BASW), have resisted moves towards closed membership, restriction of title, and the regulation of practice, and maintained strong support for non-graduate routes to qualification. Traditional concepts of professionalism have been challenged, the argument being that they are more concerned with the interests of workers than those of clients. BASW's decision to support proposals for the General Social Services Council therefore constituted a significant and welcome shift towards accepting the disciplines upon which legitimation as a profession depend. On the other hand, the opposition of the main trade union for social workers, the National and Local Government Officers' Association (NALGO) remains a stumbling block. This is not the place to rehearse the arguments surrounding these contentious issues, but it must be said that the price of resisting the inescapable disciplines of professionalization has been to weaken the standing of social work relative to other professions in the UK and to social work in other countries. The Directive has brought this home to roost.

By judging occupations against traditional yardsticks for the professions, the Directive forces social work in the UK to re-examine its stance if it wants to maintain its historic place in the social work profession in Europe and beyond. To do so, it must back proposals for a General Social Services Council and so become regulated. It must also accelerate trends towards longer qualifying courses and a larger percentage of graduate entrants, which, taken together, will ensure that a growing proportion of social work students satisfy the three year requirement (Barr 1991).

Cultivating relations with other member states

Readers may have noticed, by now, the extent to which the Directive has been considered in the UK primarily in terms of its domestic consequences. Fortunately that has not been the whole picture. A CCETSW workshop about the Directive (CCETSW 1988) included individuals from other member states and proved to be an important step in exploring wider European interests. My own study for CCETSW (Barr 1989, 1990) reinforced this. It entailed correspondence and consultations with government officials, professional associations and educational interests in the other eleven member states. The study was designed to inform CCETSW about the consequences of the single market for social work education. It put the Directive in the wider context of EC law and policy, in relation to the historical development of social work in Europe and current patterns of education throughout the twelve member states.

Other UK initiatives have also helped to build contacts and to widen debate beyond the confines of the Directive. The Association of Directors of Social Service (ADSS) has met in conference with chief officers from other member states and explored the feasibility of forging an EC-wide association with them. BASW has been active in the European chapter of the International Federation of Social Workers, not least in supporting Paul Dolan in his role as vice-president for Europe. The Social Care Association (SCA) has actively cultivated its links with the Federation Internationale des Communautes Educatives (FICE). The Social Work Education Committee of the Joint Universities Council (JUC/SWEC) has strengthened its links with the European Regional Group of the International Association of Social Workers and, in partnership with CCETSW, called UK conferences to explore European issues. The Association of Teachers in Social Work Education (ATSWE) has included contributions from other member states in its seminars and been represented at European conferences. The National Institute for Social Work (NISW) has mounted a feasibility study for a centre to promote co-operation between social work in the UK and other countries, including other EC member states.

UK delegates have been prominent in discussions about the Directive at European conferences and seminars. In addition, CCETSW has sent parties to other member states to learn about their social work education systems. As a result of these initiatives, social work in the UK has developed an extensive and growing network of relationships across Europe.

Approaches from CCETSW seem to have been the first that some ministries, professional associations and educational interests in some member states had heard about the Directive. Others were well informed. In the Republic of Ireland, for example, work to meet the Directive's requirements was already in hand, as part of the regulatory mechanisms being created to replace CCETSW (which as one of its more obscure functions had validated some courses in the Republic at the request of the colleges concerned). Irish social work teachers and practitioners were to play a prominent part in wider European discussions. Those discussions have come under the auspices of two organizations: the EC Liaison Committee of the International Federation of Social Workers (IFSW) and the European Regional Group (ERG) of the International Association of Schools of Social Work (IASSW).

Considering the directive at the European level

IFSW undertook a study (Cocozza 1989) to inform its constituent associations and the European Commission about provision of social work education in the twelve member states. Cocozza argued that the similarities were sufficiently strong to facilitate recognition of equivalence between social work qualifications across member states. Her paper was a sequel to an earlier one for the Commission (Warchawiak 1980).

A more weighty survey grew out of an initiative by IASSW (Brauns and Kramer 1986). This included descriptions of social work education in twenty-one European countries, prefaced by a lively overview. It preceded debates about the Directive, but contains much that is nevertheless relevant to them. Although beginning to date, it remains the most authoritative source of reference.

In 1989 both IFSW and IASSW held fringe meetings about the Directive during their biennial European seminars. IFSW, through its EC Liaison Committee, then decided to convene an experts' meeting. This took place in Belgium in April 1990 and included discussions with officials of the Commission. At the same time, the executive committee of the ERG, assisted by its 'Expert Network European Community Qualifications' (ENECQ), was gathering in Belgium. The two organizations met each other for the first time for several years.

Working under the umbrella of ERG, and funded by European Commission through the ERASMUS programme, the aims of the ENECQ were to review social work education in EC member states in the light of the Directive (Lavan 1991). Social work educators from the Republic of Ireland, the UK and Spain comprised the steering group. Meetings were held in six member states and involved exchange of information between social work educators from eleven of the twelve member states (Luxembourg being the exception). These meetings revealed inconsistency and confusion within and between member states as to where and how decisions were being taken about which professions would be covered by the Directive.

While government and EC officials have taken part in some of these discussions, formal consultation between government departments responsible for social work in each member state have yet to take place. One reason is plainly the difficulty in identifying which those departments are. Another is the relatively minor place that social work occupies in departments with wide-ranging briefs. CCETSW, as a unique institution wholly concerned with social work, gives the UK an advantage, but it cannot be a substitute for the DoH and other UK government departments.

Weighing the implications

Just what is the reader to make of the Directive? In spite of protracted scrutiny and debate, its relevance to social work remains unclear. Barring the Republic of Ireland, we can only speculate about the member states in which social work will be covered by it. In any case, we can only guess the number of social workers who would be affected by it as we do not know how many qualify in one member state and subsequently practise in another.

Numbers moving to and from the UK, for example, seem to be very small. Applications to CCETSW to verify social work qualifications made in other member states totalled just fifty-one between 1 April 1990 (when the new system was introduced) and 2 July 1991 (the date of the latest available figures) out of a total of 343 worldwide (15 per cent). While the figure is probably less than the total of EC social workers coming to practise in the UK, it suggests that we are still talking about little more than a trickle. In the absence of data for the outflow of qualified social workers, the general impression is that UK social workers seeking overseas experience opt presently for Australia, Canada, New Zealand, South Africa or the United States.

If the movement of social workers between member states is as low as it would appear to be, that can, of course, be invoked as an argument in favour of the Directive. By laying down the ground rules, social workers and others will know where they stand and may be more disposed to widen their experience in another member state. Time will tell. Some increase in numbers can be expected anyway as the single market gathers momentum and future generations, more conscious of their European identity, enter the profession. But much will depend upon the improvement of language teaching in schools if UK social workers practising in another country are to be credible and competent in a field where communication is of the essence.

Reports that Germany and Denmark have an over-supply of qualified social workers prompted speculation that some of them might be attracted by opportunities to work in the UK, where there is, of course, a chronic shortage, but there are few signs of this happening yet. On the contrary, the indications are that salaries and conditions of service are not sufficiently attractive, and that the cost of housing, at least in London, is an added disincentive.

CCETSW, as the UK body that has been responsible for determining the equivalence of social work qualifications awarded overseas, has rightly and necessarily taken the Directives very seriously. Even though social work in the UK is not covered by the Directive, CCETSW must now deal with applications from social workers from member states that are covered. Moreover, it must act within the wider framework of EC law and policy designed to further mobility of labour, a framework that is now much better understood and can no longer be ignored.

Recognizing this, CCETSW has already revised its policies substantially. In place of the complexities of determining the comparability of an award to the CQSW, CCETSW made an interim change of policy designed to obviate any risk of contravening EC law. CCETSW set itself the more limited, but still difficult, task of verifying that an applicant's award was a bona fide qualification in social work in the country of origin at the time when it was made, leaving it to employers to evaluate its relevance to UK practice. However, this does not address concerns regarding the need for orientation, notably in anti-racism, law and child protection, which are central to CCETSW's requirements for the DipSW. Consultations were therefore pending, at the time of writing, regarding objectives for orientation training for social workers qualified overseas and seeking to practise in the UK.

Facilitating the mobility of students and teachers

A growing minority of students take parts of their courses in other member states and may, as a result, have their horizons widened about future employment. A survey in 1988 (Barr 1989; reprinted in Cannan *et al.* 1990) found that twenty-three CQSW courses and one CSS scheme were currently engaged in co-operative programmes with thirty-one educational institutions in other member states. Eleven of these were in Germany, at least eight in France, three in The Netherlands, two each in Denmark, Ireland and Portugal and one each in Greece and Italy. The number of such programmes has almost certainly increased since then and up-to-date information is being analysed by CCETSW.

The 1988 survey suggested that one-to-one links between teachers had often grown into co-operative programmes between institutions. Reciprocal visits seemed to be getting longer, more often leading to joint activities. 'Exchange' was no longer an adequate description for a rich diversity of shared activity. Most links were either bilateral or trilateral; a few were more ambitious.

The nature of the co-operation fell into seven (not mutually exclusive) categories:

- advice by UK institutions regarding curriculum development;
- shared studies for short periods;
- reciprocal visits for study and observation, typically lasting up to two weeks;
- longer exchanges of students, including assessed practice;
- longer exchanges of teachers;
- joint curriculum development;
- proposals for the introduction of joint awards.

The first three categories were normally self-funding. The remainder were eligible for support from ERASMUS. UK teachers were universally enthusiastic about these programmes. They spoke of the enjoyment, boost to morale, stimulus and mutual reinforcement that were generated. However, each programme called for a major investment of time and energy for quite small numbers.

A CCETSW guide on links and exchanges (Cannan *et al.* 1990) described the four ERASMUS funding categories: teaching staff mobility programmes; student mobility programmes; joint development of new curricula; and intensive programmes (i.e. joint programmes for short periods). It gave examples of successful applications from social work and much practical advice in planning and executing co-operative programmes. It listed, at length, perceived advantages for students, staff, courses, the social work profession, services to clients and educational institutions. A forthcoming CCETSW paper (*In Europe 3*) by Daines describes a visit by a group of practice teachers to Angers in France in March 1990.

Post-qualifying studies offer exciting possibilities to bring together experienced practitioners from different member states. The Tilberg Institute, in The Netherlands, has offered courses in social policy for senior social work practitioners, but has experienced difficulty in recruiting viable numbers. The European Centre for Community Education (ECCE), at Koblenz in Germany, has had more success. Covering (in UK terms) both social work and youth and community work, ECCE is a consortium of European institutions whose students learn together and prepare for a common Additional Certificate in Community Education Studies.

Credit transfer

In 1987 ERASMUS launched a six-year pilot project known as the European Community Credit Transfer System (ECTS). This, as its name implies, is designed to enable undergraduates to gain credit for study in one member state towards an award in another. It applied, in the first instance, to five subject areas: business administration, chemistry, history, mechanical engineering and medicine. How and when it will be extended to other subjects remains to be seen. The introduction of modular patterns and credit transfer (Bailey 1989; Storan 1991) for DipSW programmes in the UK will make it easier to include social work, if and when the way is opened. Meanwhile, CCETSW has commissioned Steven Shardlow at the University of Sheffield to look at the implications for post-qualifying studies.

Putting Europe into the curriculum

Opportunities to study in other member states are the exception, and may remain so. Returning students are, no doubt, eager to share their experience with their peers, but this is inevitably patchy. Exchanges between teachers and joint study programmes can go further, but, for the foreseeable future, both of these apply to only a minority of courses. 'European studies' have yet to be introduced as an integral part of the curriculum for all courses.

Interest in Europe came too late to influence the drafting of CCETSW's requirements and regulations for the Diploma in Social Work (DipSW), which include no more than a 'hope' that programme providers will take the Single European Act and the Directive into account (CCETSW 1989). Such exhortation sits uneasily in a document preoccupied with preparation for the immediate demands of practice. Without a stronger lead, employers, in particular, may take some persuading that European studies should claim time and space in an overcrowded curriculum.

If the case is to be convincing, it must start by demonstrating the relevance of European studies to contemporary UK practice, including issues that are high on the current UK 'agenda', such as anti-racism, child protection, an ageing population and HIV. Comparative studies are one way to do this. They can show how Western European nations experience much the same social problems, but may respond differently. They can explore why, taking into account historical, political, legal, administrative, religious and cultural differences. Comparative study may be extended to introduce students to: ways in which such problems are being addressed at the European level; the institutions that are involved, including the European Commission, the Council of Europe and the World Health Organization's European Region; the countries that each covers; and the powers that each exercises and the impact it has. Attention can also be drawn to related rulings in the European Courts.

A second starting point is the social impact of the single market, notably that resulting from the greater mobility of people. Differences in economic prosperity within the Community will stimulate migration from less prosperous to more prosperous regions. Differences in economic prosperity between the Community and its eastern and southern neighbours will draw in immigrants, however much the EC may try to keep them out. Working with immigrants, as distinct from working with indigenous minority ethnic groups, will once again assume significance in social work practice. Working with refugees, those who arrive illegally, will be part of that.

Social workers will need increasingly to be alert to problems that people from one country may experience in living and sometimes working in another, for example young people adrift between countries, migrant workers and their families, and old people retiring to warmer climes. They will need to understand the significance of cultural, legal, linguistic and religious differences, which affect personal and social problems – problems that may become more complex and more extreme in an unfamiliar environment.

Social workers will also need to know how and where to find help, when necessary, within the client's culture in the UK and how to make contact with, and enlist co-operation from, helping services in the home member state. Records may be needed, relatives may have to be contacted and so on. It will be important for them to know about rights of domicile and employment that a citizen of the EC enjoys in another member state, and how these differ from those of migrants, immigrants or refugees from other countries.

Representatives from all twelve member states met in London in 1989 to identify issues bearing on cross-cultural practice and to enlist support to produce a handbook to help social workers in situations such as those described above (Munday 1990). This is one of the first tasks for the European Institute of Social Services established at the University of Kent.

A third starting point is preparation to work with colleagues from and in other member states. As more Continental social workers come to the UK to practise, so UK social workers will more often have them as colleagues, and sometimes carry responsibility for their orientation or supervision. Positive and informed attitudes towards social work education and practice in other member states will help to make relationships mutually enriching. UK social workers, thinking about gaining experience in another member state, may make more intelligent decisions if they have some knowledge of practice elsewhere in Europe. If and when they make the move, transferring knowledge and skills will be less difficult if their basic professional education has been within a European frame of reference.

A fourth starting point is the economic impact of the single market on individuals, families and communities. Some will experience the stresses that accompany economic 'progress', others the cold winds of economic competition. Both will have their impact on social work practice: disruption of traditional lifestyles on the one hand, relatively greater poverty and deprivation on the other.

Any case for European studies that is to stand a chance of succeeding will have to be tied to the realities of UK practice, however much European visionaries may long to raise our sights. Nevertheless, students will be introduced to social work across the Channel, and courses taking their first steps towards more wholehearted development of European studies later.

Once the case has been made convincingly, work can start to decide where such studies should be introduced – subject by subject, in college and in practice – what to include and where to find relevant learning materials.

Source materials

While there is a plethora of EC policy papers and data sources, few get close to social work practice. The outcome of the work at the University of Kent should help, while, for a UK readership, *Community Care* and *Social Work Today* publish articles about practice in other member states. More substantial literature is, however, becoming available for some topics, for example race (Institute for Race Relations 1991), and there is Dominelli's forthcoming paper for CCETSW (*In Europe 4*), plus the first European reader (Hill 1991).

No comprehensive system has yet been introduced to review social work texts and journals from other member states, to select those meriting translation, to prepare English digests of others and to lodge the remainder in an accessible UK library. A selective, annotated bibliography would be a useful first step. Unless and until teaching materials are produced and become accessible, the inclusion of European studies will remain problematic.

Taking stock

So how prepared is social work for 1992? Implications of the Directive for the mobility of social workers are still far from clear. It has, however, stimulated a timely debate about relative standards in social work education and practice, and given renewed impetus to discussions between social work interests throughout the European Community. Mutually beneficial working relations have also grown between social work courses, thanks in part to ERASMUS, which has also put credit transfer and European awards on the agenda for the future.

The knowledge base for European social work remains fragmented and superficial, and channels for communication are woefully inefficient and ineffective. It is in these areas that work is most urgently needed.

References

Bailey, R. (1989) *A Post-Qualifying Award in Social Work: the Case for Credit Accumulation and Transfer*, London: CCETSW/CNAA.

Barr, H. (1989) *Social Work Education in Its European Context: a Report to Members and Staff of CCETSW*, London: CCETSW.
Barr, H. (1990) *In Europe 1: Social Work Education and 1992*, London: CCETSW.
Barr, H. (1991) Measuring up to the EC Directive. *Issues in Social Work Education* 10, 1 and 2: 128–33.
Brauns, H.-J. and Kramer, D. (1986) *Social Work Education in Europe*, Frankfurt: Eigenveriag des Deutschen Vereins für offentliche und private Fursorge.
Cannan, C., Colman, R. and Lyons, K. (1990) *In Europe 2: Links and Exchanges*, London: CCETSW.
CCETSW (1988) *Report from the European Directive Workshop, Stoke Rochford*, London: CCETSW.
CCETSW (1989) *Requirements and Regulations for the Diploma in Social Work*, Paper 30, London: CCETSW.
Cocozza, L. (1989) *Social Work Training in the European Community*, Brussels: Commission of the European Communities.
European Commission (1989) 'Council directive of 21 December 1989 on a general system for the recognition of higher-education diplomas on completion of at least three years' duration', *Official Journal of the European Communities* 24 January.
European Community (1988) Proposal for a Council Directive on a second general system for the recognition of professional education and training (89/C263/01) which complements Directive 89/48/EEC.
Hill, M. (1991) *Social Work and the European Community*, London: Jessica Kingsley.
Institute for Race Relations (1991) 'Europe: variations on a theme of racism', *Race and Class* 32: 14–28.
Lavan, A. (1991) *Report 1990 of the Expert Network European Community Qualifications*, a document based upon a report submitted to the Commission of the European Communities, Brussels.
Munday, B. (1990) *Social Services in the European Community and the Implications of 1992*, Canterbury: University of Kent.
Parker, R. (1990) *Safeguarding Standards*, London: National Institute for Social Work.
Seche, J.-C. (1988) *A Guide to Working in a Europe without Frontiers*, Brussels: Commission of the European Communities.
Storan, J. (1991) *Credit Accumulation and Transfer for the Diploma in Social Work*, London: CCETSW.
Warchawiak, E. (1980) *Comparative Study of Training in Social Work in the European Community*, Brussels: Commission of the European Communities.

10
The future of education welfare: evolution or extinction?

Arnold Dry

The Education Welfare Service (EWS) has its roots in the final years of the nineteenth century, when school boards employed people to bring children into school. From the early days it was recognized that the home circumstances of the children were for many as significant a factor in influencing educational performance as natural ability. Accordingly the 'school board man' was frequently involved in front-line decisions regarding the balance between social control and social justice. This dichotomy has been a constant characteristic of the service and has clear parallels in other branches of social work. In recent years the service has endeavoured to identify itself more clearly with social work values, although support for such a shift is far from universal.

At the time of writing the future of the EWS is in the balance. Indifference at a number of levels has meant it has never achieved the professional coherency of other social work specialisms. Although recent child-care legislation presents an opportunity for the EWS to play a more significant part within the network of caring agencies it is part of a local government department that is being progressively undermined. The slender foundations that the service is built upon are now looking weaker than ever. This vulnerability is compounded by the inconsistent quality, structure and professionalism evident in much current EWS provision.

The lack of consistency is evident in the wide range of practice that is encountered in different parts of the country. Results of two recent surveys (NASWE 1989, 1991) endorse those of MacMillan (1977: 50) and show wide variations in numbers of education welfare officers (EWOs) employed in different local authorities. There are corresponding variations in the level of remuneration, the way the EWOs are managed and, one can deduce, in how they discharge their responsibilities. The service is still largely known as education welfare but in a number of areas, Birmingham and Oxfordshire, for example, the job title is that of education social worker. A few services, particularly in Scotland, still retain the title school attendance officer. Some have developed a clear professional identity with a distinct managerial structure, others have no functional hierarchy and still function in ways that must have changed little in the past fifty years. Beyond some regional variations there seems little to explain the difference in rates of development. Undeveloped services can be found in traditional Conservative and Labour, in rural and urban, and in large and small authorities.

The managerial structure could be one of the major determining factors. Education departments are dominated by those from teaching backgrounds, be they education officers, inspectors, or educational psychologists, and each of these groups usually has its own structure and hierarchy. If the development of the EWS is to be encouraged there would appear to be a powerful argument for it to have its own professional hierarchy. However, this would introduce a distinctly different professional perspective into the organization, which could then challenge other power structures. The reluctance of chief education officers to allow such development is understandable, but it may be the key factor in providing the opportunity and the motivation for an EWS to cultivate its professional identity. It is therefore also understandable that in areas where the EWS has no functional manager, or where such a post is afforded little status, the remainder of the service is usually poorly paid, underdeveloped and likely to function in ways that have changed little in twenty-five years.

Helping to maintain such inertia is a strong conservative element within the service itself. A traditional background for EWOs was, and still is in some parts, a career in a uniformed service. Although there has been a growth in the number of younger, perhaps more ambitious, recruits in recent years, there are still relatively few EWOs with professional qualifications in social work or a related field. A recent NASWE (1991) survey found that fewer than a quarter of field-workers or middle managers were qualified social workers, and it indicated that for many authorities such qualifications, while desirable, were not a requirement. This will be discussed later.

This pattern of piecemeal development reflects a distinct absence of coherency in the thinking of central government regarding the role and structure of the service. Twenty years ago the Ralphs Report (Local Government Training Board 1973) argued that education welfare should be developed as a social work service and some authorities responded to that recommendation. This was a view subsequently rejected by the DES, who argued that the 'services are not an extension of the personal social services' and that the 'EWO is primarily concerned to serve the child in relation to school attendance, not the whole family' (DES 1986: 1).

More recently three distinct sets of influences can be identified. The first tends to take a traditional view of education welfare and is well illustrated by the political pressure from government ministers and the DES in recent years. This has sought to curb the drift towards social work, viewing such a development as being at odds with the service's prime function of improving school attendance. Such preoccupations have often resulted in less attention being given to the important role of the service in other areas, such as special needs, school discipline and child protection, while emphasizing a punitive approach to irregular attendance. A good example of such thinking is contained in the appendix to a recent DES Circular (DES 1991), which describes the EWS as 'the attendance enforcement arm of most LEAs'. Behind this perception lies a view that truancy is an issue of law and order, linked with crime and deviant behaviour.

The second set of influences has been more progressive and has recognized the need for limited professional development within education welfare. These views have often been expressed by those located within the professional side of the educational establishment, who predominantly come from a teaching background. Clear examples are contained in the work of Her Majesty's Inspectorate of Schools (HMI). While much of their attention has focused on attendance, they have recognized that the issue is a complex one. Guidance on good practice has stressed the value of preventative work (HMI 1989a: 1). However, preventative work is described largely in terms of 'support' rather than in terms of a broader social work intervention. In addition, although they acknowledged that the service 'had developed and expanded over the years' and that the officers were sometimes known as education social workers, HMI have shown a marked reluctance to use this title in other contexts (e.g. HMI 1989b: 2).

The third influence, and one that has been generally popular within the profession, has been the implementation of the views expressed in the Ralphs Report. This envisaged the EWS dealing with a whole range of issues relating to the education and welfare of children, and had no qualms in stating that the 'education welfare officer is a social worker within an education setting' (LGTB 1973: 14). An echo of these views can be found in aspects of the Children Act 1989, and in the involvement of education welfare in areas such as child protection (DES 1988a: 2) and special educational needs. This broader role often requires structured, purposeful intervention with families related to a whole range of issues, and a professional status that commands respect and aids negotiation with schools and other agencies. Such approaches see irregular attendance at school as being the basis for intervention aimed at identifying and resolving the underlying issues, be they domestic, educational or a combination of the two, and acknowledges the need to work with parents and children on a co-operative basis.

Against this background the impact of recent legislative changes is likely to be considerable, especially that of the Education Reform Act 1988. Elements of this Act not only impinge on the direction of the service, but threaten its very existence. A central aspect of the legislation is the modification of the power structure of the education system, including aspects which, according to Maclure, introduce 'important limitations on the functions of LEAs' (Maclure 1989: ix). It is the pursuit of this objective that poses a direct threat to the future of the EWS by requiring local education authorities (LEAs) to delegate a greater proportion of education budgets to schools. The government recognized that it was inappropriate to transfer to schools funds for all the services that have traditionally been associated with the LEA. Therefore, some items were deemed to be mandatory exceptions. However, education welfare budgets were only identified as a 'discretionary exception' from delegation. This left it up to LEAs whether to continue funding the service centrally or to provide schools with an enhanced budget so that they could then choose whether or not to buy the existing service. The government clearly hoped that EWS budgets would be delegated (DES 1988b: 16). Within the framework established for local management of schools (LMS), it was indicated that the Secretary of State for Education would 'welcome' plans that involved the whole or partial delegation of EWS budgets (DES 1988b: 16).

Such delegation poses a direct threat to the EWS for a number of reasons. First, delegated budgets cannot be earmarked to ensure that they are spent on the service they are intended for. Second, if the service is bought in by a school then it is likely that the school would want provision that accommodated its own views rather than those of the child or the parents. If the school did not find the local authority EWO to its liking it could buy the service elsewhere, or employ a member of its own staff to undertake the work. Thus a service that was bought in might well find its independence compromised. Third, without reliable funding it will be difficult to provide the stability and continuity needed to maintain a viable professional service.

In spite of persistent and increasing pressure on LEAs to delegate greater proportions of their budgets to schools very few of them so far seem to find the delegation of EWS budgets attractive. One London authority has gone down that path and has delegated half of the budget. It maintains that if schools do not buy the service back then the EWS would only be involved in matters of poor attendance, and only then in pursuance of legal proceedings (London Borough of Hillingdon 1991).

Even if the EWS survives this round of the battle other aspects of the Education Reform Act are likely to present a challenge in the years to come. Of particular concern is the option for schools to become grant-maintained. This new category of schools is likely to present a considerable challenge to the viability of the EWS. Although they are freed of direct LEA control, the authority retains a continuing responsibility for ensuring the attendance of all pupils. Equally, all schools continue to have a legal obligation to notify the service if children fail to attend regularly. The challenge arises in circumstances where the EWS sees its task as not just ensuring that young people attend school, but as encouraging schools to be responsive to their educational needs. When the school is under the control of the LEA the EWS can turn to professional colleagues, such as education officers and LEA inspectors to aid them in this task. When that control is absent the service will have to depend largely on the power of persuasion and influence.

Both LMS and opting out indicate just how uncertain the future of the LEA, and by implication the EWS, is. This uncertainty is compounded by a confusion about the extent to which the LEA, and the services it provides, are concerned with meeting the needs of children rather than satisfying the demands of schools. There is a view that the LEA will rapidly become redundant. Rhodes Boyson, a former education minister, is among those who argue that they should be abolished (Fletcher 1991: 378). With increasing numbers of schools falling outside of LEA control the few remaining functions could, it is argued, be better carried out by an entirely different body outside the democratic control of local government. At the same time there are indications that the government is beginning to recognize that there are some functions that cannot be delegated to schools, and whether LEAs continue or not, some home will have to be found for them. The view on the delegation of budgets for education welfare in particular appears to have shifted from that expressed in Circular 7/88 (DES 1988b). Whereas that document determined that LEAs had to justify retaining budgets for EWSs, the recent Circular on Attendance (DES 1991) suggests that if LEAs delegated budgets they 'would need to ensure that they themselves continued to be able to perform their statutory attendance and other functions'. This is a significant change of emphasis.

In addition, there is a further problem in delegating budgets that is rarely considered. A number of the responsibilities defined in the Education Act 1944 relate to all children of school age whatever school they attend. All schools, whether local authority controlled, grant-maintained or independent, are required by separate legislation to notify the LEA when pupils attend irregularly. The precise size of the task relating to those educated outside LEA schools is rarely quantified, but with increasing numbers of schools opting out and new categories of independent schools, such as city technology colleges, being developed, it is bound to grow. It would be difficult for the LEA to fulfil its duties to such pupils if it no longer retained control of the EWS.

At the same time as the administrative context and management of the EWS is becoming uncertain, there are suggestions that the demands on the service will increase, as a side-effect of other aspects of the 1988 Act. In order to understand how this might be the case it is useful to examine elements of the thinking behind the legislation. Since 1944 schools have been managed by headteachers and governors, but in partnership with the LEA. It is the government's view that the control of the LEA, exercised through such means as budgetary and admission controls, has minimized competition, which, the government argues, is the best way of raising standards. Accordingly the Education Reform Act gives schools far greater autonomy, not only through LMS, but also by weakening LEA controls over admissions and by linking school income directly to pupil numbers. Thus, schools are being encouraged to compete with each other directly for pupils.

This may lead to some interesting developments. For example, while comprehensive schools are not supposed to be selective, popular schools will inevitably find themselves in a position of 'producer sovereignty'. According to some commentators the most attractive pupils are likely to be those of the highest academic ability who take the least effort to manage.

> If a school is to enter the marketplace and compete for 'clients' and if the overwhelming symbol of success within this marketplace is to be academic 'success', then where does this leave the child with special educational needs?
>
> (Fowler 1991: 39)

The same question could be asked for any pupil who is likely to demand additional time, effort or resources. The parents of these young people may find their choice of school restricted, and the responsibility for linking home, schools and LEA, in order to find an acceptable solution, is likely to fall upon the shoulders of the EWS.

In addition, when places for such pupils have been achieved, the parents may find that schools are less inclined to expend precious time and resources on them, as such investment is unlikely to be fruitful in terms of examination results. Similarly, poor performance in the standard assessment tests (SATs) linked to the National Curriculum may well produce alienation and disaffection. Brighouse (1989: 8) argues that the more competitive environment that will prevail among children and schools 'could be dangerous to the emotional needs of children whose needs have never been very well served by our schools'. The net result of these developments is that those pupils who already take up most of the EWOs' time could find themselves even more marginalized by schools. Inevitably such outcomes will mean an increasing burden for the EWS.

The Children Act 1989 brings with it a new responsibility for the EWS and might be seen as the most helpful change in recent years. Historically, development has been impeded by the comparatively slender legislative framework that forms the basis of its existence. The key piece of legislation has been the Education Act 1944, which empowered LEAs to prosecute parents who do not ensure regular attendance. Thus, the legislative basis for the EWS provides for a distinctly punitive and adversarial approach to poor attendance.

The secondary piece of legislation that addressed the issue of poor attendance, the Children and Young Person's Act (CYPA) 1969, while of good intent, is often exercised in similarly punitive manner. The Children Act 1989 withdraws the power to make care orders in such circumstances, but does introduce education supervision orders (ESOs). For the first time the need to tackle the underlying causes of irregular attendance is recognized and this may encourage the development of much more sophisticated approaches by the EWS. The Circular of Guidance (Department of Health 1991) establishes the framework for the application for and use of ESOs, and this echoes themes found throughout the legislation.

There are a number of reasons for seeing the new Children Act as a positive development. First, it means that care is no longer an option in cases of irregular attendance. An unfortunate legal precedent established that irregular attendance at school was itself proof of the grounds for a care order being established under the CYPA 1969, Section 1, and it was a practice to use the threat of care to coerce children into school. At times this was carried out by the court, as in the infamous 'Leeds system', where the education department was encouraged to take cases of irregular attendance directly to the juvenile court. The magistrates would then tell young people that they expected to see them back in court after a set period of time, normally two to four weeks, and if they had not attended school regularly they could expect to be taken into care. In some cases this process went on for several months. At other times the threat of care would be made informally by the EWO. Often these threats were realized: Gaffaney (1987: 7) suggests that the procedures led to 228 interim and 45 full care orders being made on school attendance grounds by Leeds magistrates in one year. When in care the remedy could be worse than the original condition.

According to Ball (1990: iv) many children were placed in community homes with education where the education was 'at best barely adequate and at worst deplorable'.

Second, the court will be required to exercise closer scrutiny of an application for an ESO to ensure that it presents a sound analysis of the circumstances and a credible justification for the making of an order. LEAs will have to ensure that their EWOs, in addition to having a measure of expertise in casework, are able to undertake proper assessments and present coherent reports.

Third, the ESO encourages a co-operative approach. An application for an ESO, and its effectiveness, depends upon developing a partnership between the parent(s), child, school and supervising officer. While familiar to some EWOs, such an approach may not be to all, particularly where punitive approaches have predominated and little account has been taken of such recent developments as client access to files.

Fourth, the order shifts responsibility from the social services departments (SSDs) to the LEA. Supervision or care orders made under the 1969 Act, even where irregular attendance was the central concern and intervention was initiated by the education department, still gave the SSD ultimate responsibility for resourcing the order and for deciding what action to take. Now if an ESO does not achieve the necessary change, then the education department and the EWS will have to take responsibility.

Fifth, the order promotes work with the whole family. The previous supervision order gave the parents a minor, often negligible role, in that advising, assisting and befriending was aimed purely at the child. The ESO, in contrast, places considerable emphasis on working with parents and helping them to help their children. This provides the EWS with the task of identifying who exactly its client is.

Sixth, the order encourages the supervising officer to act as an advocate, and this may promote a much clearer determination of the role of the EWO in relation to the school. In the past the role of the EWO within the school (DES 1986: 31; 1989: 184) was not clearly defined. Less assertive EWOs stood the chance of having their role defined by the school, rather than by their employer or by their professional standards. An integral part of the ESO is the need for the supervising officer to become aware of the educational needs of the child and to help ensure that those needs are adequately met. Thus, the task is clearly not just that of fitting children into schools, but of helping to ensure that schools provide a rewarding and stimulating environment.

The Children Act requires the EWS to develop a clearer professional identity. Over the next few years the manner in which ESOs are used will be under close scrutiny, and the relationships between EWOs and social workers will be tested more frequently. Improved management of the EWS will be required if ESOs are to be properly supervised and evaluated. Unfortunately preparation within LEAs for the Children Act is taking place in a piecemeal fashion. Department of Health funding for the new legislation is administered through SSDs, and little of this money has found its way to education. The DES has so far given very little support in this way of information, training or resources.

Assuming the EWS does undertake the necessary development to allow for the proper use of the ESO, it could well highlight the need for much wider reappraisal of the way the service operates. The structured, co-operative, time-limited intervention encouraged by the ESO is likely to prove equally applicable to cases where there is no need for legal intervention, and where the primary aim is prevention rather than cure. Thus the ESO could be the spur to the most radical and positive change yet seen in the EWS, and may help ensure that the image of the 'truancy officer' is finally banished.

In order to achieve that change of identity other issues will have to be addressed. A crucial concern is that of training, as it is in this area that the service has traditionally been weak. ESO guidance suggests that the Diploma in Social Work, or either of the qualifications it replaces, is the appropriate professional qualification for education welfare. However, the gradings survey of the EWS (NASWE 1991) found that only 22 per cent of EWOs in field-work and middle management positions are professionally qualified. Many authorities employ no qualified workers at all and where there are qualified workers these are more likely to be in management positions. Quite who is responsible for these low figures is hard to identify. Blyth and Milner (1990: iii) suggest that CCETSW, the DES and the LEAs all share responsibility. CCETSW has a legal duty to provide training opportunities for the EWS but has been reluctant to fulfil this without funding from the DES. The DES argues that it is up to LEAs whether or not they require EWOs to be trained. LEAs, in turn, display a distinct ambivalence: they may prefer qualified workers, but do not offer the pay levels and training opportunities to allow for this.

The new Diploma in Social Work is a mixed blessing for the service. It is helpful in that more flexible learning opportunities may pave the way for employers to release unqualified workers for training. The Centre for Education Welfare Studies has also demonstrated how the new Diploma can meet the training needs of the EWS. However, a difficulty then presents itself. The stricter criteria for approving agencies and accrediting practice teachers may reduce the opportunity for students to be given assessed experience within EWSs. Not one EWS received funding from CCETSW during its 1989–90 programme of agency approval. Thus there may be limited opportunities for specialist education welfare placements and fewer incentives for trainee social workers to consider a career in such a specialization.

A related issue is that of salary scales. Comparisons between the pay of EWOs and social workers in SSDs help foster the Cinderella image. Up until 1984 a separate and inferior pay scale existed for EWOs. This scale was dropped to be replaced by a determination that, while there was no national determination of the pay scales of EWOs, if they were required to work at a similar level to social workers in social services 'they should be paid accordingly' (NJC 1989). However, while some services have been able to achieve comparability, very few offer true parity. The EWS is clearly in a dilemma; without adequate pay levels it will prove hard to attract qualified workers, and while unqualified workers continue to be considered acceptable there will be little pressure on employers to improve remuneration.

The future of the service is also very much tied up with the future of local government. If LEAs disappear, either through wastage as an increasing number of schools opt out, or a consequence of legislation, what options are open for the EWS? The first is that of delegation to schools, as discussed earlier. If there is to be continuity between the holding of the legal responsibility for ensuring parents send their children to school and the managements of the services which support that responsibility, then there will need to be legislation amending the 1944 Act, transferring the LEA's responsibility over to schools. This would place schools in the position of both being a service provider and having the legal duty for ensuring their services were consumed.

A second option would be to transfer the service to social services departments. This harks back to the Seebohm Report (HMSO 1968) and was an option implemented in some authorities. However, in few cases has such an arrangement been viewed as satisfactory. Social services departments have an increasing range of statutory responsibilities that might easily lead to them failing to prioritize what schools and education departments feel to be appropriate. In addition, such a shift may weaken links with those, such as educational psychologists, advisers and LEA inspectors, who also provide support for schools and pupils, not least in areas such as special educational needs and pupil exclusion.

A third option is to give the service an entirely new structure, independent of local government and linked to the DES. This would seem the most obvious alternative if LEAs are eliminated. While the EWS may prefer to remain part of LEAs, the option of managing the service along with others that cannot easily be delegated to schools through non-elected educational boards has a number of attractions. First, it would bring greater cohesion to a service that shows a wide degree of variation in both quality and style. Second, the service would retain its links with education and thus be well placed to influence the way that schools deal with matters relating to the welfare of pupils, encouraging them to make an early response and helping them to resolve issues of poor attendance, alienation and disaffection, before they become intractable. Third, it would give the service greater security than it has at present.

A further consideration that would make this outcome attractive is linked with making the current educational reforms work in the way they are intended to. These reforms had as their focus the aim that consumers of education should have more control through increased parental choice and wider accountability. As suggested earlier there is a great danger that such choice will be the privilege of the already privileged, and that the claimed increase in influence will be, for many, illusory. If the undesirable outcome of 'producer sovereignty' is to be avoided there is a role for an independent service to act as an advocate for those who have less eloquence and less confidence, a consumer association for education. Education welfare, strategically placed between schools and parents, is ideally situated to take on such a task. In addition there are a number of different and, at times conflicting interests within education. Parents, children, schools, employers and education departments have their own perceptions as to what constitutes desirable educational outcomes. Education welfare, possessing, as it does, established links with the community and other local authority services, and with a professional commitment to look at what is best for the young person, is ideally placed to mediate between these sets of interests. To develop such a role would present the EWOs with a challenge. They would have to practise making their voice heard within their departments and within schools on issues such as special needs, exclusions, school admissions and ensuring that the system pays heed to the needs, rights and wishes of the consumers of education.

With this in mind, I would hold that education welfare has an important role to play in the future, but for the vision to be realized there will need to be some radical change.

It will require an acknowledgement from the government that unbridled market forces in education will lead to unacceptable casualties among the more vulnerable members of our school community, and a recognition that the EWS can take a key role in preventing that outcome. If the EWS is to take a lead in protecting the educational opportunities of such young people then the professional standards of the service will have to be raised and consistency improved. This could be achieved through inspection, which if carried out by a specialist branch of the HMI or Social Services Inspectorate could provide a much clearer account of good and bad practice, and through a more determined application of professional training. In this respect the DES could make a greater contribution than it does at present by giving full endorsement to appropriate courses and improved financial support through bursaries and sponsorship for individuals wishing to train.

For LEAs to realize their part within this vision they will need to recognize that while it is an important function to service schools, they also have duty to serve the public. If they acknowledge this responsibility they might also come to appreciate the key role that the EWS has the potential to fill, and set about plugging the gaps in service provision that are apparent in many parts of the country. For many this will be a sizeable task.

Last, but by no means least, the EWS itself has a contribution to make. A tradition of a hundred years of service is unlikely in itself to provide a secure basis for the future. Through its own professional organization the service will have to develop a critical attitude towards practice and a commitment to improving standards. This may be achieved through a professional code that expresses a commitment towards ethical and practical standards similar to those found in other branches of social work. Once that code is established it needs to be applied with rigour, determination and honesty. It will have to be recognized that not all members of the service will be comfortable with the kind of changes that will be required, and that taking a more assertive stance towards schools will present an immense challenge. If the EWS is able to respond to these and other challenges then I believe it has some chance of surviving another hundred years. If so it will not only be EWOs who gain, it will be those young people, often marginalized by the education system, whose true potential is never realized.

References

Ball, C. (1990) 'Spelling out the effects of truancy', *Community Care* 31, May: iv.
Blyth, E. and Milner, J. (1990) 'Opportunity Knocks for education welfare', *Community Care* 31 May: iii.

Brighouse, T. (1989) 'Which shelf for Peter and June', *Concern* Autumn: 8–9.
DES (1986) *School Attendance and Education Welfare Services, Circular 2/86*, London: Department of Education and Science.
DES (1988a) *Working Together for the Protection of Children from Abuse, Circular 4/88*, London: Department of Education and Science.
DES (1988b) *Financial Delegation to Schools, Circular 7/88*, London: Department of Education and Science.
DES (1989) *Discipline in Schools*, Report of the Committee of Enquiry chaired by Lord Elton, London: HMSO.
DES (1991) *School Attendance, Circular 11/91*, London: Department of Education and Science.
Department of Health (1991) *Consultation Paper 21, Education Supervision Order*, London: Department of Education and Science/Department of Health.
Fletcher, M. (1991) 'Straight talk from Sir Rhodes', *Education* 10 May: 378.
Fowler, P. (1991) 'LMS route may lead back to segregation', *Times Educational Supplement* 7 June: 139.
Gaffaney, P. (1987) 'The truant adjourned: not everyone approves', *Community Care* 5 March: 7.
HMI (1989a) *Education Observed 13, Attendance at School*, London: Department of Education and Science.
HMI (1989b) *Some Aspects of the Education Social Welfare Service in Oxfordshire*, London: Department of Education and Science.
HMSO (1968) *Report of the Committee on Local Authority and Allied Personal Social Services* (The Seebohm Report), London: HMSO.
Local Government Training Board (1973) *The Role and Training of Education Welfare Officers* (Ralphs Report), Luton: LGTB.
London Borough of Hillingdon (1991) *The Education Welfare Service, a Handbook of Information for Schools and Governing Bodies*, Hillingdon: London Borough of Hillingdon.
Maclure, S. (1989) *Education Reformed*, Sevenoaks: Hodder and Stoughton.
MacMillan, K. (1977) *Education Welfare, Strategy and Structure*, Harlow: Longman.
NASWE (1989) *Education Welfare National Gradings Survey 1989*, unpublished survey, London: NASWE.
NASWE (1991) 'Education Welfare National Gradings Survey 1990' *Education Social Worker* 217, March: 27–8.
NJC (1989) *Scheme and Conditions of Service*, London: National Joint Council for Local Authorities Administrative, Professional, Technical and Clerical Services.

11
Sexuality and social work organizations

Elizabeth Harlow,
Jeff Hearn and
Wendy Parkin

Although sexuality is an element in all encounters, its influence cannot be fully called to account. This is especially important in social work and social work organizations, which to some extent specialize in work on people's personal welfare. In this chapter we review current questions, themes and changes related to sexuality and social work organizations in the UK. We focus in turn on: recent debates and developments in organizational analysis; the context of social work settings; and policies and practices in social work. However, separating out each of these aspects of the subject into discrete topics has for several reasons been problematic. This is firstly and primarily because of the sheer complexity of the issues involved in sexuality and social work organizations. The subject involves a wide variety of relations between different kinds of social structures, situations and experiences, rather than any real compartmentalization of different aspects of life and analysis. Second, we are writing this chapter collaboratively, with different genders, different sexualities and different voices. Third, the area is also one of relatively rapid change in practices, policies and theoretical understandings. Fourth, the area is suffused with the problem of power. All these points mean that it is not possible to divide our discussions neatly into separate subsections. Instead there are innumerable ways in which 'general' questions of theory interrelate with more 'specific' questions about organizational settings, practices and policies. Thus this is not just a matter of the abstract structuring of writing; it is a consequence of writing about such a powerful, and yet subtle and elusive, subject as sexuality.

Power, sexuality and organizations

Both sexuality in general and sexuality in organizations are constructed through complex interplays of dominant and subordinated discourses. Within such dominant discourses, sexuality may be characterized as 'given' or 'just natural'; ideas of 'the male sex drive' or 'normal male sexuality' may be invoked (Coveney *et al.* 1984; Hollway 1984; Collinson and Collinson 1989a); 'men' and 'heterosexuals' may be located in valued positions, while 'women', 'children', 'lesbians' and 'gay men' may be unvalued, excluded or silenced. In organizations this may take the form of the domination of heterosexist work cultures, implicitly or explicitly underwritten by management. And yet within dominant discourses there is often also a conspiracy of silence around sexuality or certain aspects of sexuality. This silence may take many different forms: in specific organizational cultures; in policy, guidelines, training, and management; in organizational analysis and theories; in organizational and professional practices; in personal experiences and personal lives. Thus dominant discourses, like all discourses, depend on specific silences within them, as well as the silence of 'other' discourses.

To speak of silences in this way may seem strange. After all, it appears that there are ever-increasing discourses and debates on sexuality, particularly in social work and social welfare. This is certainly the case in relation to sexual harassment, child sexual abuse, sex offenders, people with disabilities and HIV/AIDS. However, we would treat such 'breaks in silence' with some caution. Certainly since the late nineteenth century there have been extensive professional discourses on sexuality, often informed by medical and/or moral perspectives. Professional or professionalized discourses on sexuality have been and often are ambiguous in 'breaking the silences' of the excluded and speaking *on behalf of* those who are excluded. In other words, they may be both empowering and oppressive, both liberating and incorporating. Furthermore, such professionalized discourses bring with them their own further silences: debates on sexual harassment may emphasize the tangible and the visible rather than the intangible and the invisible; those on child sexual abuse and sex offending may emphasize deviance or crime rather than the mundane or everyday; and those on people with disability and on HIV/AIDS may emphasize 'health' and 'illness' rather than other realms of experience. In these ways, such growing discourses on sexuality reproduce their own silences and their own hierarchies of value.

Moreover, sexuality is often associated with the intimate, the personal and the deeply private. This in itself works against discussion of what is meant by sexuality and how it figures for all people in all aspects of our everyday lives. While there is no one clear-cut definition of sexuality, it may be useful to think of it as a shorthand for the realm of human experiences that concerns physical, bodily desires. More precisely, sexuality refers to the social construction and social relations of physical, bodily desires, and their relationship to other areas of experience, such as health, work, consumption, violence, power and spirituality. Seen in this way, sexuality is clearly related to, yet distinct from, what is meant by gender. In most formulations sexuality is understood as an aspect of gender, or the relationship of sex and gender. An alternative, and very powerful, approach is to understand sexuality as the basis of gender (MacKinnon 1982): that is material, social relations, including sexual contacts and sexual violence, that underlie the social construction of gender, women and men.

Since the rise of modern feminism and the growth of feminist interventions in organizations, there has been increasing interest in, and analysis of, the relationship of gender and organizational life. Much of this practical and theoretical concern has focused on two main issues: the gender division of labour; and the gender division of authority, in terms of hierarchy, management and supervision. Far less attention has been directed towards what is in some ways the most obvious element of gender relations, namely sexuality in organizations (Hearn and Parkin 1987). The impetus for greater study of sexuality in organizations stemmed partly from campaigns in the 1970s and 1980s against sexual harassment in organizations (Farley 1978; MacKinnon 1979). In more recent years there has developed a wider interest in the relationship of sexuality and organizations (e.g. Horn and Horn 1982; Gutek 1985; Hearn and Parkin 1987; Hearn et al. 1989). Studies of sexual harassment have continued (e.g. Hogbacka et al. 1987), as have documentations of discriminations against lesbians (e.g. Taylor 1986) and gay men (e.g. Levine 1979).

To some extent sexual dynamics in organizations can be understood as determined by gender divisions by labour and authority. For example, the valuing of people's labour and authority by gender may be reflected or reproduced in the valuing of people's sexualities. In this sense organizations may be seen as constructing sexuality, such that we may talk of the organizational construction of sexuality. On the other hand, there are numerous ways in which sexuality in its own right affects and influences organizational life – through sexual meetings, sexual liaisons, sexual relationships, affairs, gossip, rumour, innuendo, myth, as well as sexual harassment. In this view we can refer to sexuality as a constructor of organizations or the sexual construction of organizations. Both of these processes are pervasive in organizations, and both are deeply connected with the operation of power. These connections are both crude and subtle, direct and paradoxical.

It is for these reasons that there have been a number of recent attempts to connect sexual and organizational processes in a direct way. Such concepts as 'organization sexuality' (Hearn and Parkin 1987) and 'the sexuality of organization' (Burrell and Hearn 1989) refer to the ways in which sexuality and organization can co-exist: sexual dynamics and organizational dynamics may occur simultaneously, and reciprocally define each other. These ways of understanding sexuality and organizations are in contrast to most conventional views, which see sexuality and organizations as separate, with organizations located in the public domain and sexuality residing in the private domain. Instead the interconnectedness of sexuality and organization is explicitly recognized. However, as already noted, this interconnectedness often has a distinctly paradoxical character: both sexual and organizational, both public and private, both sexualized and desexualized (Burrell 1984; Hearn and Parkin 1987). More specifically, many, probably most, organizations are dominated by (men's) heterosexuality and the 'male sexual narrative' (Dyer 1985), with an associated domination of lesbian and gay sexualities (Rich 1980; Hall 1989), and yet may also be understandable in terms of a pervasive 'homosexual subtext' (Seidenberg 1970; Wood 1987;

Hearn 1992) and women's experiences on the 'lesbian continuum' (Rich 1980). All the 'general' issues described so far are relevant to social work organizations, policies and practice.

Power, sexuality and social work settings

A female student social worker was on placement at a residential establishment with a male practice teacher who was also manager of the unit. She was wearing a V-neck blouse or T-shirt and also a locket on a chain. The locket was twisted and the male manager came and untwisted the locket, and looked down her blouse while saying, 'I like my female staff to look tidy'. The student (who wishes to remain anonymous but gave permission to use this incident) felt violated but said nothing.

This student stayed silent for fear that voicing a protest against what had occurred would make her seem stupid and would be an 'over-reaction' that would be held against her. Only in the context of a discussion on the power of sexuality in organizational politics was she more fully able to understand the abuse of power that had occurred and to voice it without feeling trivialized. In spite of the student feeling violated and sexually harassed, protest was suppressed by a combination of her powerless position in the organization and the power of the male manager.

This incident highlights the ever-present exercise of power through gender, which is crucially underpinned by the power of the male sexual narrative. The supervisor used his management position, authority and power, along with his heterosexuality, unrequested touch and gaze, to achieve concealment by silence. These issues are part of all organizational life but it could be argued that social work tasks, involving close relationships with people, are more explicitly or implicitly sexualized. Furthermore, dominant discourses on sexual harassment tend to be constructed around the tangible and the visible. This case study illustrates the point that despite and perhaps because of this, 'breaking the silence' on less tangible and more subtle forms of harassment can remain difficult. Forms of harassment that may be an intrinsic part of organizational life and power relations may continue to be shrouded in silence.

Thus constructions of sexuality in social work organizations have to be understood in the context of organizational power relations, including the location of social work and social work organizations as institutions in the public domain. At its simplest, the control of everyday life by organizations, and the way the self is defined by belonging or not belonging to an organization, are a major feature of power relations in contemporary society (Mills 1991). The positive connotations of holding organizational positions in the public world of paid work contrast with the negative connotations of inhabiting private, domestic or family worlds. In the wider context it is important to locate social work organizations in relation to these public–private divisions. Not only do men dominate in both spheres, but the public dominates the private, leading to a double domination of women (Hearn and Parkin 1987; Parkin 1989). This is especially relevant for an understanding of social work as part of state intervention into family life. Also important when looking at residential social work organizations is the recognition of unequal gender divisions of labour in both spheres and the way in which the domestic is devalued in both (Clark and Lange 1979). This contributes to a devaluing of the residential care task.

Social work tasks, though immensely varied, frequently involve issues about sexuality, both explicitly and implicitly. Relevant tasks include: family and child care work; work on sexual abuse and violence; work with sex offenders; work with adolescents; work with people with various illnesses and disabilities; work with people with HIV/AIDS (e.g. Elphis 1980; Milner and Blyth 1988). In all these and other kinds of social work an anti-heterosexist stance is important. Furthermore, in working with lesbians and gay men (e.g. Woodman and Lenna 1980; Hall 1985; Stein and Cohen 1986; Macourt 1989) on cases involving such issues as lesbian custody (e.g. Rights of Women 1984), or with people who are unclear or uncertain about their sexuality, it is especially important to avoid heterosexist 'norms' and to develop positive anti-oppressive forms of social work practice that challenge heterosexism. This has, however, been made more difficult by Section 28 of the Local Government Act 1988, which outlaws the 'intentional promotion of homosexuality' by local authorities (Evans 1989/90), and by a variety of other recent measures, including Paragraph 16 of the government's Foster Placement Guidelines and Regulations, which suggest that lesbian and gay foster parents are unsuitable (Department of Health 1990).

The range of work is only one factor as the organizational context of such 'people work' is of fundamental importance whether undertaken in prisons, hospitals, offices or residential settings. A further factor is not only the type of work, involving as it does often closely knit relationships between client and worker, undertaken in a variety of organizational settings; there are also often close knit supportive relationships among colleagues.

Social workers, their managers and clients often remain silent about sexuality, at least officially, and this is reflected in the lack of rules, procedures, management guidelines and training on the issue (Parkin 1989). There remains a strong institutional tendency to keep the issue away from official agendas. However, unofficially and informally sexuality is often a topic for conversation. In these contexts, it is not usually men's sexuality that is seen as the intrusion but women's sexuality, with its connotations of the irrational, which is seen as having no place in rational, masculinized organizations (Pringle 1989; Mills 1991). Accordingly, research on sexuality in organizations has to explore organizational silences, informal erotic hierarchies based on 'attractiveness', gossip, rumour and fantasy, and the various reasons for the construction of sexuality as a private issue in public domains.

The designation of social work, along with teaching and nursing for example, as semi-professions (Simpson and Simpson 1969) is invoking a gendered concept reflecting the power relationships between different professional groupings. In all these circumstances, there is a characteristic structure of a profession predominantly staffed by women and dominated by men. In addition, the dimension of 'people work' in social work, involving as it does questions of emotionality and relationships, increases the need to attend to sexuality as an issue for organizational agendas, guidelines and policies.

For those not conforming to heterosexual 'norms', silence around sexuality may be felt to be paramount. The desire for secrecy concerning personal life for fear of prejudice or harassment may mean an inability to join in the organization's social life and a lack of access to the informal power systems. The need to lead a double life of private and public can be stressful and debilitating. The inability to present the corporate image is not advantageous in the promotion stakes (Hall 1989). Discrimination against lesbians and gay men in social services departments was documented by the National Council for Civil Liberties as long ago as the 1970s (Ferris 1977). While some of the worst abuses of staff and potential staff may appear to have been reduced, the whole climate of local authority activity has been affected since 1988 by Section 28. It is in this context that a few authorities (including Haringey, Camden and Manchester) have developed in-service training about sexuality and heterosexism, and NAPO (1991) has produced a lesbian and gay rights training pack.

There are particular issues regarding sexuality in residential settings. Such settings are neither public nor private, but both. These settings are frequently called 'homes' but have many features of a total institution. The 'care' staff are usually female and untrained, and find their domestic role devalued in this setting as it is in the private sphere. Here is an ambiguous 'intermediate zone' (Stacey and Davies 1983) that is between the public and the private. There is both the language of the private (house parents, care assistants, cooks) and that of the public (officer-in-charge, staff rotas, meetings). They also have features of totality: surveillance and control rather than support and care. Thus the ambiguity of the setting contributes to a particular organizational dilemma that has the potential for serious, severe and prolonged exploitation, sexual or otherwise. Not only are there vulnerable clients and an emotionally charged atmosphere, there is an ambiguous setting in which the rules can change between public and private so that no one, staff or residents, is clear as to which rules are in operation. All this is conducted not in a 'home' but in a 'totality', where scrutiny of residents is at a maximum and scrutiny of staff in charge is at a minimum. The silence here is deafening but arguably more understandable when the combination of client vulnerability, emotional atmosphere, physical intimacy and ambiguity of setting all contribute to the ability of those with authority and power to keep control of organizational agendas, procedures and practices.

Social workers occupy powerful positions with their clients but are also subordinate to a predominantly male management structure. Not only do women often face problems in having career prospects discussed in supervision (Morris 1987), they are also particularly vulnerable to sexual harassment. This frequently arises from the emotional nature of the work with severely distressed clients. Comfort and support are often needed from colleagues and superiors since feelings, as well as bodies, are often bruised. Such support can often involve touch and this is an obvious arena for exploitation. It may be very difficult to refuse touch offered under the heading of support, even if it is personally unacceptable. To break the silence on this is not only to be seen as stupid, unfit for the job and over-reacting, but also to be seen as ungrateful.

Power, sexuality and social work practice

Despite the silence, sexuality may be significant not only in the policy-making and staffing of social work organizations but also in the direct practice of social work itself. That is, sexuality is an aspect of the power relations that affect social work processes. However, organizational position, age, (dis)ability, gender and race of the individuals concerned will affect the ways in which sexuality is significant. For example, sexuality as an aspect of white people's racism can be placed in an historical perspective. During the seventeenth and eighteenth centuries white Europeans writing about black African people described the men as having large penises and being particularly virile while the women were said to be particularly desirous of sexual intercourse (Miles 1989: 27). Jordan (1984) and Hooks (1982) argue that the portrayal of black African people as more overtly sexualized beings was a part of their definition by Europeans as more 'bestial' than white people, somewhat less than human, thus allowing a justification of slavery. Using as illustration the various representations of black men, Mercer and Julien (1988) argue that Western European notions of sexuality are fundamental to racism. The image of black African people as overtly sexual, closer to nature and hence uncivilized contributes to the view of black people, men in particular, as posing a threat to 'civilization' and in need of surveillance and control. In areas such as sports, where physique is all-important, black men are 'allowed', by the dominant white group, to participate and excel. Mercer and Julien, both themselves black and gay men, argue that this image of black masculinity has been 'internalized' by many black men, who then play out the stereotype. These racist and sexualized images of black people may affect the way in which social work is organized and carried out.

The ways in which racism is played out in social work varies. One of the most obvious might be the role practitioners take in 'containing' black male youth. In addition, where social work staff are involved with caring for black young people, these sexualized images of black masculinity and sexualized femininity may well influence the nature of the relationships involved, the kind of care that is offered, and the kind of activities that black young people are encouraged or discouraged from participating in. Black families may be problematized by social workers who define 'promiscuous' fathers as inadequate. Black people are not only recipients of social work interventions but are also social workers. Racism may be one of the ways in which white colleagues and clients challenge the statutory authority of black social workers. Black African and Caribbean social workers and social work recipients are not alone in experiencing the consequences of sexualized imagery. According to Mercer and Julien (1988: 133) colonial fantasies of Asian or Oriental men consist of them being seen as delicate, fragile and exotic. Parmar (1984: 75) exposes the contradictory and racist European images of Asian women, who are seen as, 'sexually erotic creatures, full of Eastern promise and on the other hand as completely dominated by their men, mute and oppressed wives and mothers'. Such popularized images of Asian men and women undoubtedly affect the social work services offered (or not offered) to Asian communities. Thus sexualized images of black and Asian men and women as an aspect of racism may affect all social work relationships irrespective of whether the black and Asian people involved are clients or social workers.

Social workers are seen as having more power than their clients and in some situations clients are more obviously dependent upon social work staff. In residential establishments older people with disabilities and children may be dependent upon residential social workers and care staff for the satisfaction of their daily human needs. The opportunity for (particularly male) social workers and care staff to exploit this relationship sexually is evident (White 1987; Parkin 1989). Scandals about ill-treatment in residential establishments are not infrequent, whether involving deprivation of older people or 'pindown' with children (Levy and Kahan 1991). Sexuality as an aspect of power relations is also evident in relationships between field social workers and their clients. Social workers visiting clients, perhaps alone in their homes, may exploit their structural power. For example, the social work approach taken may be influenced by sexual aspects of the relationship or the social worker may become involved in an explicitly sexual relationship. Hall (1987) reviews the literature on gender, sexuality and psychotherapy and, contrary to previous assertions, concludes that sexuality is an issue particularly for male therapists with 'attractive' female clients. She quotes Holroyd (1983), who suggests that 'patient–therapist sex occurs when therapists who have mental and emotional problems also have sexist views' (Hall 1987: 40). On the other hand this kind of argument downplays explanations of sexual exploitation based in individual choice, personal responsibility or structural power relations.

Those in structural positions of power are vulnerable to retaliation from those who are, or feel themselves to be, less powerful. Within the context of residential establishments staff may fear accusations of sexual abuse and this may influence the daily running of the establishments and the behaviour of residential staff. 'Any touch or show of affection is liable to be avoided. One-to-one chats in the bedrooms are a thing of the past. . . . Sexual fear has become one of the primary factors in shaping daily living' (White 1987: 63–4). In the context of field work Wise and Stanley (1990) point out that male clients may feel powerless in front of their social workers, and where the worker is female (as is most often the case) they may use sexual harassment as a means of retaliation.

The silence of social workers on issues of sexuality either with or between social work clients can have detrimental consequences. This is not only because of the opportunity to maintain and abuse power, but also in undermining or preventing the fundamental tasks of social work to provide help or care to vulnerable individuals. The daily life of residential establishments is influenced by beliefs, values and behaviour connected with sexuality, but rare is the opportunity for these to be discussed, considered and scrutinized by clients, staff and policy-makers. Within this context the sexual needs and wishes of some social work clients will go unmet because they have not been acknowledged and identified. For example, residential establishments for older people or those with disabilities will routinely offer accommodation for single people only. Bedroom doors may not be fitted with locks and there may be little opportunity for privacy. For those who are physically dependent, the support of care staff and social workers is essential for the development of sexual relationships. The failure of this to be recognized could lead to the denial of an individual's needs and wishes. Coley and Marler (1987) draw attention to the way in which mentally handicapped people are denied recognition as sexual beings. Techniques such as referring to mentally handicapped adults as boys and girls avoids having to acknowledge their sexuality. Where there is a 'risk' of sexual activity by a mentally handicapped woman, fertility has on occasions been controlled by enforced contraception or even abortion. Coley and Marler suggest that media images of the 'body beautiful' may be detrimental for those unable to see through them, and punitive attitudes towards homosexuality may go unchallenged. In such ways the failure of social workers to address sexuality and to challenge dominant myths or norms may perpetuate the injustice of gender and sexual oppression. These issues are particularly important in the residential care of young people.

White (1987) suggests that such children and young people are often unloved and insecure and may turn to sexual relationships as a means of compensation. Boys may behave in ways they believe to be essential in asserting their masculine identity and girls in particular may be vulnerable to exploitation from individuals within and outside of the residential establishment. Silence and fear about sexuality may mean that staff, although aware of children engaging in sexual relations, turn a 'blind eye' providing it is covert and in particular off the premises. Simmonds (1988) describes a situation in a residential establishment where the sexual behaviour of a teenage girl was seen as too much for the staff to deal with and she was referred to a sex counsellor from outside. This was done with little exploration as to the the best course of action, without any information about the sex counsellor, and without consulting the girl about her wishes. When the counsellor's intervention appeared to be erratic and unhelpful, the residential staff were forced to reconsider the situation. They eventually concluded that the referral had been made on the basis of their own fears, feelings and inability to discuss the issues rather than on the basis of the most appropriate course of action for the girl. The 'problem' had been removed by placing it in the hands of an outsider but the end result was that the girl had not received sensitive and considered care. Although Simmonds's work is primarily concerned with psychodynamic processes in organizations, his illustration demonstrates how fear and silence about sexuality inhibit good social work practice. Young people are prevented from discussing matters with concerned and responsible adults, and White (1987: 62) describes sex education as 'hit and miss'. Such an environment is unlikely to build the confidence of teenagers or prepare them for their future.

There is increasing interest and debate within social work on the whole area of child sexual abuse and sex offending, yet even so the failure of field social workers to identify sexual abuse in families allows exploitation and oppression to continue. Within social work the problem is generally constructed in terms of 'dangerousness' and child protection, the development of support groups for survivors of abuse and work with perpetrators of abuse. Sexual abuse is thus framed within the terms of deviance and crime rather than the mundane and everyday construction of masculinity and power relations between men, women and children.

It is important to remind ourselves that child sexual abuse was known about and addressed by the earliest social workers at the turn of the century, but the awareness was lost, ignored or forgotten by the growing profession. Contrary to the image portrayed by the popular press, social workers have not been enthusiastic about acknowledging sexual abuse, and failure to pick up clues or the turning of a 'blind eye' may occur quite frequently. Gordon (1988), using an analysis of the historical development of social work, argues that 'incest' became more visible when there was an organized feminist presence. Campbell (1988) also points out that it was two women, Marietta Higgs and Sue Richardson, who drew attention to the sexual abuse of children in Cleveland. The work of both Gordon and Campbell suggests that the silence concerning sexual abuse is more likely to be broken if women are in a powerful enough position to break it. This connects once more to aspects of sexuality and relationships of power.

Similarly, White (1987) notes that the most attention that has been paid to sexuality has been paid to 'disabled' clients – or rather people with disabilities. He suggests it is easier to consider the sexuality of 'disabled' people as 'them' than it is of the 'able bodied' and more powerful. Here within this dominant professional discourse, sexuality is being placed alongside debates on health and illness. This reproduces two further silences: the sexuality of the 'healthy', and the dissociation of sexuality and illness for those with disabilities. To put this another way, people with disabilities do not have to have sexuality constructed in terms of health/illness/disability: other frames of reference may be more liberating and empowering.

Concluding remarks

Much of this chapter has stressed the importance of giving more explicit consideration to sexuality in social work organizations and in the practice of social work. Moving in this direction may well have beneficial effects for both social workers and the people with whom they are in contact. However, in arguing for this kind of awareness in social work, it is necessary to clarify what this means in order to avoid misunderstandings, and to locate such a process in relation to power relations, as we have been doing throughout this chapter.

On the first count, giving explicit considerations to sexuality does not mean sexualizing the situation, less still behaving sexually or in a sexualized way. On the second count, the implications of giving explicit consideration to sexuality depend upon a variety of power relations, particularly, though not only, related to the politics of initiating such consideration. Who is initiating this, is it an individual or a group, and how are they located in the organizational setting? Thus, making sexuality more explicit is itself an instance of sexual(ity) politics. The attempt to make sexuality more explicit by those in positions of organizational or managerial power may itself represent a form of sexual domination.

Thus this is not a question of 'anything goes'. Equal opportunities policies cannot simply encourage equal rights for all sexualities. This is most obviously the case with regard to sexual violence towards those who are less powerful, as in the case of child sexual abuse. On the other hand, there are further complexities regarding domination between relative peers, as illustrated in debates about lesbians and sadomasochism (Ardill and O'Sullivan 1986) and 'gay macho' (Kleinberg 1987). Having said that, there are dangers that sexualities that are experienced as dominating and oppressive and that entail sexual violence could be bolstered by any kind of liberal or free market approaches. Against that it is the furthering of anti-oppressive sexualities that is at issue.

Without attention to these kinds of problems, it is quite possible that moves to give more explicit consideration to sexuality may reinforce the power of men over women, heterosexuals over lesbians and gay men, managers over workers, workers over clients. Making sexualities explicit has to be done on the terms of those in less powerful social locations and those promoting anti-oppressive sexualities. Making sexuality explicit in social work organizations is itself a form and a process of power.

Acknowledgements

We would like to thank the editors for their helpful comments on an earlier version of this chapter, and Sue Moody for typing the script.

References

Ardill, S. and O'Sullivan, S. (1986) 'Upsetting an applecart: difference, desire and lesbian sadomasochism', *Feminist Review* 23: 23–57.
Burrell, G. (1984) 'Sexual and organizational analysis', *Organization Studies* 5, 2: 97–118.
Burrell, G. and Hearn, J. (1989) 'The sexuality of organization', in J. Hearn, D. Sheppard, P. Tancred-Sheriff and G. Burrell (eds) *The Sexuality of Organization*, London and Newbury Park, CA: Sage.
Campbell, B. (1988) *Unofficial Secrets*, London: Virago.
Clark, L. M. G. and Lange, L. (1979) *The Sexism of Social and Political Theory*, Toronto: University of Toronto Press.
Coley, L. and Mailu, R. (1987) 'Responding to the sexuality of people with a mental handicap', in G. Horobin (ed.) *Sex, Gender and Care Work. Research Highlights in Social Work No. 15*, New York: St Martin's; London: Jessica Kingsley.
Collinson, D. L. and Collinson, M. (1989) 'Sexuality in the workplace: the domination of men's sexuality', in J. Hearn, D. Sheppard, P. Tancred-Sheriff and G. Burrell (eds) *The Sexuality of Organization*, London and Newbury Park, CA: Sage.
Coveney, L., Jackson, M., Jeffreys, S., Kay, L. and Mahoney, P. (1984) *The Sexuality Papers. Male Sexuality and the Social Control of Women*, London: Hutchinson.
Department of Health (1990) *Consultation Paper no. 16, Foster Placement (Guidance and Regulations)*, London: HMSO.
Dyer, R. (1985) 'Male sexuality in the media', in A. Metcalf and M. Humphries (eds) *The Sexuality of Men*, London: Pluto Press.

Elphis, C. (1980) *Sexuality and Birth Control in Social and Community Work*, London: Temple Smith.
Evans, D. (1989/90) 'Section 28: law, myth and paradox', *Critical Social Policy* 27: 73–95.
Farley, L. (1978) *Sexual Shakedown*, New York: McGraw-Hill.
Ferris, D. (1977) *Homosexuality and the Social Services. The Report of an NCCL Survey of Local Authority Social Service Committees*, London: NCCL.
Gordon, L. (1988) 'The politics of child abuse: notes from American history', *Feminist Review* 28: 56–64.
Gutek, B. (1985) *Sex and the Workplace. The Impact of Sexual Behavior and Harassment on Women, Men and Organizations*, San Francisco: Jossey-Bass.
Hall, E. (1987) 'The gender of the therapist: its relevance to practice and training', in G. Horobin (ed.) *Sex, Gender and Care Work, Research Highlights in Social Work, no. 15*, New York: St Martin's; London: Jessica Kingsley.
Hall, M. (1985) *The Lavender Couch. A Consumer's Guide to Psychotherapy for Lesbians and Gay Men*, Boston: Alyson.
Hall, M. (1989) 'Private experiences in the public domain: lesbians in organizations', in J. Hearn, D. Sheppard, P. Tancred-Sheriff and G. Burrell (eds) *The Sexuality of Organization*, London and Newbury Park, CA: Sage.
Hearn, J. (1992) *Men in the Public Eye. The Construction and Deconstruction of Public Men and Public Patriarchies*, London and New York: Harper Collins.
Hearn, J. and Parkin, W. (1987) *'Sex' at 'Work'. The Power and Paradox of Organization Sexuality*, Brighton: Wheatsheaf; New York: St Martin's.
Hearn, J., Sheppard, D., Tancred-Sheriff, P. and Burrell, G. (eds) (1989) *The Sexuality of Organization*, London and Newbury Park, CA: Sage.
Hogbacka, R., Kandolin, I., Haavio-Mannila, E. and Kauppinen-Toropainen, K. (1987) *Sexual Harassment*, Equality Publications, Series E Abstracts 2/1987, Helsinki: Ministry of Social Affairs, Finland.
Hollway, W. (1984) 'Gender difference and the production of subjectivity', in J. Henriques, W. Hollway, C. Urwin, C. Venn and V. Walkerdine (eds) *Changing the Subject*, London: Methuen.
Holroyd, J. C. (1983) 'Erotic contact as an instance of sex-biased therapy', in J. Murray and P. R. Abramson (eds) *Bias in Psychotherapy*, New York: Praeger.
Hooks, B. (1982) *Ain't I a Woman? Black Women and Feminism*, London: Pluto Press.
Horn, P. D. and Horn, J. C. (1982) *Sex in the Office. Power and Passion in the Workplace*, Reading, MA: Addison-Wesley.
Jordan, W. (1984) *The White Man's Burden*, New York: Oxford University Press.
Kleinberg, S. (1987) 'The new masculinity of gay men and beyond', in M. Kaufman (ed.) *Beyond Patriarchy. Essays by Men on Pleasure, Power and Change*, Toronto and New York: Oxford University Press.
Levine, M. (1979) 'Employment discrimination against gay men', *International Review of Modern Sociology* 9, 5/7: 151–63.
Levy, A. and Kahan, B. (1991) *The Pindown Experience and the Protection of Children. The Report of the Staffordshire Child Care Inquiry 1990*, Stafford: Staffordshire County Council.
MacKinnon, C. A. (1979) *The Sexual Harassment of Working Women*, New Haven, CT: Yale University Press.
MacKinnon, C. A. (1982) 'Feminism, Marxism, method and the state: an agenda for theory' *Signs* 7, 3: 515–44.
Macourt, M. (1989) *How Can We Help You? Information, Advice and Counselling for Lesbians and Gay Men*, London: Bedford Square.
Mercer, K. and Julien, I. (1988) 'Race, sexual politics and black masculinity: a dossier', in R. Chapman and J. Rutherford (eds) *Male Order. Unwrapping Masculinity*, London: Lawrence and Wishart.

Miles, R. (1989) *Racism*, London: Routledge and Kegan Paul.
Mills, A. J. (1991) 'Organizational discourse and the gendering of identity', Paper given at conference on 'Towards a New Theory of Organisations', Keele University.
Milner, J. and Blyth, E. (1988) *Coping with Child Sexual Abuse: a Guide for Teachers*, York: Longman.
Morris, B. (1987) 'Getting to the top', *Social Services Insight* 2, 37: 11–13.
NAPO (1991) *Lesbians and Gay Rights – Challenging Heterosexism. A Training and Information Pack for Branches*, London: NAPO.
Parkin, W. (1989) 'Private experiences in the public domain: sexuality and residential care organizations', in J. Hearn, D. Sheppard, P. Tancred-Sheriff, and G. Burrell (eds) *The Sexuality of Organization*, London and Newbury Park, CA: Sage.
Parmar, P. (1984) 'Hateful contraries. Media images of Asian women', *Ten-8* 16: 71–8.
Pringle, R. (1989) 'Bureaucracy, rationality and sexuality: the case of secretaries', in J. Hearn, D. L. Sheppard, P. Tancred-Sheriff and G. Burrell (eds) *The Sexuality of Organization*, London and Newbury Park, CA: Sage.
Rich, A. (1980) 'Compulsory heterosexuality and lesbian existence' *Signs* 5, 4: 631–60.
Rights of Women (1984) *Lesbian Mothers on Trial*, London: Rights of Women.
Seidenberg, R. (1970) *Marriage in Life and Literature*, New York: Philosophical Library.
Simmonds, J. (1988) 'Thinking about feelings in group care', in G. Pearson, J. Treseder and M. Yelloly (eds) *Social Work and the Legacy of Freud*, London: Macmillan.
Simpson, R. L. and Simpson, I. H. (1969) 'Women and bureaucracy in the semi-professions', in A. Etzioni (ed.) *The Semi-Professions and their Organizations*, New York: Free Press.
Stacey, M. and Davies, C. (1983) *Divisions of Labour in Child Health Care*, Final Report to the SSRC, Coventry: University of Warwick.
Stein, T. S. and Cohen, C. J. (eds) (1986) *Contemporary Perspectives on Psychotherapy with Lesbians and Gay Men*, New York and London: Plenum Press.
Taylor, N. (1986) *All in a Day's Work. A Report on Anti-Lesbian Discrimination in Employment and Unemployment in London*, London: Lesbian Employment Rights.
White, K. (1987) 'Residential care of adolescents: carers and sexual issues', in G. Horobin (ed.) *Sex, Gender and Care Work, Research Highlights in Social Work, no. 15*, New York: St Martin's; London: Jessica Kingsley.
Wise, S. and Stanley, L. (1990) 'Sexual harassment, sexual conduct and gender in social work settings', in P. Carter, T. Jeffs and M. Smith (eds) *Social Work and Social Welfare Yearbook 2*, Milton Keynes: Open University Press.
Wood, R. (1987) 'Raging Bull: the homosexual subtext in film', in M. Kaufman (ed.) *Beyond Patriarchy. Essays by Men on Pleasure, Power and Change*, Toronto and New York: Oxford University Press.
Woodman, N. J. and Lenna, H. R. (1980) *Counseling with Gay Men and Women*, San Francisco and London: Jossey-Bass.

12
Community work: current realities, contemporary trends

Hugh Butcher

Community work literature tends to be prescriptive and recommendatory; it is not difficult to find books and articles that suggest what community workers *should* be doing, and how they *should* be doing it. It is rather more difficult to arrive at an accurate picture of what they *actually* do, to get an overall impression about who employs them, and to gain a sense of how their work has been changing over the past decade or so.

My purpose here is to provide a review and commentary on reports and studies that *do* offer a picture of the realities of contemporary practice. Such an understanding offers two kinds of benefit: it provides an interpretive context for debates about what goals should be set in the years running up to the turn of the century, and it gives clues to the potential difficulties to be overcome by practitioners interested in implementing them. First, however, it is important to be clear about what we mean by community work. A wealth of definitions are available, but in an effort to be comprehensive, they tend to be rather lengthy (e.g. Association of Community Workers 1981; Thomas 1983; Cliffe 1985).

It will be sufficient for our purpose to say that community work involves working with people who have voluntarily come together in community groups and organizations to find answers to shared needs and problems, and promote change, thus enabling them to achieve a greater degree of control over the conditions of their lives. The focus of such work is on common concerns, developing and sharing skills, knowledge, experience and awareness, and supporting collective responses. Priority is given to working with people and communities that characteristically experience little control over the conditions of their lives – the powerless, the disadvantaged and the oppressed.

Who employs community workers and what are they employed to do?

Figure 12.1 illustrates the diversity of community work appointments, and provides a basis for discussing sponsorship and employment. Two caveats are necessary. The first is to emphasize that the diagram is illustrative and suggests the *kinds* of posts and roles to be found in public, voluntary and private sector organizations; it is not intended to be representative, still less exhaustive, or to represent a profile of community work and community workers to be found in any particular locality.

The second is that by illustrating the variety of practice in one diagram, the diversity and patchiness of provision revealed by studies of actual provision in particular localities is overlooked. With these points firmly in mind Figure 12.1 does provide a basis on which a number of generalizations can be made.

Central government sponsorship

Beginning on the left hand side of Figure 12.1 we see that public sector sponsorship of community work initiatives has come from both central and local government. Willmott identifies some central government initiatives:

> Community care is a top-down policy, originating with central government, as is community policing. Other central government initiatives are community health councils and community councils in Scotland and Wales. Community education is encouraged by the Department of Education and Science in new design schemes, and is pursued explicitly by many local education authorities.
>
> (Willmott 1989: 23)

Local government interest – the service departments

Notwithstanding central government encouragement of community initiatives it is within local government that there has been the greatest evidence of state interest in community work. Local government community workers are to be found in a range of service departments as well as in central units and support departments. Within the functional, 'service' departments the fortunes of community work have waxed and waned. The social services departments, for example, were the first to employ community workers in any numbers, and the 1970s saw a rapid expansion in the employment of workers with a community development function in this sector (see Baldock 1979). Community workers were, and are, to be found co-ordinating street warden schemes, volunteer units, special area based projects, and in some authorities are integrated into patch based and community social work teams. Major restructuring of both provision and training makes the future of community work in social services departments somewhat uncertain (McConnell 1991). It is possible that the implementation of the new community care planning arrangements will stimulate innovative approaches to enhancing the capacity of local neighbourhood networks to provide support for carers and the

146 Changing social work and welfare

Governmental

- Central policy
  - Community care
- Government initiatives
  - Community policing
  - Community education

Local government
- Chief executive's department
  - Voluntary sector liaison
  - Decentralization unit
- Recreation and arts department
  - Community development officers
  - Neighbourhood development officers
  - Play organizers
  - Community arts officers
- Education department
  - Community tutors
  - Youth and community workers
  - Community centre wardens
- Housing and planning
  - Recreation officers
  - Tenant liaison officers
- Social services
  - Community social worker
  - Voluntary work co-ordinator
  - Street warden organizer
  - Bengali community worker

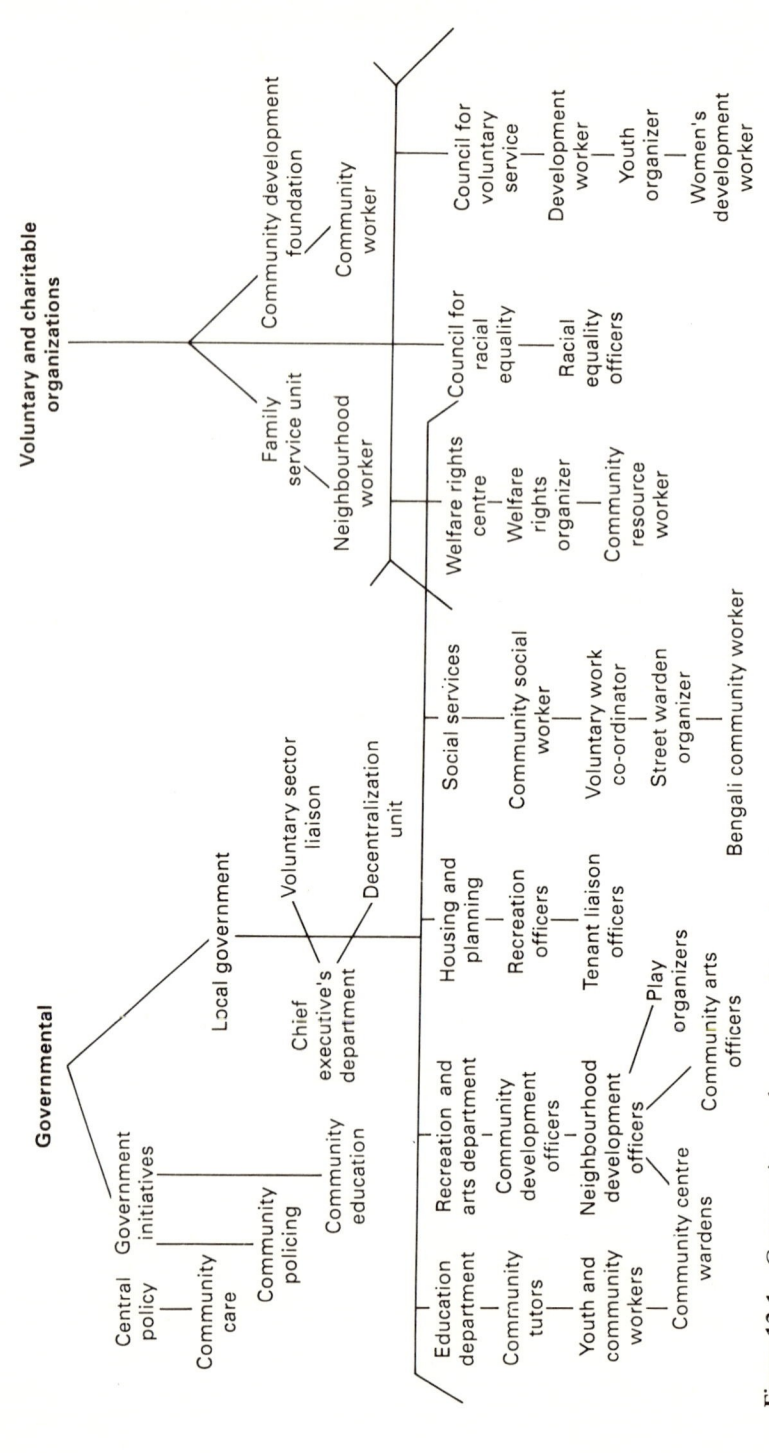

Voluntary and charitable organizations

- Community development foundation
  - Community worker
- Family service unit
  - Neighbourhood worker
- Welfare rights centre
  - Welfare rights organizer
  - Community resource worker
- Council for racial equality
  - Racial equality officers
- Council for voluntary service
  - Development worker
  - Youth organizer
  - Women's development worker

Figure 12.1 Community work: sponsorship and employment

cared-for alike, but there is little evidence of planning in this particular direction so far. Community work may be more secure within social work in Scotland, where the 1968 Social Work (Scotland) Act made specific reference to the *promotion* of social welfare as an arm of strategic social development planning. Thus in Strathclyde, admittedly the largest local authority in Europe, the social work department employs nearly three hundred community workers (Barr 1991).

Community workers are also to be found within educational and related services; here they are employed to run community centres, to work with young people and to perform out-reach roles, such as that of community tutor in community schools and colleges. Again this approach is more developed in Scotland where community work (as an element – along with adult education and youth work – of community education) is legitimated as part of mainstream post-school educational provision.

Other local government departments that have developed community work approaches include those with responsibilities in housing and urban development (e.g. tenant liaison work) and those with a leisure, recreational and cultural services remit. In Leicester, for example, Cliffe (1985) reported that the recreation and arts department employed community development officers to work with neighbourhood-based groups, and local authority leisure services departments in other parts of England have also developed interesting approaches to community recreation. Typically these have involved a movement away from a facility-based 'provider' orientation to a community-based consultative approach (Haywood and Henry 1986). Emphasis is put on targeting disadvantaged groups, the decentralization of services and user involvement in service planning.

Community work and unemployment

The second half of the 1980s witnessed efforts to explore ways in which community work could be used as an element of local authority strategies to combat unemployment and its effects. De-industrialization has led to the decimation of jobs in traditional industries, and economic depression has particularly hit small firms. This has disproportionately affected particular (working-class and black) communities, and strategies have been devised by local authorities aimed at the economic regeneration of their areas. Community enterprises have been developed as one arm of such a strategy, although the form these take varies. For example, McMichael *et al.* (1990) suggest that in England such initiatives have emphasized job creation and the stimulation of economically viable community businesses, whereas in Scotland (particularly in rural areas) community enterprise has been used as a vehicle for general community education and development.

General community development

The trend towards deploying community work not only as an aid to specific service delivery goals but also as an important element in a comprehensive approach to community development has been more in evidence within local government of late. The focus of such developmental goals has shifted. During the late 1960s and early 1970s community workers were deployed by local authorities to help them develop new approaches to 'public participation' in planning, urban renewal and public housing (Smith and Jones 1981; Boaden *et al.* 1982). The 1980s have seen a change in direction, with moves towards more broadly based initiatives concerned with decentralization, consumer advocacy and neighbourhood democracy. The implementation of explicit social and community development policies is still found within only a minority of local authorities (Broady and Hedley (1989) suggest about 25 per cent) but, where it occurs, community workers and community development strategies are generally to be found as an important component. Three broad approaches are discernible and may be called the 'going local', 'neighbourhood development' and 'enabling' strands.

The 'going local' option seeks to develop, with the assistance of those with community work skill, local neighbourhood forums (or committees or councils, the terminology varies) through which residents can become more fully involved in exercising influence and control over local government policy-making. Such initiatives may be inspired by a belief in the values of participatory democracy or the view that local policies and services will be improved if better informed by local views and priorities. They also often reflect, as Broady and Hedley (1989: 44) put it, the wish by some Labour controlled councils to 're-assert the importance of local government in the face of central government's efforts to reduce the powers of local authorities by cutting their resources and restricting their powers.' If they are to survive, local councils see the need to secure the active support of local people. This meaning of going local – of enhanced democratic participation – needs to be distinguished from the localization, or decentralization, of service administration. The two strands are often promoted in tandem (they can be mutually reinforcing), but it is only the devolution of democratic decision-making that properly involves community work skills. Decentralizing services may make them more accessible and responsive, but unless users have a greater element of control over how those services are delivered, it remains an administrative device (Hoggett and Hambleton 1987).

The second option, direct local authority support for neighbourhood development and community organization, has a well-established history. Council housing development, from the inter-war years through to the late 1950s, was often based on the ideal of the neighbourhood unit (of 10,000 or so residents), and estates were designed in ways to facilitate the growth of community networks and a sense of personal identity with a local 'patch'. Community centres were built and community associations supported as ways of encouraging social development among residents. The enthusiasm for high density, high rise construction during the 1960s and 1970s undermined such thinking, but subsequently an appreciation of the merits of smaller development has grown in parallel with a revival in local authority interest in neighbourhood development.

As one report puts it, supporting community centre provision can:

- provide direct services to needy groups, such as the elderly, pre-school children and disabled people;
- provide necessary meeting places for ... leisure activities, educational programmes, youth groups and social events;
- operate as a significant forum for local residents to articulate their needs and express them to the local authority;
- offer a focus for co-ordination between local agencies, thus helping to maximize effective use of resources.

(Association of Metropolitan Authorities 1989: 44)

By no means all local authority support for local social development is managed through community centres and associations. Support is also given for the development of community organizations founded on the common interests of participants – disabled people, women with child-care responsibilities, ethnic minority groups and so on – which cut across neighbourhood boundaries. Such organizations run mutual aid projects, articulate needs to the local authority, offer a focus for volunteering and provide a semi-autonomous base through which the local council can provide services 'in partnership'. As one local authority put it:

Community organisation enables people in a neighbourhood to take action together as a community. It includes the articulation of needs and views to the council, which can assist the authority in maximising the use of its services and resources in an efficient, economical and accurate response.

(Association of Metropolitan Authorities 1989: 44)

Third, local authorities support community work and community development at 'arm's length', via assistance for the voluntary sector in their areas. Many have an explicit policy of supporting, by grant aid and other means, the development of vigorous independent voluntary organizations and community groups, based at least in part on a recognition of the potential conflicts and contradictions that can arise from state workers directly assisting community groups with campaigning and other conflict-orientated strategies. There is, of course, a risk of co-opting 'voluntary' organizations, so that they become little more than mere agents of the local authority, leaving them with restricted scope for autonomous action, particularly in terms of campaigning activities or performing a critical 'watchdog' role for their members. Such a risk can be reduced when funds are channelled through intermediary bodies like local councils for voluntary service or councils for racial equality, and when the authority explicitly recognizes (as increasing numbers do – see AMA 1989) that pluralistic democracy must not merely tolerate, but actively encourage, independent points of influence and dissent. This in its turn involves recognizing that community workers, in supporting groups that challenge accepted policies, work in potentially exposed and ambiguous positions. Whether directly employed by the local authority, or funded through a voluntary organization, they run the risk of being seen as 'stirrers-up' of trouble. However, Broady and Hedley's enquiries found that the 'strains which this conflict of roles provokes are now increasingly recognised and accepted by many local authorities which support this kind of work' (Broady and Hedley 1989: 152).

The voluntary sector

Discussions of support for the voluntary sector's involvement in community work activity shifts the focus of our attention to the right hand side of Figure 12.1. When Francis *et al.* (1984) conducted their survey of community workers in the United Kingdom they estimated that 60 per cent were employed in the voluntary sector. Their figures date from 1983 and so whether they present an accurate picture of the situation today must be a matter of some speculation. However, there is no evidence to suggest that there has been a fundamental change in the proportion employed by voluntary organizations, although questions must be raised as to whether the funding base has not changed quite markedly. Ten years ago Francis *et al.* also found that over three-quarters of community workers employed in the voluntary sector relied on statutory sources of funding, but it is possible that the constraints on local government expenditure during the past decade has reduced this proportion. Some might welcome such a reduction on the basis that, as indicated above, non-governmental organizations should be able to challenge government policy in a genuinely independent way. Equally, grant aid, channelled through for example the urban programme, Training and Enterprise Councils, and the like (major sources of funding, often topped up by the local authorities), has distorted the work focus and objectives of organizations as they have sought to meet new and variable funding criteria. This tendency has been overlaid more recently by the increasing use of service contracts and other kinds of agreements through which the room for independent action by voluntary organizations has been further reduced.

In any event the number and type of voluntary groups and organizations supported by government funding can vary enormously. For example, Bradford MDC annually grants aid to well over two hundred community organizations, to a total of £4.6 million per annum. Not all of them employ personnel that come within our definition of 'community worker', but many do. Community organizations also fund raise through voluntary giving, approach trusts and charities, and a recent trend is to seek EC funds. The Churches are also involved in community work, and in rural areas are often the major sponsors of community initiatives. The *Faith in the Countryside* Report (Archbishop of Canterbury's Commission on Rural Areas 1990), the Mission Alongside the Poor and the boards of social responsibility of the various denominations have developed a role in rural community work, which to some extent mirrors developments that have grown out of the *Faith in the City* Report (Archbishop of Canterbury's Commission on Urban Priority Areas 1985). The Church Urban Fund, established in 1988, is a national fund-raising campaign in which dioceses across the country raise funds to be channelled to community action projects in disadvantaged city areas. By 1990 the fund was approaching its target of raising and distributing £18 million on such activities.

The diversity of the community organizations that comprise the voluntary sector makes generalizations about structures and strategies very difficult and the organizations do not, of course, necessarily have any contact with a community worker (see Knight and Hayes 1981; Taylor 1983; Bishop and Hoggett 1986; Willmott 1989). For example, Knight and Hayes tried to identify all the community organizations operating in two inner-city areas with a combined population of 13,000. They found eighteen, of which only four had been set up and run with the help of professional community workers. This compared with four that had been formed by clergymen, eight by community activists and two by people directly affected by the problem the group addressed.

In general such groups and organizations include residents' and tenants' associations, family centres, community centres, amenity groups, campaign and protest organizations and all kinds of self-help groups. Many are 'single issue', orientated to a particular disadvantaged group; others are multi-purpose, embracing a range of activities; others are umbrella support organizations such as councils for voluntary services, rural community councils and councils for racial equality.

Some generalizations

Schematic as it is, the picture of community work so far presented does enable a number of generalizations to be made. The first is to note that relatively few employed people who undertake community work are *called* community workers. If anything, this tendency for other occupations to incorporate and adopt elements of community work practice seems to be on the increase. Such 'permeation' has been noted on a number of occasions to bring with it a variety of consequences (see Munday 1980; Thomas 1983; Butcher 1986). For example, relatively few occupations that incorporate community work techniques allow those undertaking the work to practise community work full time. Certainly the Cliffe (1985) study found over seventy professional workers in Leicester with a community work brief, but these amounted to no more than thirty 'full time equivalent'.

Second, and largely as a consequence of this, most community work practitioners find themselves dispersed among a number of agencies and departmental settings. Consequently they may experience a sense of isolation from others doing similar work. In a few local authorities, and a limited number of larger non-statutory agencies (e.g. the Community Development Foundation) they are sufficiently numerous to form a team, but this is the exception. Certainly professional dispersal and organizational isolation has been one of the reasons given for attempts by some community workers to develop national and regional support networks through which knowledge and skills can be shared, support engendered and community development promoted. A working party sponsored by the Calouste Gulbenkian Foundation (1984) advocated a national centre for community development and provided evidence that such a resource, combining regional and national facilities, would have enormous potential. By working through local networks it could reach community workers employed in many different parts of the statutory and voluntary sectors. Extensive consultations and debate ensued, but no immediate action (Association of Community Workers 1986). However, by 1990 a new membership organization had been formed – the Standing Conference for Community Development (SCCD) – and was supported by grant-aid from the Voluntary Service Unit of the Home Office, with a remit to:

> act as an umbrella organisation with a membership including national organisations, regional groups, local organisations and individual community workers in order to bring together the different strands of community development activity and thus promote and develop the ideas and techniques of community development.
>
> (SCCD 1990: 1)

The commitment to 'bring together the different strands' is obviously an important development, and opportune given that policy-makers are increasingly questioning the value and techniques of community work.

What do community workers do?

Beliefs about what community workers do are prone to distortion (Barr 1991; Van Reenon 1991). Workers are reluctant to write up their work and, when they do, are prone to focus on the innovative and 'exciting' at the expense of the well-established and mundane. However, the past decade has seen the appearance of a number of studies (Davies and Crousaz 1982; Cliffe 1985; Barr 1991; Van Reenon 1991) that allow some tentative conclusions to be drawn.

The most significant generalizations to be drawn from such studies are that the bulk of community work practice is locally focused, concerned, with quite modest 'reformist' goals and 'community' led. Significantly, more than half of field-workers' time is likely to be spent in direct face-to-face work with community members (as individuals or in group settings, in pre-planned or unplanned contacts), with a minority of time spent in non-contact activities like report writing, information gathering and storage, and administration. Much time will be spent on what can be called 'resource' work, i.e. providing and managing facilities and amenities, assisting groups to obtain the financial and material means to maintain their activities and services – including assisting them in the preparation of grant applications – and provision of information and advice to assist the group in its effective functioning. It is important to expand on a number of key points regarding the activities of community workers.

The first of these is that relatively little community work is concerned with supporting high-profile campaigning activity of a confrontational and conflictual nature. Although some workers, for part of their time, may find themselves working with community organizations engaged in direct action, like picketing council meetings or rent strikes, the more usual picture is of work with groups that, if they seek to challenge the policies of decision-makers at all, limit themselves to conventional lobbying tactics, mounting the occasional publicity campaign and petition, and so forth. Group activity will, generally, be geared to maintaining some sort of service to members or to the community at large, while 'influence' tactics will be orientated to securing the necessary support and resources to do this. This in part accounts for the amount of time many community workers spend on helping groups refine their funding applications and similar activities.

Second, much community work is with groups and organizations that, for the most part, operate as autonomous and independent entities. While these may affiliate to umbrella organizations like councils for voluntary service and sometimes make common cause with other groups over specific issues (e.g. challenging a local authority on its inadequate support for the voluntary sector), the typical community organization is run by and for its members – attending to *their* recreational, welfare, accommodation and other needs. The image of the community worker as the architect or facilitator of stable, strong, long-term alliances that orchestrate local action around the pursuit of national goals is something of a myth.

Third, compared to the time and energy spent on work with and for community groups, the work of the agency-based practitioner (located in, for example, housing, social services and education departments) that is concerned with attempts to influence the politics and practice of the agency is often minimal. Community workers spend relatively little time on such activities; the majority see their primary role as enabling local groups and organizations to find their own voice or offer their own service.

A changing context

Any occupational practice, community work included, is influenced by the realities of the social context in which it operates. Pinning down the key influences at play at any time – how changing social conditions, movements in cultural attitudes and developments in public policy affect practice – is fraught with difficulties. These are further magnified when we attempt to identify the trends that shape current and future possibilities. In concluding this overview of community work I explore the consequences of some contemporary trends in four selected areas.

Private and public – re-drawing the boundaries

One of the most analysed, and significant, policy thrusts of the past dozen years has been the attempt to redraw the boundaries of the 'private' and 'public' sectors in British society (Dunleavy *et al.* 1990). A consequence of which has been the growing dominance of market values over political decision-making. This has not only challenged the very idea of local democracy, which has come under increasing pressure, but also impacted upon the practice of community workers in significant ways, some examples follow.

Opportunities for political participation. Such challenges have led to a reduction in opportunities for effective political participation at local levels.

There are fewer openings for community groups and organizations to play a participatory role in local, community-level government.

Defensive campaigns. As we have seen, local authorities fund a substantial proportion of community work (directly or indirectly) and local authority policies and practices have traditionally been significant targets for change for community organizations. Community workers increasingly find themselves in the paradoxical position of working with local campaigns to defend public services and the status of the local state, including their own jobs.

Market thinking. The growing hegemony of market thinking, of an increasing concern with outcome measures and performance indicators, and of exact targeting of resources according to bureaucratically defined needs, has a major impact on how and what community workers do. Not least they are likely to spend more time on their 'resourcing' roles, in helping community groups and organizations to make effective applications to resource holders and grant givers, and in fund raising to seed new projects and developments.

Tighter funding criteria. In both state and voluntary sectors community workers now find fewer openings for generalist project work that takes as its starting point community needs and aspirations as articulated by community members themselves. Funding from official sources has become tighter in terms of the criteria demanded, and emphasis is placed upon short-term, time-limited activities. As we have noted, the non-mandatory nature of community work tends to breed worker insecurity and the more targeted nature of contemporary funding arrangements can only serve to increase this.

Citizenship and the new volunteering

The ethic of individualism is the other side of the New Right critique of collective provision and this too has had significant implications for contemporary community work. Two examples follow.

Good neighbouring. Participation in voluntary sector activity as an expression of 'active citizenship' has been accorded renewed importance as a civic virtue, and underpins much government thinking about and support for 'good neighbouring' and community care schemes, neighbourhood watch, and other self-help initiatives. Volunteering by individuals is actively encouraged and sponsorship of community and welfare projects by the corporate business sector applauded. Community workers are given key roles in orchestrating and co-ordinating the various components of this vision of the active society.

Enabling not providing. The New Right vision of a market-orientated society has not been allowed to evolve without challenge. Although the powers of the state 'beyond Westminster and Whitehall' have been heavily circumscribed, resistance from the old and new left, and centre parties, has had implications for community work practice. Notably, attempts by authorities to develop models of 'local socialism' (Boady and Fudge 1984) have been augmented by efforts to implement decentralist forms of administration and neighbourhood democracy (Hoggett and Hambleton 1987). Community workers have been called upon to make a contribution through their skills in facilitating group action and participatory methods of working with ordinary people. Thus the language and practice of 'enabling' has entered the vocabulary of local government decision-making and service delivery; there are 'new left', 'new right' and 'liberal democratic' versions of what this means in practice, but it is significant that the term itself has for a long time been a key component of community work thinking.

Social conditions

While the social circumstances of many people have improved over recent years, many inequalities and social differences have also become more marked. For example:

A one-third–two-thirds society. Writing in 1990, Craig noted

> What's happened over the last ten years to material standards is that, broadly speaking the bottom third of the population have, in terms of income, come more and more detached from the top two thirds and the top two thirds have generally done alright. Community workers tend to work with the one third at the bottom of the pile.
> (Craig, quoted in Miller and Bryant 1990: 319)

Community workers end up both supporting locally based collective efforts to address the immediate needs of the bottom third (credit unions, self-help and mutual aid groups) and supporting campaigns directed towards forestalling the further erosion of the social wage that is so important to this group. An increasingly common focus of community work activity has involved support for schemes – top-down and bottom-up – that seek the re-integration of the casualties of current public policies into mainstream society. Employment training, housing and industrial co-operatives, community care and other initiatives represent, in a sense, the community workers' contribution to the development of the 'enterprise culture'.

The politics of difference. Alongside material inequality, increasing attention has been given to problems of marginalization, powerlessness and oppression as they relate to gender, race, sexual orientation, ability and age. Community workers have not remained immune to the developing social movement politics in these areas and there has been considerable involvement with issues of equal opportunities and anti-oppressive practice in fields such as health, housing and domestic violence. Campaigning on (finer and finer) points of social difference has significant implications for practice and some commentators have worried about how this tendency will affect the ability to bring people together to make common cause against institutional structures and cultural beliefs that lie at the heart of diverse disadvantages (Miller and Bryant 1990: 314).

Vanishing community?

Finally, has the stress on individualistic values during the past decade, along with continuing social and geographical mobility and the material changes mentioned above, effectively undermined the social basis of community activity?

Sociological evidence. Willmott has provided an excellent summary of the sociological evidence concerning the significance of local neighbourhood and 'interest' community to people's lives in contemporary Britain. His conclusion is that, in terms of social relationships and local identity, 'Most localities in present day Britain, for most of their residents, have some of the characteristics of a community of attachment. . . . Territorial communities are seldom just that and nothing more' (Willmott 1989: 18). Local ties are weaker than they used to be but to some extent their attenuation has been complemented by a parallel growth in dispersed social networks based on people's common interests, such as work, friendship and leisure. Willmott concludes that there does indeed remain a basis on which to build community-orientated practices and policies.

Social attitudes. There is no evidence that many people wish to draw away from 'community' towards a totally individualistic lifestyle. A battery of questions posed year on year for the British Social Attitude Survey is helpful here. The questions explore responses to a wide range of topics relating to individualistic and collectivist attitudes, e.g. perceptions of welfare state provision, attitudes towards trade unionism and so on. Reviewing some of the time-series data for a chapter on 'individualism' in the seventh report, Rentoul concluded: 'The major growth in private provision and private ownership over the past ten years does not seem to have led to increased support for individualism. . . . On the contrary, collectivist values appear still to be deeply rooted' (Rentoul 1990: 176).

Conclusion

It would be wrong to use reports of contemporary trends to limit discussion of options for the future. On the other hand the information to be gleaned from the studies reviewed above does provide a valuable interpretive context for appraising such options. Such factors as the professional dispersal and organizational isolation of community workers, all-party enthusiasm for promoting 'enabling' public services, widespread occupational appropriation of community work approaches, and apparent public support for maintaining a balance between 'individualistic' and 'community' values – all these, and many other features of the contemporary scene noted above must be acknowledged and taken into account when developing community work strategies.

References

Archbishop of Canterbury's Commission on Rural Areas (1990) *Faith in the Countryside*, London: Acora.
Archbishop of Canterbury's Commission on Urban Priority Areas (1985) *Faith in the City*, London: Church House Publishing.
Association of Community Workers (1981) *Towards a Definition of Community Work*, London: ACW.
Association of Community Workers (1986) *Supporting Community Development – a Report of Regional Consultations of the National Structure for Community Development Steering Committee*, London: ACW.
Association of Metropolitan Authorities (1989) *Community Development, the Local Authority Role*, London: AMA.
Baldock, P. (1979) 'An historical review of community work 1968–78', *Community Development Journal* 14, 3: 172–81.
Barr, A. (1991) *Practising Community Development*, London: Community Development Foundation.
Bishop, J. and Hoggett, P. (1986) *Organizing around Enthusiasms: Mutual Aid in Leisure*, London: Comedia.
Boaden, N., Goldsmith, M., Hampton, W. and Stringer, P. (1982) *Public Participation in Local Services*, Harlow: Longman.
Boady, M. and Fudge, C. (1984) *Local Socialism?* London: Macmillan.
Broady, M. and Hedley, R. (1989) *Working Partnerships: Community Development in Local Authorities*, London: Bedford Square Press.
Butcher, H. (1986) 'The community practice approach to local public service provision', *Community Development Journal* 21, 2: 107–15.
Calouste Gulbenkian Foundation (1984) *Making a Start*, London: Calouste Gulbenkian Foundation.
Cliffe, D. (1985) *Community Work in Leicester*, Leicester: University of Leicester Centre for Mass Communication Research.
Davies, C. and Crousaz, D. (1982) *Local Authority Community Work – Realities of Practice*, DHSS, Social Research Branch, Research Report no. 9, London: HMSO.
Dunleavy, P., Gamble, A. and Peele, G. (1990) *Developments in British Politics 3*, London: Macmillan.
Francis, D., Henderson, P. and Thomas, D. N. (1984) *A Survey of Community Workers in the UK*, London: National Institute for Social Work.
Haywood, L. and Henry, I. (1986) 'Policy developments in community leisure and recreation', *Leisure Management* 6, 7: 25–9; 6, 8: 21–3.
Hoggett, P. and Hambleton, R. (1987) *Decentralisation and Democracy*, Bristol: School of Advanced Urban Studies.
Knight, B. and Hayes, R. (1981) *Self-Help in the Inner City*, London: London Voluntary Service Council.
McConnell, C. (1991) 'Community development in five European countries', *Community Development Journal* 26, 2: 103–11.
McMichael, P., Lynch, B. and Wight, D. (1990) *Building Bridges into Work: the Role of the Community Worker*, Harlow: Longman.
Miller, C. and Bryant, R. (eds) (1990) 'Community work in the UK: reflections on the 1980s', *Community Development Journal* 25, 4: 316–25.
Munday, B. (1980) 'The permeation of community work into other disciplines', in P. Henderson, D. Jones and D. N. Thomas (eds) *The Boundaries of Change in Community Work*, London: Allen and Unwin.

Rentoul, J. (1990) 'Individualism', in R. Jowell *et al.* (eds) *British Social Attitudes, the Seventh Report*, Aldershot: Gower.
SCCD (Standing Conference for Community Development) (1990) *SCCD News* 1, June.
Smith, L. and Jones, D. (1981) *Deprivation, Participation and Community Action*, London: Routledge and Kegan Paul.
Taylor, M. (1983) *Inside a Community Project – Bedworth Heath*, London: Community Projects Foundation.
Thomas, D. N. (1983) *The Making of Community Work*, London: Allen and Unwin.
Van Reenon, L. (1991) 'Discrepancies in the working times of community workers', *Community Development Journal* 26, 3: 210–19.
Willmott, P. (1989) *Community Initiatives, Patterns and Prospects*, London: Policy Studies Institute.

13
The Community Development Project revisited

Judith Green

The 1960s – a decade of cultural change and political experimentation – was also the occasion of the official 'rediscovery' of poverty in Britain. The National Community Development Project (CDP) was launched by the government of Harold Wilson in 1969 – Britain's answer to the American War on Poverty (Marris and Rein 1974). Although the resources allocated to CDP were relatively trivial, its significance was seen as considerable by contemporary proponents and critics alike. To some of its founders it was to contribute to the moral regeneration of British society (Higgins *et al.* 1983). Others saw it as evidence of a new style of rational government (Halsey 1974: 103), while there were those who believed it was part of a more sinister plan to undermine radical political opposition (Bridges 1975; Bourne 1980; Loney 1983: 37–8).

The CDP story

The story of the establishment of CDP and its subsequent wayward career is well documented (CDP 1977b; Lawless 1979; Loney 1983; Higgins *et al.* 1983).[1]

As Lawless suggests, 'James Callaghan could hardly have anticipated the hornets' nest he let loose in 1969, in setting up the CDP, for certainly no British urban experiment has come up with so many radical and politically unacceptable proposals' (Lawless 1979: 105). Callaghan was Home Secretary under the Wilson government, which had already pledged itself to fight the newly discovered social problem of 'urban deprivation' with the launching of the Urban Programme in 1967.

CDP was intended to be

> a neighbourhood-based experiment aimed at finding new ways of meeting the needs of people living in areas of high social deprivation, by bringing

together the work of all the social services under the leadership of a special project team and also by tapping resources of self help and mutual help which may exist among the people in the neighbourhood.

(Home Office Press Release 16 July 1969)

Twelve CDP projects were established – first in Coventry, Liverpool, Southwark and Glyncorrwg, and later in Batley, Birmingham, Canning Town, Cumbria, Newcastle, Oldham, Paisley and North Shields. Despite the experimental research intentions, which should have dictated a clear strategy for choice of 'laboratories', the precise rationale for the selection of the areas was obscure; in fact some could hardly even be described as 'urban' in any strict sense in spite of the project's location within the Urban Programme. Population size varied considerably, with, for example, over 40,000 in Canning Town and under 10,000 in Glyncorrwg. Each project had an action and a research team. The action teams were employed by the individual participating local authorities, and the research teams by a university or polytechnic. The plan was that each project would operate for five years.

The total cost of this 'attack' on social deprivation was an estimated £5 million. The concept of partnership between central and local government was integral, and was reflected in the financial arrangements, with government providing 75 per cent of the costs and local authorities 25 per cent. Central government paid 100 per cent of the research costs.

CDP had been envisaged as an integrated national initiative, the intention being to co-ordinate the local action–research efforts and feed back their findings systematically into the policy-making process. However, both the original central steering group and the central research team functioned ineffectually and were soon abandoned. As a result of pressure from the local projects a new central structure was established in the form of a consultative council to act as a focus for discussion between central government and the teams. This arrangement was also to lapse in the midst of growing differences between the Home Office and the local teams over the direction of the programme.

Despairing of ever achieving fruitful and constructive dialogue with central government over the problems of urban poverty, the CDP teams turned instead to organizing their own interproject working groups, and produced a series of national CDP reports on major topics like housing and industrial change, with the help of the new central CDP Information and Intelligence Unit (IIU) set up in 1973 at the project's request and responsive to their needs. The analyses and conclusions of these reports, which were often critical of local and central government policies, proved disturbing to the Home Office and added to its growing mistrust of the monster it had created. However, the tripartite management structure within which each local team operated, with complex and confusing lines of accountability and inadequate or non-existent co-ordinating structures, meant that the Home Office could not in practice control its monster. Efforts to assert greater central control failed and, from 1975, the Home Office turned to more devious means, such as encouraging councils to withdraw prematurely from their commitments to their local projects (an opportunity that a few local authorities seized eagerly), axing the directly funded central IIU and studiously ignoring the final CDP reports.

It was not disagreements of a straightforward party political nature that led to CDP's disfavour. The Labour government that had originally set up CDP lost power in the following year to a Conservative administration under Edward Heath. Attitudes to CDP at that period were characterized by neglect, tinged with growing hostility. It was, however, another Labour government, this time with Roy Jenkins as Home Secretary, that actively sought the project's demise and openly refused to respond to the challenging analysis of poverty and urban deprivation offered by CDP.

The post-war consensus

The CDP idea was a product of the consensus politics of the immediate post-war decades. The key element of that consensus was acceptance of the mixed economy, supported by Keynesian economic management strategies and a well-developed welfare state. Both major political parties were willing to operate within the broad framework of this compromise, which was to last for the best part of a quarter of a century. Within the consensus, the dominant assumption of social policy was that problems were essentially technical and beyond the arena of political conflict; social problems were a matter for experts who would impartially define and analyse them to provide the information on which policy-makers could make rational decisions; these decisions could then be implemented in turn by other professional experts (Bulmer 1982; Loney 1983: 5). The original model for CDP was very much part of this conception of social policy.

The political consensus was underpinned by the long economic boom, which lasted from the end of the Second World War until the serious worldwide recession of the 1970s. According to Gamble, 'The end of the long boom was a profound psychological and political shock which did more than anything to invalidate the political calculations that had underlain the post-war consensus' (Gamble 1987: 193). Amidst soaring unemployment, major political debates broke out about questions of the appropriate relationship of the state with industry. The significant political divisions were not so much between the two major parties as within them. Forces inside both the Labour and Conservative Parties rejected the core assumptions of the post-war consensus, questioning the effectiveness of current modes of state intervention in industry and criticizing the welfare state as undemocratic and insensitive (Loney 1987: 14).

It was not just at the national level that important political changes were taking place at this period. The 1960s had seen, as well as marked cultural changes, a range of activities that essentially represented demands for a redistribution of power and control and for a redefinition of problems as political rather than simply to be solved by the application of professional expertise. In industry there was a renewed growth of the shop stewards' movement and grassroots activity in the workplace. Similarly the late 1960s saw a growth in community action, with the mushrooming of large numbers of tenants and action groups protesting against urban redevelopment policies like mass housing clearance and motorway schemes. Activities as apparently disparate as student unrest, the revival of feminism, and radical movements within particular professions such as social work and planning, all seemed to reflect a shared concern with bringing decision-making closer to people and challenging the myths of technical rationality (Lees and Mayo 1984: 111; Simpkin 1989). There were also more focused political protests – campaigns, marches and demonstrations about, for example, the Vietnam War – which brought political protest to the state's own front door.

The optimism underpinning CDP belonged to the cosy era of the post-war consensus. Its tasks for the state were to find new ways of solving the growing social and political problems emerging as that consensus began to disintegrate. But the project itself also reflected the developing political divisions, and in the directions it took it became for the state part of the problem rather than a contributor of an easy solution. The significance of this period of rapid transition in social and political thinking and action is captured by Waddington, himself a former CDP worker:

> 1968, as the climax of a period of substantial social and political upheaval, seems to have left a lasting inheritance in the continuing searches, on the one hand, for new forms of social and political expressions, and, on the other, for new forms of social and political control.
>
> (Waddington 1979: 41)

Redefining social problems

Three points are clear from a reading of the available accounts of CDP. First, the CDP was one of an 'extended family' of government programmes that have certain important features in common, despite their individual peculiarities. Second, the root concerns of these programmes are of central political importance (an importance out of all proportion to the trivial resources devoted to them). However, they are a disparate set of concerns and interests that cut across several major policy areas, and are only tied together by a special label under which they are represented as a unitary social phenomenon. Third, they are cheap, easy and essentially symbolic responses to these central political concerns, and operate to depoliticize fundamental issues of power and equality in our society.

The family of which CDP was a part is that of British poverty (or 'urban' or 'inner city') programmes that are area-specific. This includes the Urban Programme, which ran from 1968 to 1977, and was then re-launched as the 'New Policy for Inner Cities', in which form it still exists today, and a whole plethora of smaller and shorter-lived initiatives, such as the Comprehensive Community Programme and the Neighbourhood Schemes of the 1970s.

There was nothing new about the practice of redefining particular manifestations of basic social and economic problems in spatial terms. The inter-war years, also a period of rapid and drastic economic change, had seen the definition of a 'regional problem' requiring special 'regional' solutions – a marginal problem calling for remedial measure (CDP 1977a). The 1960s saw a revival of this process of spatial labelling with the discovery of 'urban deprivation', a definition which implied that poverty and disadvantage were marginal phenomena, largely restricted to small areas, or 'pockets of deprivation' as they were often called. In the 1970s, 'inner city problems' became the fashionable label, another catch-all phrase for a whole range of symptoms of basic social and economic inequalities that were jarringly out of place in the post-war vision of an increasingly prosperous and secure British society (Davis and Green 1979).

At issue are fundamental questions about the distribution of power and control in society, the appropriate relationship between the state and private capital, and the nature and causes of social inequalities – basic political questions, which the stability of the post-war consensus depended on obscuring. Drawing geographical boundaries to contain social problems as varied as poverty, ill-health and racial conflict had the effect of assigning them the status of special limited problems, and making them appear much more manageable. In effect, the labelling of problems as 'urban' or 'inner city' in character helped to keep them out of the political arena and transformed them into technical issues supposedly amenable to expert diagnosis and solution.

The need for geographical discrimination was a theme of a number of official reports in the 1960s: Milner Holland on London's housing, Ingleby on children and young persons, Plowden on primary education, Seebohm on the personal social services. One after another they came up with the prescription of positive discrimination towards areas of special need where deprivation appeared to be concentrated (CDP 1977b: 9–10). Contemporary with CDP, for example, were educational priority areas for educating the poor, and general improvement areas and housing action areas for housing them. For policy-makers the attraction of area-based policies was that they were seen as a means of targeting resources more effectively to greatest needs, in the context of increasing financial pressure from the Treasury.

The theoretical and empirical basis of area-based programmes has been trenchantly criticized. It has been shown that a high proportion of deprived people do not live in areas where problems are concentrated (Sinfield 1973); that not only do most poor people not live in poor areas but most of the people in poor areas are not themselves poor (Barnes 1974). Area-based positive discrimination policies will therefore deliver additional resources to many people who are not poor, while missing many who are.

The whole CDP idea was underwritten by the optimistic view of poverty as a residual phenomenon within a society basically organized so as to be able to solve all its social problems within its present structures of power, ownership and wealth. Given the original assumptions about the nature of poverty and deprivation, discussion of appropriate strategies seemed to be a merely technical matter. This raises interesting issues about how social problems are constructed, by whom and in whose interests. As Lawless says, 'there were distinct advantages in assuming deprivation to have this sort of structure'

(Lawless 1979: 110). Clearly the poor and disadvantaged do not see themselves as suffering from 'urban deprivation' or 'inner city decline', but from low pay, unemployment, poor housing, racial harassment or other quite specific social ills. In whose interest is it to bag all these problems together and label them as 'urban deprivation'? And what political processes operate to determine whose definitions of social problems will prevail? The establishment of CDP and similar programmes can be seen as a 'nondecision' in the sense coined by Bachrach and Baratz, who argue that 'the primary method for sustaining a given mobilization of bias is nondecision-making' (Bachrach and Baratz 1970: 44). Specifically it represented a choice, whether consciously made or arrived at through the 'deep structures' that are implicit within any given decision-making organization, not to tackle the various manifestations of social inequality directly at source but to reconstruct them as another smaller and more limited problem apparently amenable to limited and cheap solutions. As Edwards and Batley argue, 'the disaggregation and reconstruction of the elements of deprivation is not therefore a matter simply of semantics but has fundamental policy implications' (Edwards and Batley 1978: 241).

CDP and the Urban Programme generally have been criticized for lack of clarity in their aims and definitions of problems, and lack of systematic strategy. However, this very vagueness is arguably one of their strengths from a policy-maker's point of view. Smith has described the goals of CDP as 'nothing less than the reassertion of basic democratic ideals' and 'surrounded by a rhetoric of promise that could not conceivably be met' (Smith 1975: 200). As such, CDP represented a political commitment to address serious social problems, rather than a realistic social policy strategy. This should not be taken to mean that the CDP was merely a cynical, empty gesture. Without doubt CDP, and the Urban Programme generally, was a response to immediate and significant concerns – fears of racial conflict, urban unrest – and to a genuine desire to 'do something' about poverty and deprivation in the face of mounting evidence of its continued existence. However, the parameters of action were drawn very narrowly, both by the dominant political consensus on what was possible and desirable, and by organizational pressures and immediate constraints of financial stringency and political expediency.

The context that produced the pressure for a poverty initiative is fairly clear – it was the coincidence of two 'moral panics', in themselves symptoms of a more deep-seated historical crisis. The old fear of the urban poor and the newer concern with the impact of large-scale black immigration into white racist Britain came together and were re-packaged as the 'urban crisis'. Piven and Cloward (1972) have pointed out that the contemporary poverty programmes belong in a long historical tradition of efforts by the state to complement repressive law and order measures with more subtle management techniques to deal with the problems of social order arising from social and economic disruption. The old fears of the unknown and dangerous urban mob had been aroused by the growing incidence of violence and disorder, such as football hooliganism and vandalism. A particular concern was the perceived breakdown of traditional methods of social control of children and youth – a re-emergence of nineteenth-century fears about delinquency and violence

(Parton 1985). This was compounded by fears of racial violence, openly voiced by politicians such as Enoch Powell, who spoke of foreseeing 'rivers of blood' flowing in Britain, and fuelled by the example of the serious race riots that took place in several American cities during 1967 and 1968. As Sivanandan has argued, race was central to the construction of the urban crisis. Increasingly in social policy discourse during this period 'poverty' was used as a euphemism for racial conflict (Halsey 1974: 139).

Blaming and reclaiming the poor

The Urban Programme of which CDP was a part was launched as a direct response to fears of urban unrest and racial violence. But what sort of response was it? In *Gilding the Ghetto* (CDP 1977b) it is argued that, while ostensibly directed at poverty, the government's concern in establishing CDP was rather with the effects of poverty — in terms of the consequences for social and political order. Similarly it could be argued that the government's concern in relation to black people was not directed against racism, which was already institutionalized within the practices of state and society in Britain, but against the resultant problems for social order.

Individual pathology and inadequacy were core ideas in CDP and the Urban Programme generally. The significance of this element in early CDP thinking may be partly attributed to the project's origins in the Children's Department of the Home Office, with its concerns with inadequate parenting. The poor working-class family was not thought to be functioning very well if it was producing so many delinquents. This was linked in with the principle of the small area base through the medium of the concept of 'multiple deprivation', whereby it was assumed that the statistical fact of the relative concentrations of poor, unemployed and otherwise disadvantaged people in relatively small areas implied a common causal link between these aspects of deprivation. Furthermore, it was assumed that the causes of these various problems were to be found within the areas themselves, in terms of either the personal characteristics of individuals, or their collective characteristics — a kind of 'community pathology' perspective. The working-class community was apparently not functioning too well either. This is a more subtle version of 'blaming the victim', in which social problems are seen as caused by some failing of people, either individually or collectively. Certain theories then in vogue seemed to give credence to these views: there was the 'cycle of deprivation' by which deprivation is seen as akin to an inherited disease, 'transmitted' from one generation to the next, or the 'culture of poverty', which was crudely interpreted as meaning that the poor were trapped in particular modes of thinking and behaving that might be functional for a life of poverty but made them less able to compete in the mainstream of society. The rediscovery of the poor was accompanied by a labelling of them as a problem (Jordan 1974).

Family and community support were important themes in early thinking about CDP, and were seen, from the Home Office's point of view, as a more efficient as well as more humane strategy for preventing delinquency and other social disorders. Alongside this went a broader interest in regenerating the 'community'. This was another old theme to re-emerge in the 1960s – the loss of community in industrial society. The impact of industrial change on the nature of social relationships within society as a whole and within particular neighbourhoods has long been a theme for debate and exploration within sociology and social philosophy, and it is not surprising to find it used as an explanation for contemporary forms of social deprivation. Thus one of the aims of CDP was to be the rebuilding of local communities. This idea had great appeal as a policy aim, not least because of its vagueness and ambiguity. 'Community' has many different meanings, depending on people's social and political perspectives. Moreover, it is an unequivocally 'good' word, with warm and sentimental connotations – no one is against 'community'.

Participation or community involvement were also key themes in CDP thinking, echoing the emphasis in the American War on Poverty on 'maximum feasible participation by the poor'. Unfortunately, as with other aspects of the programme, the Home Office took the rhetoric of the American experience without due regard to the problems that had been encountered in its implementation. The enthusiasm for participation was also home-grown: the need to encourage participation and community involvement had emerged as a theme in earlier reports during the 1960s, such as Skeffington on planning. Like community, 'participation' is a problematic concept, subject to diverse views on definition and operationalization. Within the rhetoric of participation and community involvement there is room for a range of views, from the Home Office vision of happy neighbourhoods of mutually supportive people coming together with service providers to agree on solutions to problems (solutions which were assumed to be within reach, given sufficient knowledge and goodwill), to more radical demands for shifts in power and resources backed up by conflict tactics. These potential differences were papered over in early Home Office thinking about CDP, and when real problems began to emerge later out in the field the Home Office's response was simply to dump the whole experiment.

In part the idea of experimenting with participation reflected a growing interest in the application of business management techniques to service delivery. Cockburn (1977) has argued that community development was the other side of the coin of the corporate management approach. Whereas large firms try to reduce market uncertainty by controlling demand, the state uses participatory democracy and the 'community approach'. Cockburn argues that both are phases of corporate decision-making. In systems theory terms, participation and community involvement provide feedback in the form of a flow of information that can produce greater efficiency in service delivery (Cockburn 1977: 96–8). It is significant that these developments took place at a period when financial constraints loomed large in government decision-making. It was hoped that part of the pay-off from participation would be development of self-help and voluntary effort as a solution to identified problems, which would relieve pressure on state resources.

Paralleling the concern about the social consequences of the breakdown of community was a concern with the alienation of individuals from the state and the decision-making process (Wicks 1977; Lawless 1979). There was ample evidence of working-class alienation from the traditional forms of political expression, as measured by indicators like low turn-out in local elections and declining party membership. The political re-integration of the urban poor into the mainstream of society was clearly part of the agenda of the poverty initiatives. However, the problem was not simply that the poor were politically apathetic. As was noted earlier, this period had seen a considerable outburst of community action; the issue was not that the poor as a group were politically inactive, but that the action they took was not always acceptable to the state. Derek Morrell of the Home Office, architect of CDP, put the issue succinctly at a meeting to discuss setting up the Coventry CDP. The problem was, he said, 'to help the people of Hillfields to frame realistic aspirations and enable them to attain the means to realise them' (quoted in CDP 1977b: 52).

This deceptively simple formulation of the task of CDP raises huge questions about the nature of the political process, which arguably lie at the heart of the difficulties the CDPs were to experience with their sponsors. To frame the problem crudely, there are three models for understanding how changes can be achieved within a CDP area; for the sake of argument, these could be called a consensus model, a pluralist model, and a structural change model.

In the consensus model, implicit in the original Home Office view of CDP, the aim is to reach consensus about goals as early in the process as possible; then it is a technical question of how these should be achieved. This view embodies what Smith has called the 'crock of gold' assumption, that there actually exists somewhere a 'solution' to the problems that everyone can agree on, given goodwill (Smith 1975). It is also the model assumed by most local authorities who took on CDPs, and who certainly thought they knew best about the problems of the areas. Hence there were major rifts between local CDPs and their sponsoring councils, which led in some cases to the premature closure of projects.

The pluralist model accepts that conflicts of interest exist, and aims at consensus through bargaining.

> Pluralist models of change are based on the assumption that social problems arise from 'imbalances' in the democratic and bureaucratic systems. The problems are defined mainly in terms of failures of participation and representation of certain interests in the political process.
>
> (CDP 1974: 23)

The role of the state is seen as managing conflict rather than eliminating it. There is a crucial ambiguity at the heart of this model, however. Is there a crock of gold at the end of the rainbow, in terms of a solution to the problems of poverty within the existing social and political framework, or is it being argued that the process of participation is in itself sufficient to maintain a healthy democratic society? It was in response to these questions that the 'radical' CDPs opted for what was labelled the 'structural conflict' approach.

Structural conflict models of social change are based on the assumption that social problems arise from a fundamental conflict of interest between groups or classes in society. The problems are defined mainly in terms of inequalities in the distribution of power and the focus of change is thus on the centres of organised power (both private and public).

(CDP 1974: 23)

These three models do not fully reflect the complexity of the arguments involved nor the practical strategies undertaken. All twelve CDP projects accepted a 'structural' analysis of the problems of their areas as resulting from external economic and social processes. A number of projects then chose what they saw as the 'realistic' course of action, and concentrated on trying to make pluralist democracy work in the interests of getting a better deal for local people wherever possible, even if that would not cure poverty. The 'radical' CDPs, on the other hand, chose to challenge the prevailing 'mobilization of bias' and to take on issues that had been defined out of the original CDP agenda.

The Home Office had originally seen CDP, as well as a means of improving the performance of poor people in their pockets of deprivation, as a vehicle for pushing local government along in certain directions. In the context of a rapid expansion in government services, especially through the increasing size and scope of local government activities, there was a keen interest in improving efficiency in service delivery. At one level, as has already been noted, participation would, it was hoped, provide information on how effective services were at the point of delivery. Improved co-ordination in the planning and delivery of services was also a key theme, partly in the interests of efficiency and partly in recognition of the complexity and interconnectedness of the mounting social problems local authorities were expected to tackle. Again, the need to improve co-ordination of services had been a theme of earlier reports of the 1960s (e.g. Seebohm on social services) and it emerged as a significant element in early CDP thinking. Specht argues contentiously that it was the key theme in CDP, and castigates the 'radical' projects for departing from this task (Specht 1976: 9; see also Loney 1983: 52–3). While undoubtedly there was a genuine issue, as the traditional structures of both central and local government were not conducive to effective corporate planning and co-ordination, this approach begs the question of whether the services to be co-ordinated are adequate in the first place and whether the fundamental problems of deprivation can be tackled at this level anyway. Again, it could be argued that basically political questions have been reduced to technical problems.

Thus a variety of major themes were woven together in the CDP programme. The ambitiousness of its intentions, however, was not matched by either the resources put into it or the commitment the follow it through as a serious social policy initiative. Although much of the rhetoric was shared with the American poverty programmes, the actual expenditure was miniscule compared with those massive programmes: the British poverty programme was not a war but a small-scale moral crusade. The rationale for the cheapness of CDP was that it was an 'experiment' – in fact all the British urban and poverty initiatives of that period had an experimental basis, except for the main Urban Programme.

However, it was never made clear what the nature of the experiment would be or how the results would be dealt with, and there was a deliberate suppression of public debate on the results of each initiative. Loney, the most thorough analyst of CDP, has called it an exercise in 'symbolic experimentation' (Loney 1983: 17; also see Higgins et al. 1983: 85).

CDP in revolt

The previous section examined the government's intentions with respect to CDP. But all did not go according to plan. The radical outcome of CDP was not predicted at its outset, although perhaps some of the American experiences should have set warning bells clanging. Some critics foresaw a damaging process of co-option and undermining of grassroots activity; others predicted that, because of their funding arrangements and relationship with central and local government, the local projects would be severely restricted in the scope of their activities to politically uncontentious issues (Town 1973). They were wrong.

There were many reasons why CDP got out of control, including the nature of the period, which was one of profound economic and political upheaval, and the ineptitude of the government departments involved, as well as questions of personal and political biography. One major explanation must lie in the nature of the 'action–research' structure the Home Office put together, not only lacking any adequate control mechanism but also bringing together a particular combination of elements. In a way, the radical outcome of CDP was a product of the short but happy marriage of community work and social research.

Despite its explicit community development focus, it was not initially envisaged that the CDP action teams would be dominated by community workers. In the early stages, a range of professional expertise and skills were seen as appropriate, including child psychiatrists and social workers. However, the initial emphasis on individual pathology, and the accompanying narrow focus on social services, diminished as the first wave of projects got underway, leaving the primary task as creating more integrated communities supported by more integrated services. Community work had enjoyed a boom in the 1960s, largely because of its perceived role in social planning and organizing local communities to 'do business with' the state (Cockburn 1977: 110–11, Loney 1983: 20–5). Community workers therefore seemed ideally equipped for the job. But community work as a profession was already engaged in serious questioning about its role *vis-à-vis* the state and the working class. Community work had its origins in British colonialism, as a technique for controlling conquered populations after the removal of traditional sources of authority. The subsequent application of these methods to the British urban poor was initially seen as unproblematic, but towards the end of the 1960s, in the challenging mood of the times, some community work practitioners began to question whether community development was indeed a value-free and politically neutral activity.

The CDP action teams attracted many experienced community workers, skilled in the techniques of organization and direct action at the neighbourhood level, some of whom were already questioning the political basis of their professional activities. In CDP, these grassroots community workers were put together with teams of social researchers and told to do 'action–research' with the urban poor.

Social research and social science generally grew dramatically in scale and influence during the 1960s and 1970s, and in fact helped to stimulate the wider debate about poverty and urban deprivation (Higgins *et al.* 1983: 184–5). There were two distinct traditions within the social sciences. The study of social policy was traditionally empiricist, and rooted in a Fabian-type model whereby facts are uncovered by impartial scientific enquiry and relayed to policy-makers, who then make rational policy choices on the basis of this objective information (Bulmer 1982; Loney 1983: ch. 9).

Academic sociology (the other major strand within the social sciences) was undergoing considerable upheaval during this period. During the 1960s the discipline tended to be split into two sets of practices that rarely met. Sociological theory descended from a long tradition, rooted historically in concerns about the impact of industrialization on society. British empirical sociology, on the other hand, was essentially positivist and obsessed with questionnaire survey research. However, the major social and political upheavals of 1968 had prompted a search for more adequate explanations of social change. Marxism especially was a growing force within academic sociology in that period. There was a move away from the watered-down version of Marxism that had been presented for years, in which Marx figured as yet another early sociologist who happened to have a particular obsession with class. Instead, there was a move back to reading Marx's own writings at first hand, and, based on this, considerable new theoretical development. Perhaps the most crucial insight was that Marxism was not in fact 'sociology' but 'political economy', and that its significance lay in its offering theoretical tools for understanding and analysing the relationship between economic and social change. There were other newer influences shaking up academic sociology at this time – ethnomethodology in particular – which contributed to a general shift away from the previously dominant view that serious sociological research was about large-scale questionnaires, surveys and tables of figures.

Many sociologists also belonged to the cohort of academics radicalized by the events of 1968 and concerned to identify politically with the working class. The CDP provided an opportunity to get into working-class communities; many CDP workers lived as well as worked within their areas. And the researchers found that they had as colleagues community workers with years of real experience of grafting away at the grassroots level, helping working-class people to define their problems and to achieve improvements in their lives. Thus were brought together the conviction that poverty was structurally determined, the analytical skills to begin to expose the processes by which this occurred in particular historical contexts and the organizational skills needed to work for change with the poor and disadvantaged themselves.

Action-research

The 'radical' CDPs comprehensively rejected the Home Office model of the relationship between action and research. The actual working relationships within and between action and research teams were changed in an effort to move away from the model of separate and parallel hierarchical structures set up initially in favour of more democratic and collective styles of working. This can be seen again as part of the legacy of 1968 and the search for less alienated and more democratic forms of organization (Green and Chapman 1990).

The Home Office conception of action–research was also rejected for methodological reasons and on grounds of its inadequacy as a model of social change. For CDP researchers, social change was a practical problem, not merely an academic one requiring explanation (Byrne 1989: 3). They rejected as false the proffered role of the impartial expert feeding information to policy-makers so that rational choices could be made that would benefit society as a whole. They were conscious that their work necessarily involved political choices, and saw the Home Office model of policy change as depoliticizing social problems and solutions. Following the view espoused by Nicolaus – that 'the eyes of sociologists, with few but honourable ... exceptions, have been turned downwards and their palms upwards. Eyes down to study the activities of the lower classes, and the subject population – those activities which created problems for the smooth exercise of governmental hegemony' (Nicolaus 1968: 39) – CDP explicitly chose to research the activities of the powerful in order to inform the efforts of working-class people to bring about changes in their life situations and chances.

In the Home Office model, research findings would be directed upwards, to the government and local authorities; the CDP perspective entailed much more complex decisions about whom to address, how and when. Detailed and theoretically informed consideration had to be given to the form, presentation, timing and dissemination of the research output. The prime aim was accessibility and relevance to those affected by the processes being investigated. Although it is doubtful that the CDP publications were actually read by large numbers of local residents, they certainly reached a much wider and more socially representative audience than most products of academic institutions or government departments. Equally importantly, research was often used to contribute to local campaigns and actions – information about local job loss and unemployment was more likely to be used in a factory closure campaign than in a glossy report. The use of research in facilitating social change at all levels was seen as paramount.

While the major commitment was to working at the neighbourhood level, the CDPS were aware that political forces of the period offered real possibilities for change nationally. The possibility existed, for example, of influencing social change at the macro level, both by working with then powerful labour movement organizations, such as shop stewards, combines, and by entering the debate directly. The national CDP report, *The Costs of*

Industrial Change (CDP 1977a), was in part an attempt to feed into and influence the debates then raging within the Labour Party about the direction of industrial policy; the foreword was actually written by Judith Hart, then Industry Minister.

From CDP to City Challenge

The debates of the 1970s are history now. The Labour Government that came to power in 1974 on a fairly radical manifesto failed miserably either to achieve the promised redistribution of wealth and power or to manage the economy effectively along the old post-war lines. The severity of the economic crisis and the problems it generated made the previous political consensus unworkable. The scene was set for a challenge to the consensus from the right, which the Thatcher government of 1979 onwards successfully carried through, with economic and political consequences unimaginable in the CDP years. The post-war consensus was shattered as the Tories confronted key issues of power and inequality head on, by, for example, systematically undermining the political and economic position of the working class. The model of the expert with the knowledge and skills to tackle social problems was firmly rejected; policy-making became political once more under Thatcher. Despite the very different political context, however, the CDP story has lessons for us in 1990s Britain.

First, the accounts of poverty and urban decline produced by the CDPs showed, with a wealth of argument and evidence, the inadequacy of the Home Office view that the causes of deprivation were to be found within the deprived areas themselves, whether through individual pathology or in the community structures – a view that features persistently as a core idea in social policy past and present. The detailed and historically informed accounts of the impact of government policy and of wider social and economic processes give the CDP reports their strength and depth, producing in sum 'one of the most comprehensive surveys of poverty ever undertaken in Britain' (Higgins *et al.* 1983: 40).

The 'radical' CDPs collaborated to develop a powerful and influential alternative analysis of poverty, arguing that the causes of the problems identified in their areas were primarily located outside those areas, and that, moreover, far from being marginal and deviant 'pockets of deprivation', these areas typified structural processes taking place in working-class communities throughout Britain. The development and de-development of working-class communities was seen as a product of wider processes of economic and social change. The CDPs also analysed the problematic and contradictory role of the state in relation to these areas.

In retrospect it is easy to see the weaknesses and deficiencies of the CDP analysis. The accounts of urban decline can be criticized as unidimensional: the view of the state tended to be monolithic and functionalist, and issues of gender and race were neglected (Remfry 1979; Hanmer and Rose 1980; Green and Chapman 1990). To a large extent this reflects the limitations of the

COMMUNITY DEVELOPMENT WORKER
AH, HELLO SIR, I SEE YOU ARE UNEMPLOYED. I'M HERE TO GIVE YOU SELF CONFIDENCE SO YOU CAN GET A JOB!
EMPLOYMENT FIGURES
STATISTICS
NEWCASTLE'S INDUSTRY
...SO IF THERE ARE 3,000 MEN LOOKING FOR A JOB IN NEWCASTLE... ...AND 700 VACANCIES ...SOMEONE MUST BE OUT OF WORK! I MUST TELL THE HOME OFFICE ABOUT THIS!
CITY LIBRARY
LATER AT THE TEAM MEETING.....
OH YES? THEN WHY -GASP- HAVE THEY JUST CLOSED THE LOCAL HOSPITAL??
GOOD HEAVENS MRS. BLOGGS, THESE OLD SLUMS ARE WORSE THAN I THOUGHT
DAMP
HOLES
CRACKS
BUT THE COUNCIL ONLY BUILT THIS LAST YEAR! BY THE WAY PET, WHY DON'T YOU WEAR SOME DECENT CLOTHES?!
I MUST GET THIS REPORT FINISHED FOR THE HOME OFFICE
BUT...
HOME OFFICE
SLAM
REPORT
GO AWAY WE'RE BUSY PLANNING PUBLIC EXPENDITURE CUTS
CDP OFFICES
IT'S OBVIOUSLY THE GOVERMENT THAT'S THE PROBLEM!
LET'S START WORKING WITH LOCAL PEOPLE AND FORGET THE HOME OFFICE!
HOME OFFICE
I THINK WE'RE ALL AGREED GENTLEMEN. THIS PARTICULAR EXPERIMENT HAS PRODUCED THE WRONG RESULTS — LET'S FORGET IT, SHALL WE?!
H.M. GOVERNMENT NEW POVERTY PROGRAMME DEPT.
LET'S HOPE WE'VE GOT IT RIGHT THIS TIME...
BUREAUCRATS
FINAL REPORT COMPLETE

contemporary Marxist theoretical tools that the CDPs adopted to inform their analysis.

Despite these weaknesses, which I would not wish to underplay, the achievement of the CDP analysis was to move the debate on poverty and urban problems forward in major and significant directions. From then on, economic and industrial issues were firmly on the agenda of discussions about poverty and urban decline. The CDPs had demonstrated in detail the links between the macro level of analysis of economic change and localized manifestations of urban decline.

The other important legacy of CDP is its experience in experimenting with strategies for change at the local level. There were clearly many common elements in the activities of all the local projects, such as establishing welfare rights services, lobbying for particular changes in council policies and practices, and supporting tenants' associations. There were also important differences of strategy. Certain projects, such as Liverpool and Oldham, deliberately chose to operate within a pluralistic framework – working to improve the co-ordination of services at the local level, strengthening the organization of community groups and improving communications between the local authority and the community. The effectiveness of such strategies was evaluated by a number of writers (Specht 1976; Smith *et al.* 1977; Kraushaar and Loney 1978; Loney 1983) as well as by the projects themselves. Other projects were concerned to develop strategies for linking community action with broader movements and struggles (Corkey and Craig 1978; Lees and Mayo 1984). The systematic attempt to link analysis and action was also an important feature of CDP's work.

The experience of CDP still has interesting lessons for community work today, even though conditions are far less propitious, both because the broader political possibilities are more limited and because of the increasing incorporation of community work and community development within the business of urban management. Community development is not so much of a 'double-edged sword' or 'high risk strategy' (Cockburn 1977) now that it is often tied up in formal structures, with little opportunity for the relatively autonomous activity CDP was able to undertake. With CDP, central government took the lead in allocating community work a central role in combating poverty through helping to mobilize the poor. This was linked with an interest in reviving the institutions of local government. In the following decade it was within local government itself that the ideas of community development and participation were taken up most enthusiastically (Association of Metropolitan Authorities 1989), while central government was more interested in undermining and by-passing local government than supporting it. The Conservatives are not overtly opposed to community involvement, however; their particular concern is with community-based approaches to social problems that entail offloading some of the tasks previously undertaken by the state on to the 'community' (usually used in this context as a euphemism for women).

Finally, and most importantly, CDP is still relevant today because the themes that characterized official CDP thinking constantly re-emerge in new high-profile programmes to confuse and divert debates about economic and social problems. In spite of the very different political context, much of the discourse about poverty and urban problems is similar to that which produced CDP.

A stream of new programmes have followed CDP. The rhetoric surrounding each has promised a fresh start, rather than evaluating or building on previous initiatives. But the same themes continually recur, albeit with changes in emphasis. During the 1970s personal pathology fell from favour as a primary explanation of poverty, although it resurfaces from time to time. It was superseded by a growing interest in management approaches, such as area management. The Labour government's 1977 White Paper *A Policy for the Inner Cities* is often seen as a watershed in urban policy. It acknowledged the primacy of economic factors in the constellation of problems identified as inner city problems, partly influenced by the impact of the CDP analysis. The CDP message was distorted in the translation, however. While accepting that the causes of urban problems were rooted in the operations of the market, the government ignored the argument for state intervention in the market (Harford 1977: 99–101). The private sector was accorded a major role in regenerating inner cities in partnership with central and local government. There was a particular emphasis on small firms, which conveniently avoided embarrassing questions about what the larger corporations which account for most employment in Britain were actually doing in the inner cities. Another theme of the 1977 policy document was the failures of local government, and especially urban and regional planning policies.

The Conservative government that followed eagerly took up and developed these themes, stressing the central role of private enterprise in solving the problems of the inner cities, with, for example, its enterprise zones (explicitly based on the model of Hong Kong), which reduced planning restrictions and financial charges on companies operating within particular geographical areas. The government bolstered the role of the private sector and attempted to minimize that of local government with the establishment of bodies like the Urban Development Corporations to control development in particular urban areas (Stoker 1989: 123–8).

Despite the thrust to blame and exclude local government, the theme of partnership between central and local government in tackling urban decline never disappeared completely from the agenda. The structures of the Urban Programme, established in 1977 are based on the concept of such a partnership, have remained intact until the present day (although arguably it is a partnership in which local government gets the blame and central government the kudos (Sills *et al.* 1988)). Heseltine's 1991 City Challenge initiative again firmly bases urban policy on a partnership – this time between local government, the community and the private sector at the local level. The central assumption is of common interests, and it is unimportant whether this is a genuine belief or just a useful rhetorical device to conceal the real conflicts of interest. As with CDP, it is the symbolism of the programme, not the content, that really matters. Like CDP before it, City Challenge can be seen as a cynical political gesture – there is no new money, and it is neatly timed to coincide with a major financial squeeze on local government. For added political fun the government has added the element of competition, with particular cities being invited to bid for a limited number of City Challenge prizes.

Benwell in Newcastle, where I used to work as a CDP researcher in the 1970s, is one of the areas targeted by City Challenge. In the intervening decade social conditions there have deteriorated significantly. More spectacularly, it was only a month after the City Challenge announcement that Benwell, together with the former CDP area of nearby North Shields, hit the national headlines when it suffered a spate of riots involving petrol bombings and stoning of police and firemen. Will City Challenge really achieve the desired 'vision of urban regeneration' (City of Newcastle 1991) or is it yet another symbolic gesture while Newcastle burns? If it is true that history always repeats itself, it is likely in this instance that the first time is farce and the second tragedy.

Note

1 Nearly all CDP publications are available from The Social Welfare Research Unit, Faculty of Social Science, Newcastle Polytechnic. Some of the material in this chapter is drawn from Green and Chapman (1990).

References

Association of Metropolitan Authorities (1989) *Community Development: the Local Authority Role*, London: AMA.
Bachrach, P. and Baratz, M. S. (1970) *Power and Poverty*, New York: Oxford University Press.
Barnes, J. (1974) 'A solution to whose problem?', in H. Glennerster and S. Hatch (eds) *Positive Discrimination and Inequality*, London: Fabian Society.
Bourne, J. (1980) 'Cheer leaders and ombudsmen: the sociology of race relations in Britain', *Race and Class* 21, 4: 331–52.
Bridges, L. (1975) 'The Ministry of Internal Security: British urban social policy 1968–75', *Race and Class* 16, 4: 375–86.
Bulmer, M. (1982) *The Uses of Social Research*, London: Allen and Unwin.
Byrne, D. (1989) *Beyond the Inner City*, Milton Keynes: Open University Press.
City of Newcastle upon Tyne (1991) *New Challenge: New Vision. Newcastle – the West End: a Partnership in Community Regeneration*, Newcastle: City of Newcastle upon Tyne.
Cockburn, C. (1977) *The Local State*, London: Pluto Press.
CDP (1974) *Interproject Report*, London: CDP IIU.
CDP (1977a) *The Costs of Industrial Change*, London: CDP Interproject Editorial Team.
CDP (1977b) *Gilding the Ghetto*, London: CDP Interproject Editorial Team.
Corkey, D. and Craig, G. (1978) 'CDP: community work or class politics', in P. Curno (ed.) *Political Issues and Community Work*, London: Routledge and Kegan Paul.
Davis, B. and Green, J. (1979) 'State policies and the new sweatshops: the flipside of the industrial strategy', Paper given at annual conference of the Conference of Socialist Economists.
Edwards, J. and Batley, R. (1978) *The Politics of Positive Discrimination*, London: Tavistock.
Gamble, A. (1987) 'The weakening of social democracy', in M. Loney *et al.* (eds) *The State or the Market*, London: Sage.

Green, J. and Chapman, A. (1990) 'The lessons of the CDP for community development today', delivered at the OU/HEC winterschool: 'Roots and branches: community development and health'.
Halsey, A. H. (1974) 'Government against poverty in school and community', in M. Bulmer (ed.) *Social Policy Research*, London: Macmillan.
Hanmer, J. and Rose, H. (1980) 'Making sense of theory', in P. Henderson, D. Jones and D. Thomas (eds) *The Boundaries of Change in Community Work*, London: Allen and Unwin.
Harford, I. (1977) 'The inner city – whose urban crisis?', *The Planner* July: 99–101.
Higgins, J., Deakin, N., Edwards, J. and Wicks, M. (1983) *Government and Urban Poverty*, Oxford: Blackwell.
Holman, R. (1970) *Socially Deprived Families in Britain*, London: Bedford Square Press.
Jordan, W. (1974) *Poor Parents: Social Policy and the Cycle of Deprivation*, London: Routledge and Kegan Paul.
Kraushaar, R. and Loney, M. (1978) 'Requiem for planned innovation: the case of the Community Development Project', in M. Brown and S. Baldwin (eds) *The Yearbook of Social Policy in Britain*, London: Routledge and Kegan Paul.
Lawless, P. (1979) *Urban Deprivation and Government Initiative*, London: Faber and Faber.
Lees, R. and Mayo, M. (1984) *Community Action for Change*, London: Routledge and Kegan Paul.
Loney, M. (1983) *Community against Government*, London: Heinemann Educational.
Loney, M. (1987) 'Introduction', in M. Loney et al. (eds) *The State or the Market*, London: Sage Publications.
Marris, P. and Rein, M. (1974) *Dilemmas of Social Reform*, Harmondsworth: Penguin.
Nicolaus, M. (1968) 'Sociology liberation movement', speech made to the convention of the American Sociological Association, reprinted in T. Pateman (ed.) *Counter Course*, Harmondsworth: Penguin.
Parton, N. (1985) *The Politics of Child Abuse*, London: Macmillan.
Piven, F. F. and Cloward, R. A. (1972) *Regulating the Poor: the Functions of Public Welfare*, New York: Vintage.
Remfry, P. (1979) 'North Tyneside Community Development Project', *Community Development Journal* 14, 3: 186–9.
Sills, A., Taylor, G. and Golding, P. (1988) *The Politics of the Urban Crisis*, London: Hutchinson Educational.
Simpkin, M. (1989) 'Radical social work: lessons for the 1990s', in P. Carter, T. Jeffs and M. Smith (eds) *Social Work and Social Welfare Yearbook 1*, Milton Keynes: Open University Press.
Sinfield, A. (1973) 'Poverty rediscovered', in J. B. Cullingworth (ed.) *Problems of an Urban Society 3*, London: Allen and Unwin.
Smith, G. (1975) 'Action research', in M. Bulmer (ed.) *Social Policy Research*, London: Macmillan.
Smith, G., Lees, R. and Topping, P. (1977) 'Participation and the Home Office Community Development Programme', in C. Crouch (ed.) *British Political Sociology Yearbook 3*, London: Croom Helm.
Specht, H. (1976) *The Community Development Project: National and Local Strategies for Improving the Delivery of Services*, London: National Institute for Social Work.
Stoker, G. (1989) 'Inner cities, economic development and social services: the government's continuing agenda', in J. Stewart and G. Stoker (eds) *The Future of Local Government*, London: Macmillan.
Town, S. W. (1973) 'Action research and social policy: some recent British experience', in M. Bulmer (ed.) *Social Policy Research*, London: Macmillan.

Waddington, P. (1979) 'Looking ahead – community work into the 1980s', in D. Thomas (ed.) *Community Work in the Eighties*, London: National Institute for Social Work.

Wicks, M. (1977) 'Social policy for the inner cities', in M. Brown and S. Baldwin (eds) *Yearbook of Social Policy in Britain*, London: Routledge and Kegan Paul.

14
Professional practice and public controversy: discourse and transracial adoption

Derek Kirton

Straddling as it does the sensitive areas of child-care and 'race', transracial adoption (TRA) has become one of the most contentious issues in contemporary social welfare. In the apparent absence of 'conclusive' research on its efficacy, debate between supporters and opponents has come to resemble something akin to trench warfare.

Johnson (1991) offered a review of contemporary issues related to race, child-care and social work. This included a historical background and a political analysis of 'race' in relation to British child-care policy, particularly with regard to substitute family care. That article provides an important context for my concerns here. These rest primarily with the relationship between professional social work practice in the area of 'race' and placements, and its handling as a (periodic) matter of 'public controversy'. Examination of the relationship comprises two parts. The first is an analysis of early newspaper coverage of the 'Croydon case', to date the media's biggest TRA story. The second focuses on the results of a survey that attempted to gauge the effects on adoption policy and practice of government guidelines issued following the Croydon case. Of particular interest are the varying discourses within which debates on TRA are conducted in the respective realms of professional and private.

The development of TRA in Britain was closely associated with a discourse of liberal values captured in the British Adoption Project's quest for families possessed of 'broadmindedness', 'sense of public service' and 'no more than a minimal amount of mild prejudice' (Raynor 1970: 68, 129). In line with the assimilationist policies of the day, racial identity figured, if at all, as implicitly problematic, to be 'accepted' (Raynor 1970: 143).

Black liberation struggles that rejected the sham of integration and liberal paternalism, favouring 'autonomy' and pride in black identity, were predictably opposed to TRA, which was portrayed as 'cultural genocide' (Mandell

1973: 60) and 'internal colonialism', a new form of slave trade in children (Stubbs 1987: 478). Such language was never likely to become part of mainstream adoption discourse but, translated into more 'acceptable' forms, opposition to TRA came close to being conventional wisdom (at least officially), particularly in metropolitan areas. The new discourse emphasized black children's needs for a sense of 'culture' and 'identity' and for learning to 'cope with racism'. White families were seen as either unable to meet those needs, or able only with great difficulty and sacrifice (Small 1986: 92). Such arguments were also applied to children of 'mixed parentage', seen as black within a racist society (Bagley and Young 1982: 91; Cheetham 1982: 87). Received variably by existing transracial adopters (Austin 1985), the new orthodoxy was also subjected to a strong ideological counter, with attacks on the 'banning' of transracial placements (Kerridge 1985; Stubbs 1987: 479) and the alleged condemnation of black children to institutional care (Dale 1987). 'Same race' placement policies were also declared to be 'politically motivated', part of a conspiratorial 'anti-racism' (Lewis 1988: 116).

Reporting the news

On 24 August 1989, adoption and 'race' became national news, its elevation prompted by an Appeal Court verdict allowing Croydon Council to remove a seventeen month old warded boy of mixed parentage from his white foster family and place him with a black family for adoption. Alongside features on radio and television, what generally became known as the 'mixed race baby row' occupied over 500 column inches in the following week's national dailies, with several front page stories and leader comments (and some thirty published letters from readers).

Notwithstanding its other assets in terms of newsworthiness – a 'tug of love', 'human interest', legal controversy and social worker involvement – there is little doubt that the key factor propelling the story on to front pages and into leader columns was that of 'race'. 'White mum told to give up black baby' (*Daily Mirror*), 'Black baby torn from a white family's love' (*Daily Express*) and 'Mixed race baby must go to black home' (*Guardian*) were typical headlines (all 24 August 1989). Given the relatively limited interest of TRA itself for a mass (predominantly white) readership, newsworthiness depended upon wider signification, with the deeming of white parents as 'unsuitable' signalling the 'hijacking' of an emotive and symbolically important area of decision-making.

It will be argued here that the public discourse on TRA of journalists and readers was deeply rooted in 'common-sense racism', drawing selectively upon an ethnocentric child development discourse and the wider social aims of 'integration'. The central aspect of this largely covert racism is the denial of racism itself, and thereby the rendering of notions such as culture, identity and coping mechanisms as irrelevant, and those who propound them as misguided or even conspiratorial.

The under-protection and over-policing of black communities are mirrored in media practices that tend to under-report transgressions against those communities while over-reporting the supposed threat they represent (Gordon and Rosenberg 1989: 21). Similarly, while reporting of racism in the child-care system has been negligible, the Croydon case with its 'white victim' received extensive coverage, which emphasized the 'threat' of 'same race' placement policies. The *Daily Express* (31 August 1989) simultaneously published the results of a 'race survey' that (courtesy of some mental gymnastics in interpretation) was said to explode 'the myth that whites are the main source of discrimination and intolerance'. For our purposes, the paper's introduction to the survey is instructive.

> The survey comes in the week of the Notting Hill Carnival which ended in violent clashes and follows the Salman Rushdie affair and the outcry over a white mother being forced to give up her mixed-race foster baby.

Thus the removal of the child is set alongside the 'racial violence' of Notting Hill and anti-Rushdie protests.

The underlying assumptions of common-sense racism may also help to explain the extraordinary weight of hostility levelled against the judgement and 'same race' policies. Not only was condemnation virtually unanimous within this public discourse, it was frequently vitriolic. Terms such as 'racist', 'fashionable dogma' and 'thoroughly disturbing' all appeared in leader columns, while letter writers declared themselves 'appalled', 'horrified', 'dismayed', and 'never so angry' as at this 'diabolical' decision.

'White eyes' (Hall 1981) dominated coverage, evident not only in the contributors to debate, but also in that the major concerns addressed were those of white people. Ostensibly the point at issue, the needs of black children received little mention. The exoneration of white society from imputed racism figured much more prominently, as did the counter-attack upon 'anti-racism'. Whether focused on the individual judgement itself or on the placement policies it was taken to represent, public discourse questioned the main planks of its professional counterpart.

Initial reporting of the case served to establish, first, that the Appeal Court verdict was based solely on race: 'Because she's WHITE and he'd be better off with a BLACK family' (*Daily Star* 24 August 1989). With the judge's description of the foster mother's 'admirable care' widely quoted, the apparently bizarre removal hinged on the view that, in the words of a senior social worker, the boy is 'seen as black in society'.

'Love is all you need'

Characterized as above, and in the context of reporting on 'race', the judgement clearly provided a soft target. 'Love' was declared to be the crucial missing element by MPs, editors and letter writers. In ordering his enquiry into the case, David Mellor, then a minister at the Department of Health, warned that 'love knows no racial barriers, nor should we seek to erect any' (*Daily Mirror* 26 August 1989). Intentionally or not, the contrast made between 'love' and 'race' tended towards an either/or view, implying that black families had little to offer beyond their skin colour. The near total lack of interest in the boy's prospective adopters did little to challenge this view.

Bonding and identity

'Love versus race' also featured under the more sophisticated guise of 'bonding versus identity'. Perhaps the least threatening concept in 'professional' discourse, the notion of identity was granted at least some recognition. A spokesperson for Families Forever argued that adoptees 'need a confident belief in themselves as black people. No matter how much love and affection a white family have, it is difficult for them to create that in a black child' (*Daily Mail* 24 August 1989). Yet this recognition was in the main grudging. Some letter writers were keen to deny any racial aspect to identity: 'The child may well have an identity crisis, but don't we all' (letter to the *Daily Mail* 30 August 1989). Meanwhile, the *Daily Express* (25 August 1989) transformed the testimony of Croydon's director on possible difficulties in adolescence into a confirmation of racial stereotypes, claiming that social workers had wanted 'to spare the woman the anguish of seeing her foster son turn against her as an angry black adolescent!'

If identity gave at least some logic to a 'same race' placement, it was the 'bonding' of foster mother and child that should have rendered it inapplicable in this case. For a *Guardian* leader writer (29 August 1989)

> it should not be assumed that because it is normally right to assign black children to black families, it is equally right to remove black children from non-black families with whom they have formed real bonds.

The treatment of 'bonding' drew from discourse on child development, with support from 'expert witnesses'. The *Observer* (27 August 1989) explained that some child-care experts felt that 'same race' policies 'had gone too far and become a tyrannical piece of political dogma, used to justify the most cruel and inhumane decisions.' Several child psychologists and psychiatrists were quoted during the week's coverage, emphasizing the 'irreparable damage' of separation and declaring the arguments on identity as based on 'flimsy evidence' (*Observer* 27 August 1989), merely 'fashion, fantasy and polemic', and questions of discrimination as 'pure speculation' (*The Times* 25 August 1989).

Of experts and alleged experts

The newspapers' preferred 'experts' were, to my knowledge, all white and with one exception drew their expertise neither from issues of 'race' and child-care nor from issues of substitute family care (the consequences of which I return to below). Supporters of 'same race' placements were dismissed by the tabloids as 'alleged experts'. Even the 'quality' *Observer* (27 August 1989) could barely desist from mocking comparison:

> While the BAAF welcomed the decision and a black children's pressure group called it 'wonderful', a *leading* child psychologist condemned the

decision as Nazi-like and a *distinguished* child psychiatrist called it 'institutional child abuse'. [My emphasis]

Far from the usual association of expertise with detached judgement, we are treated here to something more akin to 'rent-a-quote'. No one would deny the importance of bonding. Yet in reporting of the Croydon case it was used primarily as a stick to beat the advocates of 'same race' placements. Ignorance of social work practice in adoption was alarmingly widespread, with even most of the 'experts' apparently unaware of the differences between fostering and adoption (including the use of pre-adoptive foster placements).

In view of the enormous importance attached to 'bonding', one might also ask why there has been so little media and expert outrage over the separation of large numbers of black and poor working-class children from their families.

White parents and black identity

An arguably more sophisticated defence of TRA involves acceptance of the 'particular needs' of black children but disputes the necessity of 'same race' placements in meeting them. In the *Sunday Times* (27 August 1989), Tizard, a researcher and herself a transracial adopter, argued that showing sensitivity to racism and its effects was the crucial factor, but added that 'there is plenty of evidence that white parents can do this, while not all black parents do.' Yet what of the application of this line of argument to the Croydon case?

Not one commentator questioned the foster mother's ability to meet the child's needs in terms of identity and the like. This crucial silence becomes more significant when set beside the testimony of the foster mother and her husband. 'I never looked at him and saw a black little boy' (*Daily Mail* 25 August 1989). 'We do not think of him as coloured . . . just as a person'. 'Unless we explained to people that he was fostered, people thought he was one of us' (both *Observer* 27 August 1989). Such comments scarcely indicate awareness of racial identity, and might even appear as a somewhat alarming 'denial'.

The proof of the pudding

Not surprisingly, one of the major defences of TRA lay with its 'success stories' – celebrities such as Daley Thompson and Bruce Oldfield, the adopted daughter of an earl and countess, and a Grenadier guardsman whose mother had 'wanted him to go to a white family to have a better chance in life' (*Daily Express* 25 August 1989). The preferred reading of such scenarios highlights both the 'success' of, and black support for, TRA, rather than the arguably more pertinent question of why better chances depend on membership of white families (Ely and Denney 1987: 10). This line was supported by letters from the transracially adopted and, much more commonly, transracial adopters. The dominant message was of the irrelevance of 'race', with racism at most a minor irritation.

> We have tried to bring up our daughters to believe that, in Britain at least, the colour of one's skin is irrelevant and that it is the person that is

important. Are we to presume that we are naive in our belief and that we should have taught them to have different expectations because of the colour of their skin.

(Letter to *The Times* 31 August 1989)

Acknowledged difficulties in TR placements were extremely rare. Only in the *Guardian* (28 August 1989) did negative personal testimony appear, with one person describing how her 'protective' foster parents none the less operated double standards – making racist jokes, discouraging her from mixing with other black people and even using living with them as a threat (see also Bagley and Young 1982: 88–91; Ely and Denney 1987: 164). A TR adoptee also wrote (*Guardian* 31 August 1989) to complain of letters from 'uninformed people who obviously are not black and have not been adopted by white people, but who speak authoritatively about situations they know nothing of.' Throughout the coverage, no mention was made of the not unusual attempts of black children in care 'to become white', even by self-mutilation (Cheetham 1982: 80; Ely and Denney 1987: 171).

Mixed parentage and identity

Surprisingly perhaps, though not in the light of more generalized opposition to 'same race' placements, relatively little attention was paid to the boy's mixed parentage. While the *Daily Mail* and, seemingly, its letter writers referred to him as 'half-caste', most papers moved freely between 'black' and 'mixed race'. Where the latter appeared, an 'even-handed' treatment was used implicitly to deny the significance of 'race' and racism. Echoing several letter writers, the *Daily Mail*'s Lee Potter (30 August 1989) dismissed the 'humbug' about the boy's black roots, asking 'what about his white roots?' The *Daily Mail* (31 August 1989) also used the judgement to ask 'how far will this go?', raising the spectre of children 'with only a quarter ethnic minority blood' being placed in black families. Notwithstanding the real dangers of crudity in ethnic matching, such arguments, quite apart from their lukewarm attitude to black families, appear to have less to do with the needs of children than with ownership. One-way traffic, it seems, only becomes a problem when threatened with reverse.

Making the connections

Wider debate on the judgement overwhelmingly dismissed opposition to TRA as groundless and somewhat sinister. As Murray observes, any attempt to look at British culture and institutions from a black perspective brings the press on to the offensive, 'exonerating British society from imputations of racism and re-affirming British values and "way of life" ' (Murray 1986: 9). The consensus to be upheld against the conspirators is of Britain as a tolerant society; of support for common sense as against dogma; the humanity of ordinary people as against the ideology of the politically motivated and their allies. Where black people challenge this view or may be suspected of doing so, white versus black also becomes an underpinning theme.

Exposing the threat

In so far adoptive children are a sought-after resource and black parents are chosen in preference to white, 'same race' placement policies can easily be portrayed as entailing positive discrimination, offending both the cruder common-sense racism of the tabloids and the more subtle liberalism of the quality press. Several critics described the policies as 'racism' or 'reverse racism' (more of which below).

To the extent that racism is 'taken for granted' or merely 'common sense', the onus of proof lies squarely with the critics – in the case of TRA, to prove it harmful beyond reasonable doubt. Only *The Times* and the *Guardian* carried articles that looked briefly (and with little obvious sympathy) at the critique of TRA. A *Guardian* leader (29 August 1989) quoted Tizard declaring that it rested on 'unproven theories by black social workers in America' – an evocative message.

Combined with a wider absence of discussion on racism in the child-care system, this paved the way for the battle to be fought out on the more favourable ground of political extremism. In the 'quality' press, the latter lay in the perceived rigid implementation of an otherwise acceptable policy (*Independent* 29 August 1989). More bluntly, the *Daily Mail* (24 August 1989) dismissed policies based on 'fashionable dogma', while the *Daily Express* (25 August 1989) talked of children 'being sacrificed on the altar of ideology'. Links with 'extremism' were taken furthest by the *Daily Mail* (25 August 1989), which, having emphasized the origins of 'same race' placement policies with left-wing councils, gave this theme a cruder, more personal twist, blaming 'socialists like Indian-born Patrick Kodikara' and referring to his 'liaisons with white women and the resulting mixed-blood children'.

If the link with 'extremism' and various political bogeys represents one strand of the counter-attack, a second revolves around the capture and inversion of the language of critique. Opponents of TRA are variously described as 'racists', 'ghettoizing' child-care and operating a 'colour bar' and the policies of 'apartheid and Nazism'. However nonsensical, the words are chosen for maximum effect, attempting to utilize the moral weight gained for such words by anti-racist struggles against those who would claim lineage from such struggles. The term 'racism' is widely used, but implicitly attached to those who are 'making race an issue'. Loss of any association with prevailing power relations and the visibility of challenge combine to produce the 'paradox' that racism is something black people inflict on white (Murray 1986: 2). While a letter writer (*Guardian* 29 August 1989) attacked social workers for 'making society more racist', the *Daily Express* (25 August 1989) contended that

> the public must be thoroughly bemused. Wasn't it the intention of race relations legislation . . . to make us a colour-blind society? Yet now we are

told to believe that in the emotionally fraught area of adoption, colour is of paramount importance.

Conor Cruse O'Brien in *The Times* (29 August 1989), traced the success of 'same race' policies to an unholy alliance between black and white racists: 'Black racists object to white people adopting ... black babies. White racists ... don't much care for that kind of carry-on either.' From this stance, there is only 'racist' opposition to TRA. Only one letter, from the Commission for Racial Equality (CRE), was published challenging this misuse of the term 'racist' (see Fletchman-Smith, cited by Ely and Denney 1987: 122).

The term 'ghettoization' was used on several occasions (including a *Times* leader, 25 August 1989). Shorn of any structural context, it appeared to arise automatically from a 'concentration' of black people. As with the charge of 'racism', the appropriateness of terms such as 'apartheid' and 'Nazism' was taken as self-evident. 'I detest the application in Britain of South African and Nazi laws' (letter to the *Daily Express* 30 August 1989). The *Daily Express* (25 August 1989) claimed that social workers, supported by the CRE, had 'formulated their own version of the Nazi Nuremburg laws' dressed up in 'facile psychological patter'. Child psychologist Newsom spoke of a 'Nazi attitude, saying that only pure Aryans count as white' (*Observer* 27 August 1989). Such remarks display a remarkably convenient ignorance. Apartheid and Nazism move from a power-maintaining 'separatism' to what is in one sense its direct opposite, namely a defensive use of 'separatism'. Of course, there will be shared elements between the two – the importance of 'race' and classification, possible 'essentialism' (Gilroy 1987: 64–7) etc. But to invert basic meaning requires a grotesque racist logic. Whatever else, 'same race' policies are hardly concerned with exclusion from Aryan purity, any more than they are part of a strategy for black domination!

Set against the evils of apartheid, Nazism and the ghetto are the virtues of integration. Conceding in a rare moment that racism was an unpleasant fact of life, the *Daily Express* (25 August 1989) argued that the best chance to overcome it occurred 'when a coloured child is introduced to a white family' (or indeed 'a white child to a coloured family'). An ex-judge spoke of TRA as 'bridge-building' (letter to *The Times* 30 August 1989), while a vicar bemoaned the way in which 'same race' placements served to widen the material gap between black and white (letter to the *Daily Mail* 30 August 1989). Aside from its fit with the worst aspects of the 'child rescue' tradition, one curious feature of such 'social engineering' is the apparent ignorance of the small scale of adoption, let alone adoption of black children and those of mixed parentage. The idea that placement policies (notwithstanding any symbolic power) would have any significant effect on 'race relations' is hopelessly out of touch with reality. Even if such engineering were possible, it might be asked why children who have already faced difficult experiences should be 'used' in this way.

The 'guidelines'

Following a Social Services Inspectorate investigation into the Croydon case in January 1990, whose conclusion was that the council was not found to be

Professional practice and public controversy 187

operating 'a "same race" placement policy as a pre-condition or rule of thumb', a letter was sent to Directors of Social Services on 'Issues of race and culture in the family placement of children'. This was effectively a set of guidelines that sought to address the concerns raised by the Croydon case (Utting 1990).

The letter gave a supportive prominence to the main elements within recent 'professional' discourse. Agencies were to demonstrate cultural awareness and sensitivity, facilitate children taking pride in their cultural heritage and understand the effects of discrimination. However, the 'other things being equal' endorsement of 'same race' placements (S.9) was immediately followed (S.10) by a warning that 'guiding principles are valuable only insofar as they are applied with proper consideration for the circumstances of the individual case.' The letter stated that no one factor should override all others (S.8), and that care should be taken to avoid 'simplistic assumptions of similarity between different ethnic groups', particularly by the umbrella use of the term 'black' and 'black family' (S.6). As for children of mixed ethnic origin, they were to 'be helped to understand and take a pride in both or all elements in their cultural heritage'.

The document can be viewed as a compromise. The main thrust of recent social work practice towards 'same race' placements is endorsed, but this is hedged with warnings against over-zealous pursuit, and in political terms 'watered down'. Ethnicity is given a markedly higher profile than race, while racism itself is not mentioned (with only occasional references to prejudice and discrimination).

The survey

In early summer 1991, a small-scale postal questionnaire was sent by the author to a cross-section (geographically and between state and voluntary sectors) of adoption agencies. The questionnaire sought information on: (a) any changes of policy, procedure or documentation arising from the letter; (b) any perceived influence on placement decisions; (c) changes in writing/ presentation of reports to panels or courts; and (d) any related changes linked to implementation of the Children Act. The major purpose was to gauge in 'broad brush' terms the impact of the letter (and the preceding Croydon controversy) on adoption policy and practice, its 'discourse' and placement outcomes. In all, thirty-five (just under 50 per cent) adoption agencies replied to the questionnaire, with the range of starting points and responses suggesting that they were fairly representative of their peers.

Findings

Changes of policy, procedure or documentation

Twenty-one of the thirty-five replies indicated 'no change' in the relevant areas, although some comments were made about formalizing or otherwise supporting good practice. Among agencies reporting changes, the most common development appeared to be that of strengthening the focus on race and ethnicity. Six reported formulating policy where previously none had existed. Specific developments included: the introduction of ethnic monitoring and greater use of race within forms; more specific questions on ethnicity and culture on application forms (and in one case removal of a general question on TR placements); greater efforts at recruiting black/minority ethnic adopters; casting the net wider to secure 'same race' placements; ensuring that agency and panel personnel better reflected the ethnic composition of local populations; and in one case the establishment of a support group for existing transracial adopters. On 'flexibility', two agencies referred to the introduction of time limits for seeking ethnically matched placements.

Within a broad adherence to ethnic matching with flexibility, there were none the less readily apparent differences in interpretation of 'flexibility'. For several (particularly metropolitan) agencies, the Department of Health's letter was taken as strengthening existing 'same race' placement policies, and flexibility was confined to exceptional cases. Several agencies indicated that they had made no, or at most a handful of, TR placements in recent years. Given the letter's clear targeting of 'rigid' policies, this might be regarded as a selective reading (more of which below).

At the opposite end of the continuum were those who placed considerable emphasis on 'flexibility'. One policy statement, having noted it as an ideal, said of ethnic matching 'this will not, however, be seen as an overriding consideration'. Alongside possible ideological objections to strong 'same race' placement policies, it was evident in some cases (particularly in predominantly 'white' areas) that emphasis on flexibility reflected (perceived) difficulties – described by one respondent as 'formidable' – in appropriate family finding.

Two replies highlighted the problem of combining flexibility with strong commitment to ethnic matching. One expressed concern that the new guidance might serve to weaken such commitment, creating loopholes for avoiding or curtailing the search for suitably matched placements. Another spoke of the difficulty of genuinely operating flexibility in a tiny minority of cases without appearing to lack commitment to 'same race' placements.

Perceived influence on placement outcomes

The links between 'words and deeds' are of course manifold, and agencies were asked whether any of the above changes had actually influenced individual decisions on child placement. Most of those agencies indicating such changes chose to interpret 'influence' in general rather than specific terms, looking at the basis of discussion and decision-making rather than concrete variation in placement outcome. Of the former, the most common response was to increase commitment to ethnic matching, with in two cases mention made of greater efforts to match in short-term placements. There were also, however, some moves towards 'flexibility', couched in terms of avoiding unacceptable delay. None of these agencies reported any different outcomes, although one agency did comment on how a local test case court ruling had been taken to confirm the importance of 'same race' placements. The relative lack of reported change in outcomes may, of course, reflect its hypothetical nature and concerns over publicity, even with the promise of confidentiality. Four references were made to internal conflicts between (some) area social workers and their adoption counterparts, with the former being seen by the latter as less committed to 'same race' policies.

Only one agency mentioned a specific case, namely where white foster carers were attempting to adopt two children of mixed parentage, a plan opposed by the adoption unit but supported by area social workers. The (adoption unit) respondent stated that area staff had used the Department of Health guidance as support and expressed the view that the white family concerned also felt the guidance to be supportive of their application.

Changes in reports to panel and courts

In the area of report writing, notified changes tended towards a strengthening of professional discourse. Twelve of the thirty-five replies indicated a stronger focus on issues of race and ethnicity in report writing. (This was particularly so in agencies where race had previously taken a fairly low profile.) 'Race issues could no longer be ignored.' 'The guidance has served to increase awareness of the issues.' In at least two replies, this requirement was seen as useful in dealing with the more recalcitrant social workers, who were lukewarm on the importance of ethnic matching. Greater (and more formalized) focus on the issues is clearly not synonymous with increased support for 'same race' placements. However, such comments as did indicate the effects of such a focal shift tended to confirm the link: 'Workers are now being more specific in the way reports are written. They feel more confident in recommending same race placements both to the panel and in court.'

'Race', placement and the Children Act 1989

Although the Act introduces some significant changes to adoption law (White et al. 1990: ch. 11), the latter is of course currently the subject of a wider review. The Croydon case was important, however, in that the associated controversy prompted a late addition to the Act (Schedule 2, para. 11) requiring local authorities in recruiting foster carers to 'have regard to the different racial groups to which children within their area who are in need belong'.

From those agencies citing specific developments in relation to their Children Act planning, the most often mentioned (referred to by twelve agencies) was that of a thorough incorporation of relevant issues – variously of 'race', language, culture and religion – into training. The broadening from 'race' may be interpreted both as a sign of greater sophistication in thinking on children's needs and as a means of diffusing some of the hostility aroused by the terminology of 'same race' policies. One referred to this as updating its policy. Efforts at recruiting more foster carers and adopters from minority ethnic groups were mentioned by eight agencies, while a further five referred to attempts to recruit more such workers and panel members. While again the underlying message of comments suggested that any movement would be towards strengthening 'same race' policies, two agencies argued that the likely effect of the Act would be greater flexibility.

Conclusions

In interpreting the findings of the above survey, its limitations – brevity, impressionistic nature and reliance on the view of an agency spokesperson – should be acknowledged. The purpose was a modest one, namely to gain a broad view of the impact of Department of Health guidance and indirectly of the fierce battle fought out in the media over 'race' and placement policies. Earlier, it was argued that the public discourse on TRA was infused with 'common-sense racist' assumptions, centred on a denial of the importance of 'race' and racism in adoption. The Department of Health's investigation can be seen as a political response (doing something) to public or media 'outcry'. The subsequent guidance letter represents a delicate balancing act between the newly dominant professional discourse about identity, culture and discrimination and the critique of 'same race' placements (the latter dealt with in the various warnings against rigidity and crudeness).

With regard to the impact of the guidance on policy and practice in adoption agencies, the findings here are suggestive of continuity, with relatively minor changes in most agencies, and those predominantly in the direction of strengthening 'same race' placement policies. It is perhaps not surprising that agencies should fail to recognize themselves as being rigid or crude. However, as we have seen, there did appear to have been moves in the direction of more sophisticated matching. How then can we explain the 'paradox' of an apparent strengthening of commitment to 'same race' placement policies?

For the purposes of argument, a useful distinction can be drawn between agencies according to their previous position on the issue of 'race' and placement. What is clear is that in several cases where such issues were low profile (with greater likelihood of TR placements), the guidance served as a benchmark, with agencies feeling obliged to raise the profile by giving more serious consideration to issues of 'race', ethnicity and so on. While some doubtless took comfort from the emphasis on flexibility, this was none the less combined with a basic recognition of the ideal of ethnic matching. From those previously strongly committed to 'same race' placements, there was little indication that the guidance would serve to weaken this commitment (although one respondent expressed such a worry). A number of such agencies chose a minimal interpretation of flexibility, i.e. as applicable only in exceptional circumstances, while welcoming the broader endorsement of 'same race' placements.

In the meantime, TRA has periodically re-surfaced into the public arena, with social work practice receiving consistently hostile treatment (*Daily Mirror* 6 February 1990; *Daily Express* 18 December 1990; Channel 4's *Black Bag* 9 April 1991).

What can be gleaned from developments since the Croydon case? Perhaps the most obvious point is that the ideological battle over TRA has become, to a considerable extent though by no means exclusively, one between those within the social work profession and those outside. It is argued here that their respective positions continue to hinge on attitudes towards 'race' and racism, with public discourse (supported by some members of the child-care establishment (Black 1990) indignantly denying their importance, and its professional social work counterpart utilizing its relatively insulated 'space' to give them prominence. It would seem as if the periodic media/public abuse over TRA has had little effect on the thinking of most social work agencies, who, while clearly embattled on this issue, appear prepared to stand by the new orthodoxy (and presumably await the next episode of 'public outrage').

References

Austin, J. (ed.) (1985) *Adoption: the Inside Story*, London: Barn Owl.
Bagley, C. and Young, L. (1982) 'Policy dilemmas and the adoption of black children', in J. Cheetham (ed.) *Social Work and Ethnicity*, London: George Allen and Unwin.
Black, D. (1990) 'What do children need from parents?', *Adoption and Fostering* 14, 1: 43–5.
Cheetham, J. (1982) 'Some priorities', in J. Cheetham (ed.) *Social Work and Ethnicity*, London: George Allen and Unwin.
Dale, D. (1987) *Denying Homes to Black Children*, London: Social Affairs Unit.
Ely, P. and Denney, D. (1987) *Social Work in a Multi-racial Society*, Aldershot: Gower.
Gilroy, P. (1987) *There Ain't No Black in the Union Jack*, London: Hutchinson.
Gordon, P. and Rosenberg, D. (1989) *Daily Racism: the Press and Black People in Britain*, London: Runnymede Trust.
Hall, S. (1981) 'The whites of their eyes: racist ideologies and the media', in G. Bridges and R. Brunt (eds) *Silver Linings*, London: Lawrence and Wishart.
Johnson, M. (1991) 'Race, social work and child care', in P. Carter *et al.* (eds) *Social Work and Social Welfare Yearbook 3*, Milton Keynes: Open University Press.
Kerridge, R. (1985) 'Fostering apartheid', *Spectator* 6 July.
Lewis, R. (1988) *Anti-racism: a Mania Exposed*, London: Quartet.
Mandell, M. (1973) *Where Are the Children?*, Lexington, MA: Lexington Books.
Murray, N. (1986) 'Anti-racists and other demons: the press and ideology in Thatcher's Britain', *Race and Class* 27, 3: 1–19.
Raynor, L. (1970) *Adoption of Non-white Children*, London: George Allen and Unwin.
Small, J. (1986) 'Transracial placements: conflicts and contradictions', in S. Ahmed *et al.* (eds) *Social Work with Black Children and Their Families*, London: Batsford/BAAF.
Stubbs, P. (1987) 'Professionalism and the adoption of black children', *British Journal of Social Work* 17: 177–90.
Utting, W. B. (1990) 'Issues of race and culture in the family placement of children', Circular C1(90)2, London: Social Services Inspectorate, Department of Health.
White, R., Carr, P. and Lowe, N. (1990) *A Guide to the Children Act 1989*, London: Butterworths.

15
Trust in the future: an examination of the changing nature of charitable trusts

Alison Harker

The world of charitable trusts is known by few people. Those who are part of it may know individual trusts well but even they are unlikely to have an overview. It is, in many respects, a private world. There has been little written about trusts though they have attracted more attention recently as the funds they provide become more important and as government has begun to focus attention on their monitoring and control.

This chapter looks at charitable trusts and examines the changing world in which they operate. It does not look at any individual trusts in detail nor does it examine their investment practices.

Anyone who has sought funding from charitable trusts will testify to their idiosyncratic nature. This has been of benefit to many trying to develop new ideas and fresh approaches. It has worked to the detriment of others. Whatever an individual organization's experience is of charitable trusts, they are an important potential funding source for the voluntary sector in the United Kingdom and, as such, cannot be ignored. They can also be important for individuals. Trusts report an overwhelming increase in the number of requests for financial assistance from social workers on behalf of those who no longer are or perhaps never were eligible for assistance from the state.

The most recent figures available showed that the total income of the United Kingdom voluntary sector is estimated to be £15 billion annually (based on an estimate of £12.6 billion in 1985). This amount is three times the income of the agricultural sector of the economy, which in 1988 was £5.4 billion or 1.5 per cent of gross domestic product. Charitable trusts and donations contributed approximately £2 billion to the income of the voluntary sector. The philanthropic input from the main trusts amounts to about £250 million. Considerable amounts can be paid in grants to voluntary organizations. The *Guide to the Major Trusts* gives several examples of grants made by the largest trusts of £50,000 and above. The Tudor Trust, the largest charitable trust with a general welfare brief, has made a number of grants of this size. This policy was applauded by Luke Fitzherbert in his introduction to the 1991 edition of the Guide when he refers to 'the splendid work of the Tudor Trust' (Fitzherbert 1991). But trusts with a lower grant-making income can make grants of equal importance to the recipients, if smaller in size. The Trust for London makes grants of up to £5,000 but targets small groups, many of whom may have had little if any money previously.

There are approximately a hundred trusts that currently make grants of over £500,000 per annum. It is trusts in this range that are the main focus of this article. In the context of a hard pressed voluntary sector charitable trusts have long been an important source of finance. However, there are questions about which voluntary organizations benefit from trust funds. Getting money from trusts can be seen as an art, a science or merely a game. It is those who know the rules who profit. The others lose out. The words of Richard Hoggart in his autobiography, albeit in a different context, are apt: 'It is the old English story: to him that hath shall be given; for him who know what he needs provision shall be made abundantly; and that provision in that form and style, will keep out those who need it more, but don't know they need it' (Hoggart 1990: 72).

The nature of trusts and the grants they make

Charitable trusts are many and various. It is hard to generalize as they operate so differently. Some fund individuals but this chapter only considers those that make grants to organizations. Some trusts are small bodies making small grants, perhaps with very tight restrictions on what they fund and where. These include local and parochial trusts. Others have substantial income and make grants on a national and even an international level.

Each charitable trust will have its own interests and priorities for grant-making. These may reflect the personality or commitments of the trust's founder or those of the members of the trustees who currently make decisions upon applications. They may have been established long ago and never reviewed or they may have been revised at regular intervals. Charitable trusts are autonomous bodies which are in the control of trustees, who are the decision-makers about all the trust's business. Unlike for local authorities, there is little pressure on charitable trusts to spend all their money by the end of each financial year for there is no rule whereby unspent money is taken back and withheld next year. However, the Charity Commissioners are concerned to ensure that trusts do not accumulate unnecessary income which ought to be spent upon their charitable objects.

The older trusts for the most part were endowed; that is to say, there was an initial endowment which was invested; and the interest is used for grant-making purposes. More recently trusts have been established to distribute the funds accrued from large media and public appeals. There are also trusts whose finance derives from particular family businesses and family members may be heavily involved in running them.

The nature of a trust will frequently be reflected in the make-up of the board of trustees. The board may consist of members of the particular family that originally established a trust. The trustees of the Wates Foundation include several family members. Unusually the board may consist of people nominated by public bodies or include invited members; the City Parochial Foundation is such a body, whereas the Joseph Rowntree Charitable Trust's board of trustees comprises members of the Religious Society of Friends (Quakers). Trusts are not political bodies and are unlikely to include among their trustees practising politicians. There may be staff employed but it is unlikely to be a large number. In some cases the trust administration is carried out by a firm of solicitors. Administratively, charitable trusts are small bodies and few employ staff with direct voluntary sector experience.

By nature charitable trusts, with notable exceptions, will be reactive rather than pro-active bodies. They do not have a tradition of targeting or of seeking applications. The onus is very firmly upon the organization seeking funding to make the running. Traditionally they have seen their role as pumppriming: viewing themselves as bodies that can initially fund new ventures, which if successful go on to seek long-term monies from statutory bodies. It is a route tried and successfully tested by many now large and well-established organizations. This is a role that might be said to have been usurped by the pumppriming initiatives of central government in recent years. The latter has introduced a series of schemes into the voluntary sector, initially using government money but designed to be funded in the longer term by other bodies, including trusts.

This role has not been totally accepted by the trusts themselves. Trusts are proud of their independence and their non-political nature and do not easily slot into any role defined for them. Many have resisted the pressure to reconstitute cuts made by statutory bodies, and to fund areas they identify as clearly a statutory responsibility. Of course there does not exist in the world of charitable trusts sufficient money to pick up all the schemes whose funding has been cut, but it is the principle rather than the financial considerations that is important to trusts. Nevertheless, there is extreme pressure on trusts and they are facing dilemmas in trying to stick to their pumppriming role. Neuberger expressed the concern felt by many trusts that 'they are being asked to plug gaps left by changes and diminutions in government funding in a way they have not been asked over the past thirty years.' She asked

> whether it is right for charitable foundations to pick up the tab where government, national or local, has ceased to fund. On the one hand it is simply taking the government's work away from it, allowing it as it were, to get away with ceasing to fund essential services for sectors of the population. On the other, by not picking up the tab, the service users suffer from the closure of their familiar service.
>
> (Neuberger 1991: 3)

For Hazell (1991: 14) the position is clear: 'the remedy for trusts who object to the reversal of roles is simply to sit on their hands.' Although trusts may have common views, they operate independently from each other and follow traditional and individual ways of working rather than adhering to a policy agreed by all.

Where grant-making bodies are reactive, there is a certain sameness about the nature of the funding made and who will receive it. Money can be sought and received for anything that is charitable and trusts have a wide variety of interests. Increasingly grants can be and are made for both capital and revenue expenditure. They do like innovative projects but it is a fallacy that they will never fund existing work, or rescue organizations in trouble. Taylor, the former Director of the Gulbenkian Foundation, described how 'A rising proportion of our grants are now for "tanking up", to keep the recipients alive while they wander in arid regions looking for an oasis to settle beside, meanwhile collecting any chance rainfall, drinking from dew ponds and hiring a water diviner' (Taylor 1991: 9).

A long standing practice has been only to accept applications from bodies registered with the Charity Commissioners. However, increasingly they are willing to accept applications from non-registered groups via a registered charity. Moreover, a few trusts will consider applications from groups whose constitutions clearly indicate they have charitable purposes and who are in the process of seeking registration with the Charity Commissioners. But the common belief is that charitable registration is necessary in order to approach trusts for funding.

This reactive way of operating favours certain groups. It benefits those who are well organized, part of networks, in bodies that receive information, have a certain level of resources and 'know their way around'. It favours those that have a name (and a history) and a good command of English, and are working on sympathetic causes. It excludes those who do not have access to certain resources and information.

Knowing about which trusts to contact means knowing about the various directories of trusts and how to make an application. Even organizations that are registered charities (and in December 1988 there were 164,534) frequently do not know that they hold the key to opening many potential funding doors. Burkeman of the Joseph Rowntree Trust expresses an interesting view: 'Perhaps because those who run trusts in the United Kingdom have in the past tended to be rather elderly gentlemen of a culture not given to self-exploration still less self revelation, very little has been revealed by endowed foundations about those people or the way they work' (Burkeman 1991: 7).

As a result, international aid agencies can attract funds to work abroad with refugees but refugee communities in the United Kingdom can experience great difficulty in attracting funds. Although trusts indicate they will make grants over a limited period, in fact some organizations have been grant-aided by trusts over many years. It is not unusual to find that some large, established bodies have consistently received grants for one purpose or another over a twenty or thirty year period.

As Davies of the Allen Lane Foundation said, 'Grant-making trusts seem, at present, an invisible and frequently unapproachable group. Many trusts want it that way' (Davies 1989: 245). It certainly means that organizations that are intent on making applications to trusts must be determined, resourceful, informed and able to 'play the funding game'.

The all-important relationships

When I was in a position of seeking money for projects with which or for which I worked the relationship that mattered was that with the local authority. There was a particular one with the officers, which was different to that with local councillors who might be prepared to support a funding application. There was also a relationship of sorts with the officers at the Regional Office of the Department of the Environment, who had a special interest in the Urban Programme, which was a useful source of funds. I imagine that for a small organization it was fairly unusual to have such a contact.

Relationships with charitable trusts were confined to written communication. This was frequently one-way. That is to say, I wrote and never received a reply. Occasionally my letter elicited a welcome cheque accompanied by a brief covering letter. I was never asked for more information and never visited in response to a request for funding nor indeed after funding was agreed. When more money was needed I would have great deliberations with myself about whether I could re-approach a trust that had previously made a grant; was I being cheeky doing so? Would it be seen as greedy to ask for what we needed? Should we not ask for a portion and hope to make up the balance somehow? I know my experience was not unique.

Relationships with trusts were in marked contrast to that with the local authority, which was open and easy. Yet trust funding for a small struggling project was vital, particularly when trying new developments. It was also important in a voluntary sector that mainly survived on short-term funding and was strongly encouraged by the statutory bodies to find alternative sources of income. These bodies had little accurate knowledge of trusts and certainly had no relationship with them.

Since then funding for the voluntary sector has become more difficult and increasingly organizations have had to turn to charitable trusts. This has led to changes in the relationship between the two. It has also been a factor in the improvement of inter-trust relationships, as several might be approached by the same organization.

Whereas it is true to say that some of the major foundations do have relationships with government departments, civil servants and even ministers, there is probably only a tiny number that have any contact with local government. It should be remembered that most large trusts will have a national brief or, if they operate in a restricted geographical area of benefit, they are likely to cross the boundaries of several local authority areas. Thus the prospect of establishing and maintaining relationships with local authorities is a huge and daunting task.

Sadly, it is not always the case that small is beautiful. Money attracts money and it is bigger organizations with high levels of income that can raise more and that have relationships with trusts. Although the situation might be improving for smaller bodies and communities they can still lose out. This is true of black and ethnic minority groups and, particularly, of migrant and refugee groups. As few trusts would have staff or trustees from these communities their needs can more easily go unrecognized.

Establishing relationships between grant makers and grant receivers is not solely dependent upon personal contact, although this is important. There are ways in which grant-making trusts can establish systems whereby relationships with the beneficiaries can be made and grants can be disbursed and used as effectively as possible. The recent report of a working party established by the National Council for Voluntary Organisations is helpful, as it gives consideration to the way funders provide grants to voluntary organizations and the relationship between those who give and those who receive grants.

> The way in which an organisation provides grants has an important impact on the effectiveness of voluntary organisations. We believe that funding will be more effective if it rests on a properly considered policy which lays down criteria for selecting voluntary organisations to whom grants are made and deciding the method of grant giving. . . . Without an agreed policy the practice of a grant giving organisation will be haphazard and probably ineffective. Such a policy should be made publicly known, so that those voluntary organisations which might obtain grants will apply for them, and, equally important, organisations with no chance of success will not waste time and effort in making applications.
> (NCVO 1990: 35)

The report goes on to say: 'Effective grant giving involves more than establishing a policy and then deciding on paper between various applications for grants. A relationship also needs to be established between the funder and recipient!' (NCVO 1990: 36). For a relationship to be established between funder and recipient changes in the way many trusts currently operate are necessary, but there must be an understanding and acceptance of why change is needed.

Why change?

Within the world of voluntary activity in this country major changes have taken place and will continue to do so. Such shifts reflect those that take place in society and give rise to new needs. As changes have occurred, some of the older organizations have sought to meet the emerging needs by the appointment of new staff or the establishment of units attached to a core body. However, newer organizations have also emerged to address the needs of the communities they represent. They are mainly black or minority ethnic groups and self-help groups. The membership is frequently female although members may not see themselves primarily as women's groups. The services they provide address the needs of particular communities, which are being ignored or inadequately served by the wider community. Included among them are refugee and migrant groups.

These groups form the new voluntary sector. The needs they address are basic and their brief is often health and welfare, although a cultural and religious element may be included. Their services are both supplementary and complementary to those provided by statutory bodies and the traditional white voluntary sector. They are rarely funded by sources outside the particular community but they are serving important needs and helping sizeable sections of it, and deserve financial assistance to do so.

Across London and in other major cities there exist a plethora of black and minority ethnic organizations providing care for their elderly by visiting schemes, luncheon clubs, drop-in facilities and translation and interpreting assistance. Organizations run child-care schemes and after-school clubs; provide supplementary education schemes for children at evenings and weekends; help with homework; provide coaching in English, maths, science and other subjects; and teach their own history and mother tongues. Community organizations run holiday schemes, youth projects, employment and training projects, and events to celebrate their own culture and to ensure that their children can discover and be aware of their own identity. There are schemes by women for women to learn English, to learn how 'the systems' work in this country, to reduce their isolation and support each other. There are groups that develop arts and music. There are legal advice projects using the services of volunteer solicitors and barristers. There are housing schemes designed to meet the needs of particular groups. Among the refugee communities organizations exist to assist newer arrivals: they go to the airport to collect new refugees, find them accommodation, help them to sort out legal tangles, accompany them to the Home Office, try and secure an income, education, and medical treatment. Some regularly visit detainees in centres and support them on release.

Most of this activity continues thanks to practical and financial input by individuals in the communities. It is not a transitory phenomenon. Many organizations have been running on a shoestring for years. Yet the services being provided are vital. They are not duplicating existing work, they are filling gaps. There is no doubt that many of these schemes are pioneering and carried out in response to a clearly perceived need. It is frequently the type of work that charitable trusts looking for innovative schemes might love to fund, yet few do. So what is it that prevents them from doing so?

One reason is that the traditional structure and method of operation of most charitable trusts militates against there being ready contact. The organizations may not know that charitable trusts even exist. It is ironic that many groups have secured charitable status but have never known the potential funding doors that this might open to them. The staff employed by trusts are unlikely to be from black and minority ethnic communities. They are unlikely to have experience of working with black and minority groups or indeed to know the issues facing the different communities. This is also true of trustees, who are predominantly white and male. It is hardly surprising given this situation that such groups are not funded to any great extent by charitable trusts.

If traditional structures and ways of operating are the only deterrent to bodies meeting new needs, then it would appear that there is resistance to change. It is important to focus on the reasons, but initially the type of changes necessary should be identified.

How change can be achieved and what happens when some trusts begin to make changes

It is naive to think that changes can be achieved across the board in the world of charitable trusts, and innovation should not be sought merely for the sake of it. The changes necessary concern the accessibility and clarity of information made available to all the voluntary sector. All trusts might begin to publish their policies and procedures, and details of which organizations they grant aid. This is basic information and guidance for grant seekers. They can establish timetables for considering applications and publish these. They can begin to monitor the grants they make, if only in terms of the types of organizations and geographical areas they cover. They can begin to publish their annual accounts.

What happens when some trusts start to make these kinds of changes? Inevitably, when policies are stated and a more pro-active stance is adopted applications from targeted groups appear, new relationships are made, new communities, new work, new needs and new cultures become known. For trusts it can be an interesting and exciting exercise for staff. It can be stimulating for established trustees to consider different types of organizations and applications and to meet new trustees and advisers, who are knowledgeable about the areas targeted for funding and whose experience is vital to ensure responsible grant-making. It can be equally important for those trustees or advisers who may be new to the world of trusts but whose input may have a positive spin-off for organizations within the communities they represent.

One London-focused trust has deliberately targeted and prioritized small groups in certain communities in the metropolis and adopted a programme of concentrating on a different set of boroughs every year over an initial period. The result has been that resources have been made accessible to many groups previously excluded from funding opportunities because of their size, lack of development and lack of knowledge of potential sources. The Gulbenkian Foundation has adopted a policy of 'seeking out new and pioneering forms of activity to support' and, as Taylor puts it, 'we try to pick good 'uns when odds are long before other trusts place their bets'. As a result 'few of the recipients feature in the donations lists of other trusts' (Taylor 1991: 8).

Trusts do no need massive resources to carry out changes. Important changes that will benefit the voluntary sector can be made by small trusts with few resources and at little cost. It is a question not solely of money, but also of commitment to responding to the changing needs in society and having structures that are sufficiently open and clear to encourage and allow appropriate applications to be made by all sections of the community.

Why change is resisted

Organizations that have undergone policy changes with consequent practice alterations know the upheaval that can result. Arguably trusts as small organizations could make changes more easily than many others. However, there is a moral pressure on trusts to spend as little as possible on administration and charges. Any increase in the volume of applications received by trusts would entail extra staff appointments as would any programme of visiting and local research.

Many trusts adhere to loose policies that are related to a series of interests. They may not have been reviewed for years. As trusts have in the main only recently begun to communicate with each other it is not surprising that many are unaware of each other's interests and priorities. Targeting would require making tighter policies and operating in the knowledge of what others are funding and what needs exist. By their very structure most trusts will be removed from the local areas and issues into which they direct funds. It is only if they deliberately seek out local contacts or seek advice from those with local knowledge and experience that grant-making can be targeted. Several trusts are now employing staff in the geographical areas where their grant-making is focused. The Baring Foundation has for some years employed locally based staff in several parts of the country. The staff are responsible for visiting applicant groups, processing the subsequent applications and preparing them for trustee decision on whether or not a grant will be made. This is a practice that must be developed if the imbalance of funding which exists between London-based organizations and those outside is to shift and if grant-making is to be fully informed. Other trusts ensure that staff visit applicant groups across the country. Some trusts now target a proportion of their funds at Northern Ireland, for example.

The issues of evaluation and monitoring are key factors in trusts being informed and open to changing their policies, procedures and practices. It can be through proper monitoring and evaluation of initiatives funded that decisions can be reached on where more funds ought to be directed, and good practice can be identified. Applicants for funding need to monitor and evaluate their own work and report the outcome to the trusts providing the funds, in the same way that increasingly they have to do for other funders. It is in their own interests to monitor and evaluate in order to establish and maintain good practice. By implication, this means that the terms of any evaluation exercise are agreed between trust and applicant at the outset, and this necessitates the formation of a professional relationship between the two parties, as *Effectiveness and the Voluntary Sector* (NCVO 1990) recommends.

Monitoring and reviewing of applications should not be confined to the applicants. Trusts must review and monitor their own grant-making and practice if they are to be sure they are responding to new needs and taking accounts of new development.

Both the Carnegie UK Trust and the City Parochial Foundation undertake quinquennial reviews and set new policies and priorities for the next five years. The Barrow and Geraldine S. Cadbury Trust holds an annual residential meeting of staff and trustees 'to review grant trends over previous years and confirm or revise policies' (Wilson 1991: 33). Those trusts undertaking such an exercise report similar findings:

> evaluation of the foundation's own performance over and above that of the recipients of its grants, during the past quinquennium;

bonding between trustees and with their staff as they determine future priorities;

policies which result from a careful and rational process;

the transmission of these decisions to the foundation's constituencies with the implication that the quality of applications rises accordingly.

(Wilson 1991: 33)

Although these are positive factors, beginning to evaluate clearly requires time and resources, and many trusts need to be persuaded of its importance. Others are already convinced. In a fast moving world, major changes can rapidly disappear from sight and may not even be anticipated. Writing of the City Parochial Foundation's quinquennial review 1987–91, Cook points out: 'we did not anticipate the abolition of the Inner London Education Authority with all its consequences, nor the upsurge in the number of refugees coming to London, nor the developments of what has become known as cardboard city' (Cook 1991: 18). Add to this the fact that the income of many trusts is increasing, as are the demands made upon them, and monitoring and reviewing becomes more important than ever.

If changes are to take place in the world of trusts, there must be a will to change and to operate more openly. There are signs that however jealously trusts guard their independence and their freedom to act, or not, there is a growing expectation in several quarters, including government, that they should be more publicly accountable (House of Commons Committee of Public Accounts 1991). This means at least publishing their annual accounts to show where their funds have been spent. The existence of the recently formed Association of Charitable Foundations indicates a willingness on the part of at least some charitable bodies to share experiences and look at issues of common concern. Such co-operation must be beneficial for all parties.

The implications of change

Charitable trusts are justifiably proud of their role as funders of pioneering work. In a climate of major change for voluntary organizations and ever-increasing needs coming to the fore, it is more important than ever before that trusts can be accessible and open to potential new applications and new ideas.

Achieving changes in the ways trusts operate and broadening the types of bodies they fund need be neither too problematic nor too traumatic. To become more open about policies, procedures and practices will not necessarily 'open the floodgates'. On the contrary, it may cut down on the number of inappropriate applications received. Charitable trusts exist in the majority of cases to fund the voluntary sector yet they have little to do with it other than in the capacity of grant maker. This reactive role means that knowledge of changes within the sector and those issues that have a bearing upon it is either negligible or obtained only through the narrow focus of a grant maker. Few trusts have within them a detailed and personal experience of voluntary sector activity and operation. It can be argued that an input from the voluntary sector or at least established channels of communication with it are important if trusts are to respond to felt and unmet needs and identify gaps in provision where pioneering work is needed. Advisory bodies made up of representatives of all areas of the voluntary sector may have a significant role to play in the future for charitable foundations. The implications of this for the voluntary sector are that grant-making by trusts may become more informed and professional. Trust funds may also be more accessible to all of it, not just an already advantaged section.

If trusts are to be accessible to potential applicants they must adopt a pro-active stance. This means publicizing themselves and their interests and explaining how to make applications. It means being clear about what may be funded and what definitely will not. It means being open and responsible and flexible. It means having timetables for grant-making that are helpful. In practical terms, it probably means appointing more staff or using the services of locally based personnel. It means monitoring and evaluating practice and policies. It also means some re-allocation of resources.

Underlying all of this is the basic premise that charitable trust funds exist to be spent responsibly, not preserved indefinitely. They are to be spent in assisting the voluntary sector to continue its work and to develop, which is the purpose for which trusts were originally set up. Charitable trusts exist not for their own benefit but to benefit the charitable sector, of which voluntary organizations are a major part.

References

Burkeman, S. (1991) *Report for the Years 1988–90*, York: Joseph Rowntree Charitable Trust.
Cook, T. (1991) 'Quinquennial reviews: City Parochial Foundation', *Foundations 1*, London: Association of Charitable Foundations.
Davies, G. A. (1989) 'Grant making trusts in a changing society', in L. Fitzherbert and M. Eastwood (eds) *A Guide to the Major Trusts*, London: Directory of Social Change.
Fitzherbert, L. (1991) 'Introduction', in L. Fitzherbert and S. Forrester (eds) *A Guide to the Major Trusts*, London: Directory of Social Change.
Hazell, R. (1991) 'Role reversal', *Trust Monitor*, London: Directory of Social Change.
Hoggart, R. (1990) *A Sort of Clowning*, London: Chatto and Windus.
House of Commons Committee of Public Accounts (1991) *Monitoring and Control of Charities in England and Wales*, London: HMSO.
National Council for Voluntary Organisations (1990) *Effectiveness and the Voluntary Sector*, London: NCVO.
Neuberger, J. (1991) 'Better giving', in *Foundations 1*, London: Association of Charitable Foundations.
Taylor, L. C. (1991) 'Gulbenkian Foundation, Annual Report of 1986', in *Foundations 1*, London: Association of Charitable Foundations.
Wilson, A. (1991) 'Afterword', in *Foundations 1*, London: Association of Charitable Foundations.

16
Policy-making in the probation service: a view from the probation committee

Simon Holdaway and Greg Mantle

In recent years the government has turned its attention to the reform of the probation service and expressed an intention, so ministers argue, to bring probation to 'centre stage' within the criminal justice system (Home Office 1991). The reasons for this are diverse. Certainly, the growth of the prison population during the 1970s and 1980s begged questions about the alternatives to imprisonment and consideration of 'supervision and punishment in the community' (Home Office 1990a). Whatever meaning might be attributed to these notions of punishment and supervision, probation officers were identified as the personnel who could respond to and balance within their work the needs of offenders, the public and the courts.

Although the addressing of offending behaviour is now a feature of much probation work, it is undertaken against a historical background of ideas that probation is no more or less successful a means of reducing offending behaviour than any other penal disposal (McIver 1990). The so-called 'nothing works' doctrine (Martinson 1974; Brody 1976) created a situation where the probation service tended to rest content with interventions primarily related to its social work base, mainly by casework and the offering of help to offenders (Bottoms and McWilliams 1979).

When a government is keen to demonstrate a strong commitment to tackling crime, as well as requiring all public sector institutions to prove their efficiency and effectiveness, an appeal to offering help to offenders can appear to be and may, in truth, be a rather haphazard rationale for probation work. Precisely what amounts to an offer of help to an individual and its effectiveness as a penal intervention are difficult to assess. From the perspective of a policy-maker, the reduction of offending appears a more immediate, effective, focused, measurable and potentially achievable objective. A determination developed within the Home Office to ensure that area probation services would be planned with a greater degree of clarity and rationality.

In 1984 the Home Office required all probation areas to define their priorities in a written statement (Home Office 1984a). Other requirements to develop action plans within a framework of financial management followed (Home Office 1988b; Audit Commission 1989; Humphrey 1991). This move towards a restatement of the purpose and function of the probation service required chief probation officers to become proficient in management methods based on the setting of clear objectives for policies and the monitoring of outcomes for effectiveness and efficiency. Area probation services were to become more accountable for their work. The notion of rational management has been central to these themes of change.

Importantly, probation committees have been included in the plans for the reform of the probation service. In this chapter we will analyse how far these committees have contributed to the general direction of change towards rational management required by the Home Office. This analysis will be based on the findings of a two-year research project during which seventy-seven members of probation committees working in five probation areas and their respective chief probation officers were interviewed.[1] While a keynote for change within the probation service has been rational planning, the role of the probation committee in policy-making and in the management of area probation services, we shall argue, has been marked by uncertainty and ambiguity.

Probation committees

Probation committees are not a well known institution. Each of the fifty-six area probation services in England and Wales has a probation committee with a membership of magistrates, elected by local benches. An area with a continuing London borough or metropolitan district within its boundary is required to co-opt a councillor to the committee. Furthermore, all committees may co-opt up to a maximum of one-third of its total membership but few have done so. Magistrates form the majority membership of most probation committees and related sub-committees. At the time of the research all fifty-six committees were chaired by a magistrate. Judges serving courts within a probation area are also represented by colleagues. Each probation committee, therefore, has a diverse membership but, importantly, one dominated by the magistracy.

Probation committees are the statutory employers of probation officers. Their members also have a duty to ensure 'the efficient running of an area probation service', which requires involvement in the determination of policy. In fact, our interview data indicate that probation committees have not initiated policy. The local impetus has mainly come from chief probation officers, working within a framework of statute and Home Office guidelines. Committee members are of course able to submit agenda items that could lead to policy initiatives, but this is rare.

The extent of debate about policy issues varies from committee to committee. In one of the five areas researched, sub-committee review panels had considerable involvement in the development of policies related to their specific areas of responsibility. When major documents about the reform of the probation service have been published, committees and chief officers have often organized 'discussion days'. Main committee agendas, however, are full and discussion time for an item is strictly limited. We were often told about the large volume of papers members had to digest before a meeting and of the considerable knowledge of probation work required to understand them fully. This situation limits the extent to which main committees are able to determine policy.

Chief officers' reports about specific areas of probation work, including evaluative and related statistical materials, are to be found in committee papers. These are rather different sources of information from evidence gained from monitoring by agreed indicators directly related to policy objectives. The point here is that very few committee members have interpreted their monitoring work in these terms. Overall, we found that they understood the dominant meaning of their role to be 'oversight': guidance if staff strayed too far from expectations and a lay monitoring of professionals on behalf of the courts and, more widely, the public.

Within this context, chief officers recognized a responsibility to account to their committee for their performance and members felt they too had ultimate control over senior managers. However, such power was latent, limited in most part by the relationship between the chief probation officer and the chair of the probation committee.

We will argue that the dominance of magistrates as members has had an effect on the ways in which probation committees have interpreted their statutory duties, especially to ensure the efficient running of an area probation service. To develop this argument it is first necessary to review how the content of probation rules has tended to promote ambiguity about the purpose and function of a probation committee rather than giving a more secure foundation for the creation of rational planning within probation areas.

Probation rules

First, ambiguity is created by the requirement of probation rules that a probation committee should ensure the 'efficient running of an area service'. 'Efficiency' is not a notion that can be operationalized readily. It could be efficient, for example, to breach all clients who, without good excuse, fail to keep a second appointment with a probation officer. The question of how effective this might be in the longer term is another matter. It could be efficient for an area probation service to curtail or end its work in the civil courts, where it deals with complex issues about the custody of and access to children involved in matrimonial disputes and related problems. How effective this would be for the people caught up in these problems is another matter.

Efficiency is one valid criterion for the assessment of human behaviour within organizations. It is not the only one, however, and at times will conflict with other equally viable criteria of direct relevance to probation work. The requirement that a probation committee ensures the efficient running of an area service poses as many questions and dilemmas as answers about how policies should be developed.

Ambiguity and uncertainty about the purpose and function of a committee follow, ambiguity and uncertainty compounded by the diversity and complexity of probation work itself. It is not easy to define the core function of probation work – is it casework, groupwork, serving the courts, crime prevention, reducing re-offending, offering social work help to offenders or another function? Who, furthermore, are the key staff of an area probation service when decisions about policy have to be taken? In a recent study of policy implementation within a probation area, May (1991) has described the different perspectives of senior management, middle management and fieldworkers when a single change of policy was introduced. There is not one but many views about priorities for policy and practice within each area service. Questions about whose view should prevail when probation priorities and objectives are discussed are complex.

Second, the stipulation of probation rules that probation committees should ensure 'the efficient running of an area probation service' implies the involvement of committee members in the task of management. This is not the day-to-day management carried out by chief officers but the setting of a direction, perhaps through agreeing policy objectives for an area service, the definition of performance indicators, systems of monitoring outcomes from various interventions and so on. Certainly, the Home Office and probation professional associations, not least the Central Council of Probation Committees (CCPC), have taken this view. As long ago as 1984, David Faulkner, Deputy Under-Secretary at the Home Office, described in a speech to the Central Council the work of probation committees in these terms:

> It would be a natural part of our job to make sure not only that you have set the right objectives and priorities for your Area Services, but also that your managing director – your Chief Officer – has been given clear directions to work towards their achievements.
>
> (Home Office 1984b)

The question of how far committees should be involved in the management of area services was raised again in the government's *Supervision and Punishment in the Community* (Home Office 1990b). In their response to this document the CCPC concluded that a committee should indeed

> be functioning as an effective board of management of the local services. As such it should be planning ahead, making appropriate policy decisions in the interests of the service, overseeing management and holding it to account to the many interest groups and agencies we have identified earlier.
>
> (Central Council of Probation Committees 1990)

The task of management requires particular knowledge and skills, which committee members should possess if they are to fulfil the purposes outlined by Faulkner and endorsed by the Central Council.

Policy-making in the probation service   207

The main criterion for membership of a probation committee, however, is membership of the magistracy. Appropriate knowledge and skills required to ensure the efficient running of an area probation service may be diverse, and they may be contestable. At the moment, however, they are not directly related to the formal criterion for election to a probation committee. Some magistrate members of probation committees are no doubt highly qualified to be involved in the governance of the probation service, but their election to committees has been fortuitous rather than the intended outcome of the application of probation rules. Summarizing the view of most chief probation officers interviewed in our study, one put it that 'What I find very difficult is the haphazard way in which people are put forward for membership of the committee without any account of what the needs of the probation service are.'

During interviews, some committee members said that the skills and knowledge that they brought to their work were certainly relevant but incidental rather than intentionally related to the governance of their probation area.

> If you sit on a board of directors you look for one chap [!] who is good at public relations, one for government, one who'll be able to keep an eye on the accountants and so on. We're not appointed like that so you have to find a way of drawing on the experiences of a group of people who come together almost accidentally and that to me limits the usefulness or authority of the probation committee.

This system of election places a further limitation on the manner in which committees approach policy issues. Magistrates are elected to a probation committee by their local bench, an arrangement that tends to stress a parochial view of committee work. Magistrates are not elected because they have a comprehensive view of the needs of a probation area and the priority to be afforded to the various issues facing its staff. Although a probation committee is in law a corporate body in its own right and not a body to which the representative views of local benches are brought for debate, members interviewed frequently took a rather different view: 'They (my fellow magistrates) are the people who elected me and I can't shrug them off and adopt a new role when I get to committee.' Or, as another member explained, 'I represent the Bench who appointed me and to whom I report back at either our half-yearly or annual meeting.'

Probation rules create a probation committee membership that, in terms of the recognized knowledge and skills possessed by members, is not necessarily suited to the fulfilment of its mandate.

A magistrate's perspective

Members have tended to serve their probation committee as magistrates rather than people with skills in finance, personnel work, policy evaluation and so on. 'We are producing the policy more by describing the reactions of magistrates and judges than we are sitting down poring over figures and saying "Well, we have got that much less or that much more".'

Specific skills and knowledge about managerial tasks a probation committee might employ were not the only ambiguous features of committee work identified during our research. The following member argued that probation rules did not help a committee to define an overarching purpose for an area service. 'Efficiency' is not a sufficient basis to sustain values appropriate to working with offenders and other probation tasks. The onus to develop probation work based on particular values therefore falls, if to anyone, to the committee chair and long-serving members.

> The duties of the probation committee as set out in regulations are so vague and general that I think it is difficult to produce any great philosophy. I think that philosophy depends very much on the interaction, principally of the chairman and perhaps the vice-chairman, the most senior colleagues and obviously the chief probation officer and his most senior colleagues.

However, committee members developed a distinctive perspective within this context of their work. The central feature of this was the relationship they perceived between the courts and the probation service.

We asked members: 'What are the main purposes of the probation service?' 'Serving the courts', 'rehabilitating offenders', 'reducing re-offending' and 'providing alternatives to custody' received the most frequent mentions. When we differentiated between answers from sentencer and non-sentencer members of committees, 85 per cent (66) of the former and 45 per cent (11) of the latter group mentioned 'serving the courts' as the main purpose of the probation service. These purposes, which are orientated towards the work of the magistrates' courts, were related to key tasks performed by the probation service. When asked to rank various probation service tasks in an order of priority, sentencers listed the preparation of social enquiry reports as the second most important. The emphasis here was on providing background information about offenders rather than making recommendations for sentencing, which was the business of magistrates. Again, the relationship between the probation service and the courts is evident.

In response to a question about whom they represented on their probation committee, 35 per cent of magistrate members in our sample saw themselves as representatives of their respective benches. A further 30 per cent said that they represented the wider magistracy on their committee or had a dual responsibility to their bench and the magistracy. Again, this is a partial interpretation of membership because, although election to a committee is from benches in petty sessional areas, members do not have a formal mandate to represent those benches. The committee is responsible for the whole of the work of an area probation service and in law a corporate body in its own right. No doubt views from different benches may at times be wise advice but they are not integral to decision-making about probation area policy.

These findings do not indicate that the magistrate members of committees we interviewed failed to recognize that they held some sort of managerial responsibility. Lacking a clear mandate and drawn from a membership that does not easily lend itself to policy-making and other managerial tasks, however, these magistrate members brought to committee assumptions that formed a perspective on the purpose of the probation service and its work.

A central feature of this perspective is the view that the probation committee is a forum to facilitate liaison between the probation service and the courts.

> A policy on juvenile justice was recently issued to members of the committee who took it back to their benches and in one or two areas there was distinct unease which was fed back. The policy has now been redrafted and the bench will probably be much happier.

Liaison could be interpreted in this rather specific manner when a particular policy was proposed or, as these members explained, in a more general sense,

> to help spread the word about the probation service. To sell probation to our colleagues, which is no mean task. There will always be a tension between sentencers and probation. I think ignorance, that I think the committee as a whole and individual members try to break down. . . . My personal view, I think, is from the role I see myself playing. Profiling the probation service for my local bench. Taking my work from the committee back to the bench and explaining, trying to explain and trying to profile what has been done very successfully by the probation service.

These views form part of what we call the 'assumptive world of the sentencer'. This notion refers to a series of assumptions about the nature and purpose of the probation service and its work, the role of the probation committee and of the magistrate member. Issues for consideration by a probation committee are interpreted through these assumptions and afforded a priority according to their adjudged relevance. Issues of direct relevance to the work of the magistrates' court are likely to be given a higher priority than, for example, crime prevention schemes. This assumptive world (Young 1977) bears resemblance to what Parker *et al.* (1989) in their research about sentencing called 'the professional ideology of the lay magistrate', which includes 'ideology, attitudes and opinions' associated with work in the courts and in particular the relationship between the bench and the probation service.

A further feature of the sentencers' assumptive world – and a key one of relevance to the involvement of committee members in policy-making – concerns the transfer of an approach to decision-making thought suitable for the magistrates' court to the forum of the probation committee. This is a case-by-case approach to decision-making, which has its virtues but is limited when matters that span a number of issues, cases or the whole of a probation area's work are considered. Policy prescribes general rules that should be applied to particular cases. When a view is taken that an agenda item for discussion is understood as a discrete item it becomes far more difficult to develop policy. This became particularly clear when we discussed policies on race issues during interviews with the magistrates.

Race issues

During the past decade there has been considerable development of race issues policy within the probation service, largely stimulated by national probation and other bodies, including the National Association of Black Probation Officers (Central Council of Probation Committees 1983, 1987; NACRO 1986, 1989, 1991; Association of Chief Officers of Probation 1988; Home Office 1988a). Our research indicates that probation committees may have delayed rather than assisted any progress that has been made. An important part of an explanation for this situation concerns the structure and function of the assumptive world we have described (Holdaway and Allaker 1990).

Racial prejudice and discrimination may well be lodged within the policies and practices of organizations like area probation services. The distinctive feature of race should not be neglected. However, structures of racial inequality are mediated through particular views of the world held by members of organizations, which are not necessarily or directly related to perceptions of race *per se*. This is where the assumptive world of the sentencer is of importance.

An assumption that each case is unique makes it very difficult for sentencer members of committees to perceive any threads of continuity that link similar cases or those that on first sight appear to be of different types. A case-by-case approach, for example, does not sit easily with one that finds a thread of discrimination running through magistrates' decision-making. The development of race issues policy, like all policy, requires a broader appreciation of an organization that includes general principles, and related objectives and strategies to achieve them. The development of race issues policy requires an understanding of organizations that extends beyond the case-by-case approach. Chief probation officers, however, identified a rather different perspective among committee members:

> There is a resistance, particularly from sentencers on the committee who have this judicial framework that deals with each case on its merits. To be able to think in terms of the differential experience of different groups, to be able to make the transition from being judges and magistrates to being employers and policy-makers is actually quite a leap on their part.

Magistrate members therefore tended to sit more securely in a probation committee seat when their work was related to the magistrates' court. One magistrate made the point in a clear manner when asked about the extent to which social enquiry reports may contain an element of bias.

> No I don't think there is any truth in that at all. And all this business of blacks being put into prison. When one sits sentencing it makes not the blindest difference what colour they are and I think you have to look at the different offences and the nature of those offences, the seriousness of those offences, before you start saying, 'too many blacks in prison'.

When asked about the types of race issues policies within his probation area another member of the same committee did not mention special field-work services, monitoring arrangements for social enquiry reports or any other probation policy. He reverted to his experience of the courtroom.

> Well I think that we certainly try to make sure that people who come, I can only talk about it from the court's point of view, making sure that when

people come before the court that if they are in difficulty with language then steps are taken to make sure there is an interpreter, whether it be at worst a relative or at best an independent one. Making sure a probation report is discussed properly and thoroughly. I think talking to the defendants and their families, trying to put across the way the legal system works.

When views like these, which include clear assumptions about the ways in which magistrates sentence people from different ethnic groups, are brought to a probation committee difficulties arise. In one area where we conducted interviews a research report about sentencing practices in one of its magistrates' courts had recently been published. The evidence presented in the report indicated that there were differential patterns of sentencing for the different ethnic groups brought before the court. The report came to the probation committee and, as the chair explained,

Well, this report was presented to the committee and had a full discussion. I think there were concerns at the committee – like there were in [mentions town] where the research was carried out – that they didn't feel as sentencers themselves that they were discriminating. They forgot that they were members of the probation committee. Once again, they put their magistrate's hat on.

These and other committee members sifted the information contained in committee reports through the assumptions they brought to discussion. The focus of discussion about the race issues policy has therefore tended to be based on: an understanding of discrete items, rather than corporate, policy issues; a forum of liaison between the magistracy and the area probation service rather than the needs and problems of a probation area as a whole; and the individual views of sentencers rather than those of members of a committee with managerial responsibilities.

When they were asked about race issues policy within their probation area, members' initial response was usually a comment about the recruitment of staff from minority ethnic groups to field-work and managerial posts or the ethnic composition of their probation committee. The monitoring of objectives and other wide-ranging features of race policy were rarely mentioned. The emphasis was on probation committees as employers of probation staff rather than managers or directors of an area service.

These views of committee members can usefully be compared with those of chief officers who, when describing their work on race issues policy, more readily cited injustice, discrimination and other types of unfairness within the criminal justice system in general and in the probation service in particular. Within committees the development of race issues policy has, with some exceptions, largely been the province of chief officers' work, prompted by the professional associations and other national bodies, including the Central Council of Probation Committees, the Home Office and NACRO. Being dominated by magistrate members, committee discussion has been seemingly directed towards the particular concerns of the courtroom and sentencing. The meaning of efficiency has been constructed within an assumptive world that is somewhat at odds with the notion of rational management promulgated by probation's professional associations and the Home Office.

Explanations

Probation committees are now under review. The latest Home Office document about the future of the service has posed many questions about the future reform of committees (Home Office 1991). The Home Office has committed itself to new probation rules that will provide committees with 'clearly defined responsibilities for planning, objectives and monitoring of performance' and stated that 'the respective roles of probation committees and chief officers should be clearly defined' (Home Office 1991: 9). The size of committees will be reduced to around fifteen but it is suggested that 50 per cent of the membership be retained from the magistracy: 'the sentencer members (i.e. judges and magistrates) should be reduced to 50% of the total membership; that the other 50 % of the membership should be co-opted under guide-lines laid down by the Home Office' (Home Office 1991: 9).

Many of these proposals are to be welcomed. There is certainly good sense in rewriting the rules defining the purpose and duties of probation committees, in reducing their size and in forming a new committee membership. The new memberhsip should reflect the skills and knowledge required to clarify policy objectives and to monitor them, which are not simply managerial and financial in character but also encompass the values upon which policies are based. There is also a key role for a committee to play as a buffer between the centralizing tendencies of the Home Office and the potential for control of a probation area by a chief officer. Committees can ensure that the accountability of area services is rendered effective. Our research leads to these conclusions.

Several ambiguities remain in the published Home Office document, however. The most important is, what is the function of magistrate members on probation committees? If they are to fulfil a managerial role of the type we describe – formulating and monitoring policies within an area probation service – committees require members with skills in management by objective setting, financial accounting, the monitoring of performance, raising questions about the values implicit within area probation policy, employment practices and so on. Unless skills and knowledge are defined precisely by the Home Office we can envisage a situation where it is erroneously assumed that, say, a headteacher possesses planning skills, an accountant possesses financial skills related to the public sector, and so on. A probation service moving into a new role within the criminal justice system needs and deserves a more effective system of governance than that.

There is no doubt that some representation from the magistracy should be maintained within committees. However, the Home Office proposal that half of a committee membership of fifteen should be drawn from sentencers, with, as the Home Office paper says, an enhanced role for judges, could, on the basis of our evidence, retain the dominance of a sentencer's view and, potentially, lead to conflict between sentencer and non-sentencer members. This 50 per cent sentencers' membership of committees follows a recommendation by the CCPC made in their response to the Home Office Green Paper (CCPC 1990: 5). More attention needs to be given by the Home Office to the ways in which the assumptive world of the magistrate that we have identified has in the past and will in the future continue to make an impact on probation committees' consideration of policy.

Whatever reforms the Home Office settles on, constraints will remain. There is an inherent ambiguity about the purpose of the probation service. It will always have to find a creative niche between tensions of care and control, between reactive and pro-active initiatives, and so on. The outcomes of probation interventions will always be unpredictable to some extent, just as they are for other 'human service organizations' (Mintzberg 1979). Furthermore, factors such as the external environment of area probation services restricts and constrains policy-making by the reduction of resources; societal structures of inequality will have some bearing on the behaviour of both probation staff and clients. Allowing for this context of work, suitable reforms could still bring to probation committees a significant measure of managerial planning to develop the work that has already been initiated by chief officers.

The model of rational, corporate management that is so keenly advocated by the Home Office assumes a view of human beings working within organizations who read policy directives and, within margins implement them. A central notion of Home Office reform of the probation service has been 'efficiency'. This is a notion that is not readily meaningful to the staff of an area probation service and to the members of their probation committee. We have demonstrated how the magistrate members of probation committees create an 'assumptive world' that rationalizes for them the ambiguities and uncertainties of their committee work. Whatever membership is decided for probation committees by the Home Office, attention will have to be given to the ways in which policy is filtered through particular assumptions brought by members to the probation committee agenda. If magistrates and judges remain the dominant members of committees, we now have a clearer understanding of how this will affect the determination of future probation service area policies.

Note

1 ESRC Grant R 000 23 1183 refers. The research was about the role of probation committees in policy-making, especially in crime prevention and race issues policies. We are grateful to the committee members and chief probation officers who took part in the research. Special thanks are due to Ieuan Miles, Secretary of the Central Council of Probation Committees, and his colleagues, who generously supported our work.

References

Association of Chief Officers of Probation (1988) *Anti-racism Policy Statement*, Wakefield: ACOP.
Audit Commission (1989) *Promoting Value for Money in the Probation Service*, London: Audit Commission for Local Authorities in England and Wales.

Bottoms, A. E. and McWilliams, W. (1979) 'A non-treatment paradigm for probation practice', *British Journal of Social Work* 9: 152–202.
Brody, S. R. (1976) *The Effectiveness of Sentencing: a Review of the Literature*, London: HMSO.
Central Council of Probation Committees (1983) *Probation: a Multi-racial Approach*, London: CCPC.
Central Council of Probation Committees (1987) *Black People and the Probation Service: Towards Racial Harmony*, London: CCPC.
Central Council of Probation Committees (1990) *Probation: the Key to Change*, London: CCPC.
Holdaway, S. and Allaker, J. (1990) *Race Issues in the Probation Service: a Review of Policy*, Wakefield: Association of Chief Officers of Probation.
Home Office (1984a) *The Probation Service in England and Wales*, London: HMSO.
Home Office (1984b) *A View from the Home Office: Address by Mr David Faulkner, Deputy Under-Secretary of State, Home Office*, Annual General Meeting of the Central Council of Probation Committees, London: CCPC.
Home Office (1988a) *Probation Service Policies on Race*, Home Office Circular no. 75/88, London: HMSO.
Home Office (1988b) *Punishment, Custody and the Community*, London: HMSO.
Home Office (1990a) *Crime, Justice and Protecting the Public*, London: HMSO.
Home Office (1990b) *Supervision and Punishment in the Community*, London: HMSO.
Home Office (1991) *Organising Supervision and Punishment in the Community: a Decision Document*, London: HMSO.
Humphrey, C. (1991) 'Calling on the experts: the financial management initiative (FMI), private sector management consultants and the probation service', *Howard Journal of Criminal Justice* 30, 1: 1–18.
McIver, G. (1990) *Sanctions for Serious or Persistent Offenders: a Review of the Literature*, Stirling: Social Work Research Centre, University of Stirling.
Martinson, R. (1974) 'What works? Questions and answers about prison reform', *The Public Interest* 23: 22–54.
May, T. (1991) *Probation: Politics, Policy and Practice*, Milton Keynes: Open University Press.
Mintzberg, H. (1979) *The Structuring of Organizations*, Englewood Cliffs, NJ: Prentice-Hall.
NACRO (1986) *Black People and the Criminal Justice System. A Report of the Race Issues Advisory Committee*, London: NACRO.
NACRO (1989) *Race and Criminal Justice*, London: NACRO.
NACRO (1991) *Black People's Experience of Criminal Justice*, London: NACRO.
Parker, H., Sumner, M. and Jarvis, G. (1989) *Unmasking the Magistrates: the 'Custody or Not' Decision in Sentencing Young Offenders*, Milton Keynes: Open University Press.
Young, K. (1977) 'Values in the policy process', *Policy and Practice* 5: 1–12.

17
Force for change or optional extra? The impact of research on policy in social work and social welfare

Jan Pahl

There is certainly a common assumption that research is a force for change. Many researchers claim that their work deserves to be funded precisely because the results will inform policy, and many policy-makers assert that their policies have been validated by research. The White Paper, *Caring for People*, commented that research in the community care field:

> has produced impressive work in terms of quality and relevance for both policy makers and service delivery agencies. The Government believes that this successful record of research-based innovation will be needed just as much in the future as in the past.
>
> (Secretaries of State 1989: 46)

On the other hand, there is also a deep pessimism about the links between research and policy and a suspicion that in reality research is more of an optional extra. Most of the readers of this book will be able to list examples of expensive research projects that have failed to make any impact whatsoever on either policy or practice. In her study of the aims and outcomes of social policy research, Thomas quotes a researcher – 'If research findings confirm policy makers' own beliefs they accept them. If not, they still accept that they are true, but they do nothing' (Thomas 1985: 87) – and a policy-maker – 'Policy is about things to which there is no clear answer. You can't settle political questions by research' (Thomas 1985: 89).

In this chapter I shall examine the links between policy-making and research, drawing out some of the incompatibilities between the two activities and analysing some of the qualities that characterize influential research. The underlying hypotheses will be, first, that research has an impact on policy and, second, that the closer the researcher is to the policy-maker the more influence the research will have. I shall focus on the research process, and in doing so will make suggestions as to how those carrying out research, at both local and national levels, can contribute more effectively to policy debates and practice developments.

Definitions and assumptions

Setting out to examine the impact of research on policy raises many questions. What do we mean by 'research' in this context? What sorts of 'impact' might we expect? And how broad should be our definition of 'policy'?

The word 'research' can have different meanings. At one extreme a journalist may spend a few days doing research for an article; at the other a team of professional researchers may spend years carrying out a sophisticated evaluation study. Both may help to shape the views of policy-makers. At a local level, in particular, some of the most influential research is that carried out by practitioners and clinicians, while at the national level the researchers whose work influenced the television play *Cathy Come Home* probably had more impact than most of the academic experts on housing at that time.

We have to limit the topic in some way. In this chapter I shall be concerned with research of two main sorts, both of which have had to pass the test of peer review. First, I shall be concerned with research supported by the main funding bodies, such as the Department of Health, the Department of Social Security, the Economic and Social Research Council, the Joseph Rowntree Foundation, the Mental Health Foundation and so on: in all of these cases the research is subject to the scrutiny of outside referees, both when the proposal is agreed and when the final report is received. Second, the chapter will be concerned with enquiries undertaken by research officers and practitioners working within local health and social services departments: here the scrutiny by managers and fellow practitioners is of a rather different sort, but it can be just as demanding as far as the researcher is concerned.

Research can take many different forms. It may, for example, be descriptive or evaluative, may last a few months or many years, may aim to solve immediate problems or to increase long-term knowledge and understanding. In commissioning and using research, policy-makers often do not grasp the significance of the academic discipline from which the researcher comes. The same research topic will be tackled in very different ways by, for example, an economist, a sociologist, an anthropologist and a policy analyst.

The process by which research makes its 'impact' on policy is often far from clear. Researchers may cherish the hope that their results will be seized upon by policy-makers and incorporated into the next ministerial speech. Official statements may even foster the same theory. Thus the general aim of the Department of Health's programme of health and personal social services research is described as: 'To provide objective information for Ministers as a basis for developments in health policy, improvements in public health, and increasing efficiency and effectiveness in health and personal social services' (Department of Health 1990: xiv). In practice, however, things are far less clear. Those who have interviewed policy-makers have discovered that they often find it hard to identify research that has had an impact on their thinking. Weiss concluded that those who are responsible for policy-making

> have great difficulty disentangling the lessons they have learned from research from their whole configuration of knowledge. They do not catalogue research separately; they do not remember sources and citations. With the best will in the world all that they can usually say is that in the course of their work they hear about a great deal of research and they are sure it affects what they think and do.
>
> (Weiss 1986: 219)

If research is diverse and its impact unclear, the term 'policy' is equally hard to define. Taking a broad perspective one could say that for many people their welfare is profoundly affected by the policies of those responsible for the level of mortgage repayments, the price of season tickets, the availability of contraception, the provision of child-care facilities and the location of Sainsbury's. However, again we have to limit the topic. Since the word 'policy' is derived from the Greek word *polis*, meaning 'the state', this chapter will focus on the policies of the state, at local, national and, increasingly, international levels. Policy may be made by elected Members of Parliament or local councillors, by policy-makers and planners in the Department of Health or in local authorities, or by professionals in their capacity as advisers to the local or national state. There is an important distinction to be made between *policy*, as explicit intent, and *practice*, which covers the implementation of policy and what professionals actually do in the course of their work. Researchers may set out to influence both policy and practice, but in this chapter I shall be concerned with the former more than the latter.

Incompatibilities between research and policy-making

There are many ways in which research and policy-making are incompatible activities: exploring this may help us to see how research can become 'more useful' (for policy-makers) or achieve 'greater impact' (for researchers). First, each has a different *relation to the political process*. If researchers are to influence policy they must be tuned in to the political issues of the day, but if they do this too well they risk losing the critical stance for which they are valued. Research is valued for being 'objective', as in the Department of Health statement above. In truth research is no more value free than policy-making: perhaps the crucial difference is that researchers have to make explicit the values on which their work was based and the methods by which their results were achieved (Becker 1970). This in itself can make research uncomfortable reading for policy-makers.

Second, research and policy-making have different *objectives*. Research tends to complicate issues by making them appear more ticklish than they first appeared, whereas the art of policy-making lies in simplifying things to the point where action becomes possible (Booth 1988). Research aims at clarity, while policy-making requires ambiguity. As Keynes observed: 'There is nothing a government hates more than to be well-informed, for it makes the process of arriving at decisions much more complicated and difficult' (quoted in Higgins 1980: 197). Research inevitably produces information: yet policy-makers dislike having too much information, or the wrong sort of information, because it complicates the difficult process of reaching the level of agreement necessary to make policy.

Third, research and policy-making operate on different *time-scales*. This is not simply because policy-makers work to short and demanding deadlines, while good research can take many years to complete. It also reflects the different patterns of employment. If policy-makers were out of a job once a particular policy was decided, while researchers remained in post even though a particular project had been completed, the situation would be very different.

Fourth, researchers and policy-makers are likely to be responsible to different *interest groups*. The values of policy-makers tend to reflect the values of the hierarchy within which they work, while researchers may see themselves as bound to reflect the views of a range of interest groups. A good example of this dilemma is described in the pluralist evaluation by Smith and Cantley (1985). More dangerously, researchers may take on a special responsibility to report the experience of the powerless. The current emphasis on researching the views of service users sounds good when research is planned, but when the results are critical of current provision managers may disown what they originally welcomed. Perhaps there is a law which says that 'the larger the number of interest groups represented in any research report, the less likely it is that any one interest group will take the report seriously'.

Fifth, researchers and policy-makers have different expectations about the *products of the research*. Researchers are likely to favour a substantial report that does justice to all their hard work, while policy-makers prefer the executive summary. In their survey of in-house research in social services departments Barnes and Wilson showed that while 86 per cent of projects ended in a final report, only half produced a summary report; even though half of the projects were intended to make an impact on professional practice, only 4 per cent produced results in the form of training materials (Barnes and Wilson 1986: 21). These results suggest that researchers need to give much greater attention to dissemination. There may be a particular problem for those whose results relate to social work practice. Social work is often described as a practice-based profession, where the transmission of information and expertise has a large oral component; research, by contrast, is essentially a written activity, where success is traditionally measured by publications rather than by oral communication.

Sixth, researchers and policy-makers may have incompatible views on the *scope of policy recommendations*. Some researchers do not see it as part of their job to make recommendations. Even when they do put forward proposals for policy, researchers are often naive about the world into which those recommendations must go. In an article considering 'the unfulfilled promise of policy research' Higgins concluded that the real problem for social scientists involved in policy research is not how to gather knowledge but how to present that knowledge, once assembled. She concluded that the promise of policy research has been unfulfilled because of a failure to recognize that this is a political and not a technical problem (Higgins 1980: 205). Some recommendations may be politically unacceptable, while others may be politically impracticable. For example, in the 1970s about seventy researchers were involved in the programme of research that set out to examine the concept of transmitted deprivation. The underlying message from the researchers was that the problems they had identified could only be tackled in the context of the wider society. Yet as the final summary report on the programme acknowledged, most policy-makers lack the power to achieve grand changes to the basic structures of society (Brown and Madge 1982).

So the marriage between research and policy can only be regarded as a partial success. Their incompatibilities include their different relations with the political process, different objectives and different time-scales; they tend to be responsive to different interest groups, and they often hold different expectations about the products of the research and the scope of any policy recommendations. Given their incompatibilities, how is it that they continue to associate with each other?

How and why might research influence policy?

The processes by which research does, or does not, make an impact on policy are mysterious, which is perhaps the reason why there have been many attempts to identify the different strategies which researchers might adopt. For example, Thomas distinguished between the *insider model*, where the researcher knows and works with the government machine, the *gadfly model*, where the researcher seeks to challenge the government machine, and the *limestone model*, where research results are simply left to find their own way through the fissures in the system (Thomas 1985). Researchers may choose rationally between these models, but it seems more likely that they simply adopt the one that best suits their temperament. A rather similar typology, and one to which I shall return as the story unfolds, was proposed by Rein (1976). He distinguished between three approaches:

1 The *consensual approach*, in which the policy-maker poses the questions and the social scientist provides the answers. This may appear to be the most promising strategy as far as policy-makers are concerned. On the other hand the questions may not be answerable, or the researcher may not be interested in playing so narrow a role.
2 The *contentious approach*, in which the social researcher assumes the role of witness to the failings of policy-makers and service providers. This may be enjoyable for researchers, but tends to be unpopular with policy-makers, who shoulder enough criticism without contracting for more.
3 The *paradigm-challenging approach*, where the researcher steps beyond the bounds of received opinion to bring a new vision to the definition of problems and the possibilities for action. This may be the most rewarding role for researchers but, in the short term at least, it delivers least of all to policy-makers.

These different approaches are discussed in more detail by Booth (1988), who also points out a fundamental process that persistently cuts the ground from under the feet of the social scientist. In so far as the insights and findings of social science research are judged to be of interest and use, they tend to be absorbed into the language of everyday discourse and appropriated as 'common sense'. Thus yesterday's research may have influenced today's policy, without the policy-maker being aware of its influence.

In considering why research might influence policy we must start by recognizing the many influences brought to bear on policy-makers. Research plays only a minor role in a play in which the main parts are surely taken by the economic interests of the government of the day, the priorities of dominant interest groups, the media scandals that shape public opinion and so on. In the next sections I shall consider three areas where researchers have been active and where policy has been made over the past twenty years. Before attempting to trace the connections between research and policy, it may be useful to elaborate on the influences that shape policy. There are many of these, but they can be subsumed under three main headings:

1 The *economic interests* of the government of the day, or of the state, the capitalist system or whatever. This approach assumes that the policy process at both local and national levels is essentially about making choices over the use of resources. As long as economic policy is defined as more fundamental than social policy, economic rationality is likely to predominate. As one policy-maker said, when asked about the impact of research, 'Government's ultimate aim is not to maintain the purity of truth but the existence of the state' (Thomas 1985: 92).
2 The *priorities of dominant interest groups*. Here the assumption is that the political process is essentially pluralist. Dominant interest groups must include the upper class and the business community, though these can be subsumed under the previous heading. For the purposes of this chapter more significant interest groups will be the powerful professions, such as medicine and the law, influential pressure groups, and the most long-standing dominant interest group of all – white, middle-aged men.
3 *The mass media and public opinion*. Identifying these as influences on policy also assumes a pluralist approach to the political process, but here the influences on that process are seen as more diffuse. Both the mass media and public opinion are hard to define precisely, but there is no doubt that on occasions both have brought about significant changes in policy and both have brought down governments.

To sum up this section, researchers may play many different roles, adopting, for example, a consensual approach, a contentious approach or a paradigm-challenging approach. Policy-making may be shaped by many different forces, including, for example, the economic interests of the government, the priorities of dominant groups or the pressure of the media and public opinion: researchers may make an impact by adding weight to one or more of these influences. So what can we say about the impact of research on policy? Let us explore this question in the context of three areas of policy, all of which are important for the welfare of large numbers of people.

Force for change or optional extra? 221

Case study 1: reducing long-stay provision in hospital

Whatever the cause of the change the facts are not in doubt. In 1961 every day nearly a quarter of a million people (221,000) woke up in a mental illness or mental handicap hospital; by 1984 this figure had been reduced to 137,000 (Central Statistical Office 1970, 1987). The reasons for this change are complex and debatable. Any explanation has to acknowledge the role of new drugs in controlling mental illnesses and epilepsy; it would also have to assess the relative importance of the resettlement of old long-stay patients in the community, the refusal by hospitals to accept new long-stay patients, and the reduction in the average length of stay, which is replacing long-stay with 'revolving-door' patients.

Any brief account of the reduction in the numbers of long-stay patients in mental illness and mental handicap hospitals will inevitably be selective and over-simplified, but there are certain key landmarks. In 1957 the Royal Commission on the Law Relating to Mental Illness and Mental Deficiency (Cmnd 169) recommended a shift in emphasis from hospital to community-based care, and suggested the use of the term 'community care' instead of 'supervision'. During the years that followed a number of influential research studies were published. Perhaps the most widely known name is that of Goffman (1968). The concept of the 'total institution' has shaped the thinking even of those who have never read *Asylums*. The richer environment provided for disabled children living in more domestic settings, as opposed to hospital wards, was documented convincingly by King *et al.* (1971). The regimented 'batch living' endured by people living in long-stay hospitals was given widespread publicity through the work of Morris (1969) and Oswin (1971). The reports on the scandals that erupted in, for example, Ely, Farleigh, Whittingham and South Ockendon Hospitals added the pressure of public opinion to the pressure coming from research (Martin 1984). In addition the Campaign for Mentally Handicapped People set new standards by which provision could be evaluated when it brought the PASS and PASSING techniques to Britain (Tyne 1982). Other organizations were active in pressing for change.

Throughout the 1970s health authorities complained that it was impossible to transfer long-stay patients from hospital to community care without bridging finance. The new community services could not be developed as long as resources continued to be tied up in hospitals. As late as 1981, when I began research on services for children with learning difficulties, families were still being offered permanent places in hospital for their disabled teenagers: the hospital gates did not close to new patients until two or three years later. The change was brought about by the creation of a mechanism by which joint finance monies were made available by regional health authorities to district health authorities and social services departments (Department of Health and Social Security 1981, 1983). In effect every patient leaving hospital was provided with a 'dowry', which began at over £9,000 per annum and rose in line with inflation, and which could be used to purchase care in the community. As far as health authorities were concerned it became financially prudent to

Table 17.1 Average daily occupied beds in mental illness and mental handicap hospitals (thousands)

	1961	1966	1971	1976	1981	1984
Mental illness	159	145	132	109	96	89
Mental handicap	62	64	65	59	52	48

Source: Central Statistical Office (1970, 1987).

move the less dependent patients out of hospital. As far as families were concerned, two classes had been created. Those who had placed their children in hospital found that they had thereby acquired a lifetime endowment; those who had kept their children at home often found that the promises of community care were hollow.

So what does this brief case study tell us about the impact of research on policy? The reduction in the numbers of patients in long-stay hospitals has certainly been dramatic, as Table 17.1 shows. Many of the most powerful influences on policy were in evidence in the course of this particular policy change. It was always in the long-term economic interest of central government to close the big, expensive long-stay hospitals; after 1983 it was also in the short-term interest of local and health authorities to begin to move their long-stay patients out. Various powerful interest groups, such as the Campaign for Mentally Handicapped People, campaigned for the change; only some hospital-based psychiatrists fought a rearguard action on behalf of their patients and perhaps their own professional power. The media exposed a number of scandals in long-stay hospitals. However, it is impossible to say for sure whether research had an impact on policy. The period of time is so long, the influences on policy are so many, that direct causal links cannot be made. Certainly research played its part, in terms of both rigorous evaluative exercises and vivid ethnographic studies. The first studies to assess the experience of those who had moved out of hospital reported that, in general, people benefited from, and preferred, life in the community; in addition, the new pattern of services cost less to provide (Knapp *et al*. 1991).

The story of the run-down of long-stay hospital provision suggests that any relation between research and policy is not linear but circular, since clearly policy also has an impact on research. The 1957 Royal Commission and the Act that followed it preceded the research of the 1960s and 1970s, while the research done in those decades informed the policy changes of the 1980s. Figure 17.1 sets the idea out as a simple model, which might be described as the research–policy process. Of course the model is a simplification. However, it suggests something of the relationship between policy-making and research, while indicating some of the other influences on both. The model postulates that research has an indirect effect on policy, for example by providing information to pressure groups and to the media, while policy affects research, not only because researchers want to study the issues of the day, but also because those issues re-appear among the priorities of funding bodies.

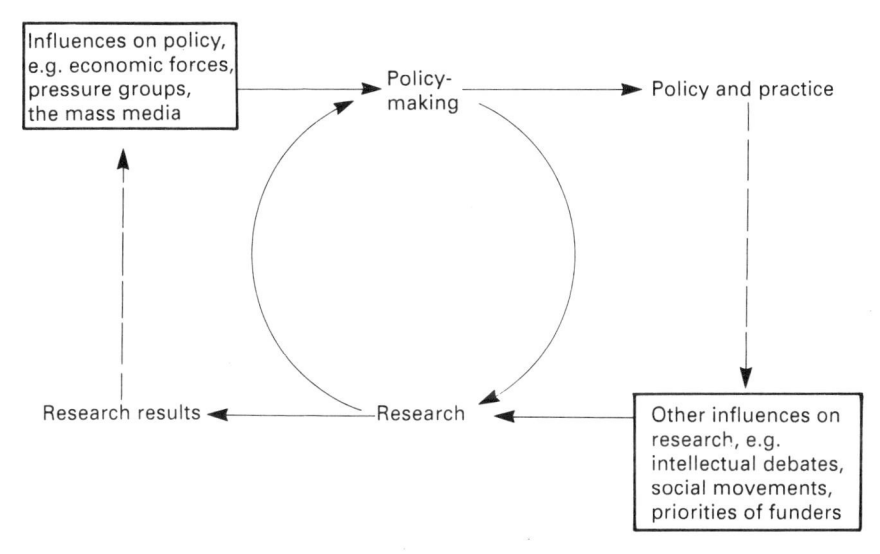

Figure 17.1 The research–policy process

As the hospital closure policy was put into practice it became clear who would bear the costs: the families who will care for the rest of their lives for those who in the past would have gone into hospital. In the next case study I shall examine the issue of caring and of providing support to carers.

Case study 2: research on carers and caring

Throughout most of the 1970s 'caring' was largely invisible; the word 'carer' was no part of professional discourse in the health and social services, nor was it to be found in government documents on provision for elderly, mentally ill and mentally handicapped people. There was, of course, research on caring for elderly and disabled people, but the terms 'families', 'relatives' and 'supporters' were used for the people who did the work of caring. Table 17.2 shows the entry of the word 'carer' into the English language as documented in some of the dictionaries of the time. I could find no dictionary reference to the word 'carer' before 1984. In the mid-1980s it began to appear, but was usually listed as a variant of the word 'care'. Not until 1989 did 'carer' achieve the status of

Table 17.2 The appearance of the word 'carer' in some English dictionaries

'Carer' does not appear in	'Carer' listed under 'care' in	'Carer' listed on its own in
Shorter Oxford 1952	Longman 1984	Oxford 1989
Hamlyn 1971	Chambers 1986	Shorter Oxford 1990
Chambers 1972	Collins 1988	
Penguin 1986	Cassell 1989	
Reader's Digest 1989		

an entry in its own right. What part did research play in all this and what has been the impact on policy?

In its original form community care policy had envisaged a significant role for public services in maintaining highly dependent people outside institutions. By the late 1970s this was changing. Under the twin pressures of public expenditure constraints and an ideological commitment to reducing the role of the state, the emphasis shifted from statutory to informal and voluntary provision (Baldwin and Twigg 1990; Parker 1990). At the same time the women's movement was drawing attention to gender inequalities in society.

The first research studies on carers and caring were carried out mainly by feminists, who argued that 'community care' was a euphemism for care by women, and that it was costly, both financially and in terms of time, work and stress. A significant landmark was the paper presented by Finch and Groves, in a sunny college garden in Cambridge, to the 1979 conference of the Social Administration Association. This argued that current policies for community care would intensify the inequalities already experienced by women because of the demands that caring makes on the carer (Finch and Groves 1980). In the next few years the nature of those demands was documented.

In a small, but influential, time budget study Nissel and Bonnerjea (1982) showed that husbands typically gave little help with caring, even when the person cared for was their own parent. In terms of time spent the husbands averaged eight minutes per day, in contrast to the 139 minutes the average wife spent caring. An earlier study had already found that most mothers caring for a child with a mental handicap received very little help with the work of caring: fathers did a small amount, while kin, friends and neighbours did initially nothing (Wilkin 1979). The most detailed and methodologically sound study of the economic effects of caring was that carried out by Baldwin (1985). This showed that mothers caring for disabled children at home were less likely to have a paid job than the mothers of a control group of normal children, despite the greater costs of caring for disabled children. Levin *et al.* (1983) showed that caring was also associated with increased levels of strain. Following a group of carers over time, it was found that the mental health of those who continued to care declined, while those whose elderly relative had died, or entered residential care, had improved.

Throughout the early 1980s the evidence coming from research was used, and was extended, by a number of significant pressure groups. For example, the Equal Opportunities Commission funded and published a series of studies of carers. A quarter of the carers in one study had given up paid work, or reduced their hours of employment, as a direct result of caring for an elderly or dependent person (Equal Opportunities Commission 1980). Another very effective pressure group was the Association of Carers, which publicized the burdens on carers and fought for policy changes that would benefit them (Oliver 1983).

By the end of the 1980s there was a substantial literature on carers and caring: one review listed over 200 references on the topic (Parker 1990). What part did research play in making the carer visible? Important evidence comes from the *Social Sciences Citation Index*, which lists the majority of articles

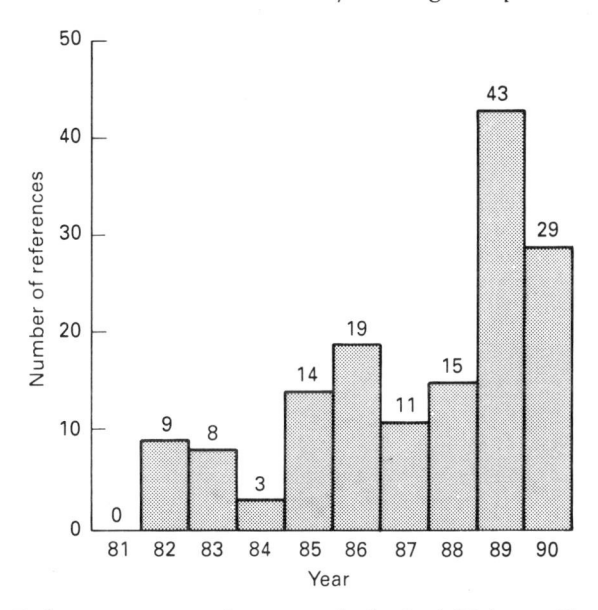

Figure 17.2 References to research on carers in the *Social Sciences Citation Index*

published in English, indexing them under topics. As Figure 17.2 shows, the word 'carer' did not appear in the index in 1981 or in any year before that. After that the trickle swells to a steady stream. Taken together, Table 17.2 and Figure 17.2 suggest that the researchers led the way in introducing the word 'carer' into common usage. Confirmation of this comes from the *Oxford English Dictionary*, which defines the word's current meaning as 'a person whose occupation is the care of the sick, aged, disabled, etc.: one who looks after a disabled or elderly relative at home, esp. one who is therefore unable to work' (Simpson and Weiner 1989). The dictionary notes that the word is derived from the old English word meaning 'sorrow, trouble or grief'. It also lists the first appearances of the new word, quoting an article in *Age and Ageing* in 1978 and *The Times* of May 1982.

What policy changes have occurred during ten years of research? Certainly the word 'carer' has passed into the language, and no policy statement on community care can now ignore the topic. Thus in 1988 Sir Roy Griffiths, in his agenda for action on community care, stated:

> Publicly provided services constitute only a small part of the total care provided to people in need. Families, friends, neighbours and other local people provide the majority of care. . . . [These] proposals take as their starting point that this is as it should be and that the first task of publicly provided services is to support and where possible strengthen these networks of carers.
>
> (Griffiths 1988: 2)

The new visibility or caring must be counted as an achievement. But what did the policy-makers see when they looked at carers? The carefully gender-neutral language of Sir Roy Griffiths's statement, and its blurred phrases ('families, friends, neighbours . . .'), are typical of many official statements.

Caring for carers is now government policy, but what does it mean in practice? Probably the most significant advance during the 1980s was the change in the social security regulations that allowed married women to claim the Invalid Care Allowance. Research may be said to have played a part, by informing the campaign fought by the Equal Opportunities Commission, but the crucial test case took place in the European Court in 1986. Other forms of support for carers are expanding slowly: they include respite care, sitting services, home care, carers' support groups and so on. However, provision for carers is still patchy, and one review of research in the field concluded that 'Carers remain relatively invisible in the policy formulations of agencies' (Twigg et al. 1990: 67).

It is interesting to compare the impact of research on carers with the impact of the evaluation of the Kent Community Care Project, which was carried out in the Personal Social Services Research Unit at the University of Kent. The Kent Community Care Project implemented a new approach to providing long-term care at home for frail elderly people, by the decentralization of resources to front-line field-work staff in social services. The research suggested that the project provided a cost-effective service that had helped to keep some elderly people out of residential care and had improved their quality of life (Challis and Davies 1986; Davies and Challis 1986). Compared with the control group there were benefits for carers, but again the greatest improvements were experienced by carers whose elderly relatives had died or entered residential care. This research was funded by the Department of Health and Social Security and the Personal Social Services Research Unit worked closely with Kent Social Services Department and later with the other departments who set out to replicate the project; the results were disseminated through a regular newsletter that was sent to every local authority in the country. The Kent Community Care Project is very widely known and has provided a model for the new pattern of services that is developing following the National Health Service and Community Care Act of 1990.

Comparing the impact of the research on carers with that on the Kent Community Care Project tends to confirm the hypothesis that the closer the researchers are to the policy-making process the more impact the research will have. The Kent research was carried out for central government, in collaboration with local government, and the results were disseminated very effectively to policy implementers and professionals in the field. The research addressed questions that were of great interest to key policy-makers, and the results of the research were in line with the direction of current government policy.

By contrast, the early research on carers was carried out mainly by feminists, and its general approach aimed to challenge existing paradigms and assumptions. The Department of Health and Social Security, to its great credit, also funded much of this research, but some of the most influential early work was done by tenured university lecturers who did not have particularly close links with policy-makers (Finch and Groves 1983). The researchers made it clear that giving carers financial compensation for their work would be expensive:

Force for change or optional extra? 227

inevitably major policy change in this area would be perceived as against the economic interests of the government and would involve a substantial transfer of resources from men to women, that is from tax-payers to carers. This may explain why, in terms of changing policy, the research on carers has had only a modest impact. However, in terms of the way we talk and think about caring its impact has been far-reaching.

Case study 3: research on day services for elderly people

In the third case study the focus shifts from the national to the local level, in order to extend the analysis of the impact of research on policy into a different context. In 1985 I was asked by Medway Health Authority to undertake a study of day services for elderly people in the district. At the time Medway had just set up and funded a full-time research post at the University of Kent and I had been appointed to fill it. The day services study was just one of many with which I was to be involved over the next few years.

The aim of the study was to monitor the existing day services provided for elderly people in the Medway Health District and to make recommendations for future developments in provision. The study was planned in close collaboration with the elderly health care planning team, which included representatives not only of health service planners and professionals, but also of the social services department and local voluntary organizations. The first report on the study, which ended with thirteen recommendations for action, was presented to a special meeting of the elderly health care planning team two years later. Thus those who planned the study were also those who were in a position to implement the recommendations when the study was completed.

A year or so later I was asked by the health authority to assess the impact of the study, and of the first report, in terms of identifiable changes in the services. Copies of the first set of recommendations were sent to all those who might have had a responsibility for implementation, with a request for information about what had actually happened. The request was sent out by the director of policy and planning, and not by the researcher. The replies showed that considerable progress had been made in some areas – and none in others. One advantage of research in a local setting is that it is much easier to trace its impact on policy.

Some recommendations had been implemented in full or in part. These included a major re-organization of the transport arrangements at the day hospital, weekend opening at some day centres and an expansion of the chiropody service. Even where recommendations had not been implemented there had often been gains from the research. For example, recommendations 12 and 13 were as follows:

> The *skills and experience of elderly people* who attend day services are a neglected resource. Those who run the services should assess the strengths, as well as the weaknesses, of each client so that his or her talents can be used for the benefit of all.
>
> *Representation* Those who use day services often have a very different perspective from those who provide services. All day centres should make

sure that the views of their clients are heard, by, for example, having management structures on which patients/clients are represented.

When the replies came back it seemed that these recommendations had provoked considerable debate: 'staff at many centres said that they welcomed suggestions from clients about the running of the services and commented that the research report had been useful, and sometimes controversial, in stimulating discussion of this issue' (Pahl 1988: 81).

The focus of this study was essentially local, and the recommendations named specific day hospitals and day centres. However, the study also produced results with more general relevance. Data about each elderly person were collected both from him or herself and from a member of staff. The questions were similar but the answers revealed enormous discrepancies. For example, in only 26 per cent of cases did the staff member and the service user give the same reason for the elderly person's attendance at the day facility and in only 35 per cent of cases was there agreement about what constituted the elderly person's most troublesome impairment (Pahl 1989).

What lessons can be drawn from this one small study about the impact of research on policy? First, the study underlined the value of close links between policy-makers and researchers. When those responsible for policy have been involved in planning the research, and when the results are reported directly to the relevant decision-makers, the research is much more likely to make an impact (Mugford *et al.* 1991). Second, the impact of research can take many forms, including the creation of a more informed context for policy-making and a more reflective approach to service delivery. Third, there is a great value in funding the researcher, as Medway does, rather than the research project. Any project can be divided between the stages when the research is planned, when it is carried out and when it is disseminated: unfortunately in many cases only the middle stage is funded. The lessons of research often continue to be relevant for years after the report is written and ways must be found to make the researcher available to policy-makers. Finally, locally initiated research is not necessary parochial. Facing the continuing tension between research, policy and practice can focus the mind more powerfully than is the case when the links between the three are more ambiguous and diffuse.

Policy research: swimming with the current or diverting the stream?

Clearly research can be a force for change. However, the case studies also suggest an important distinction between two different approaches to policy research. The first approach might be described as swimming with the policy stream: examples are the research on patients leaving long-stay hospitals and my own work on day services for elderly people. Here the researcher works within the policy framework, and research becomes part of the process of policy development. There are clear strategies that this sort of researcher can adopt in order to make greater impact on policy (for a more extended discussion see, for example, Booth 1988; Richardson et al. 1990). Researchers who want to make an impact on policy should:

- aim to answer the questions facing policy-makers;
- involve policy-makers in the research at every stage;
- plan good research that will produce robust results;
- complete specified reports and publications on time;
- achieve a balance between doing good research and meeting deadlines;
- take responsibility for disseminating the results of the research;
- target dissemination to specific audiences.

The second approach might be described as diverting the stream: this means that the researcher challenges the policy framework of the day, as the research on carers challenged taken-for-granted assumptions about the nature of family obligations. Only research that is independent and critical can point up the contradictions between economic interests and social welfare, question the priorities of dominant interest groups and expose the fashions of the mass media. In the short term this sort of research may be disregarded, or defined as trivial or irrelevant. However, in the long term this may be the research that makes the greatest impact of all.

References

Baldwin, S. (1985) *The Costs of Caring*, London: Routledge and Kegan Paul.
Baldwin, S. and Twigg, J. (1990) 'Women and community care: reflections on a debate', in M. McLean and D. Groves (eds) *Women's Issues in Social Policy*, London: Routledge.
Barnes, M. and Wilson, T. (1986) 'The internal dissemination and impact of in-house research in social services departments', *Research, Policy and Planning* 4, 1-2: 19-24.
Becker, H. (1970) 'Whose side are we on?', in H. Becker (ed.) *Sociological Work*, London: Allen Lane.
Booth, T. (1988) *Developing Policy Research*, Aldershot: Avebury.
Brown, M. and Madge, N. (1982) *Despite the Welfare State*, London: Heinemann Educational.
Central Statistical Office (1970) *Social Trends*, London: HMSO.
Central Statistical Office (1987) *Social Trends*, London: HMSO.
Challis, D. and Davies, B. (1986) *Case Management in Community Care*, Aldershot: Gower.
Davies, B. and Challis, D. (1986) *Matching Resources to Needs in Community Care*, Aldershot: Gower.
Department of Health and Social Security (1981) *Care in the Community: a Consultative Document on Moving Resources for Care in England*, London: HMSO.
Department of Health and Social Security (1983) *Health Service Development, Care in the Community and Joint Finance*, Health circular HC(83)6/LAC(83)5, London: HMSO.
Department of Health (1990) *DH Yearbook of Research and Development*, London: HMSO.
Equal Opportunities Commission (1980) *The Experience of Caring for Elderly and Handicapped Dependants*, Manchester: EOC.

Finch, J. and Groves, D. (1980) 'Community care and the family: a case for equal opportunities', *Journal of Social Policy* 9, 4: 487–511.
Finch, J. and Groves, D. (eds) (1983) *A Labour of Love: Women, Work and Caring*, London: Routledge and Kegan Paul.
Goffman, E. (1968) *Asylums*, New York: Doubleday and Sons.
Griffiths, R. (1988) *Community Care: an Agenda for Action*, London: HMSO.
Higgins, J. (1980) 'The unfulfilled promise of policy research', *Social Policy and Administration* 14, 3: 195–208.
King, R., Raynes, N. and Tizard, J. (1971) *Patterns of Residential Care*, London: Routledge and Kegan Paul.
Knapp, M., Cambridge, P., Thomasson, C., Beecham, J., Allen, C. and Darton, R. (1991) *Care in the Community: Evaluating a Demonstration Programme*, Aldershot: Gower.
Levin, E., Sinclair, I. and Gorbach, P. (1983) *The Supporters of Confused Elderly People at Home*, London: National Institute for Social Work (republished in 1989 as *Families, Services and Confusion in Old Age*, Aldershot: Gower).
Martin, J. (1984) *Hospitals in Trouble*, Oxford: Basil Blackwell.
Morris, P. (1969) *Put Away*, London: Routledge and Kegan Paul.
Mugford, M., Banfield, P. and O'Hanlon, M. (1991) 'Effects of feedback on information on clinical practice: a review', *British Medical Journal* 303: 398–402.
Nissel, M. and Bonnerjea, L. (1982) *Family Care of the Handicapped Elderly: Who Pays?* London: Policy Studies Institute.
Oliver, J. (1983) 'The caring wife', in J. Finch and D. Groves (eds) *A Labour of Love: Women, Work and Caring*, London: Routledge and Kegan Paul.
Oswin, M. (1971) *The Empty Hours*, London: Allen Lane.
Pahl, J. (1988) *Day Services for Elderly People in the Medway Health District*, 2nd edn. Canterbury: Centre for Health Services Studies.
Pahl, J. (1989) 'Day services for elderly people: misunderstandings and mixed metaphors', in J. Norton (ed.) *New Approaches to Day Care for Elderly People*, London: Age Concern Institute of Gerontology.
Parker, G. (1990) *With Due Care and Attention; a Review of Research on Informal Care*, London: Family Policy Studies Centre.
Rein, M. (1976) *Social Science and Public Policy*, Harmondsworth: Penguin.
Richardson, A., Jackson, C. and Sykes, W. (1990) *Taking Research Seriously*, London: HMSO.
Secretaries of State (1989) *Caring for People: Community Care in the Next Decade and Beyond*, London: HMSO.
Simpson, J. and Weiner, E. (eds) (1989) *Oxford English Dictionary*, Oxford: Clarendon Press.
Smith, G. and Cantley, C. (1985) *Assessing Health Care: a Study in Organizational Evaluation*, Milton Keynes: Open University Press.
Thomas, P. (1985) *The Aims and Outcomes of Social Policy Research*, Beckenham: Croom Helm.
Twigg, J., Atkin, K. and Perring, C. (1990) *Carers and Services: a Review of Research*, London: HMSO.
Tyne, A. (1982) 'Community care and mentally handicapped people', in A. Walker, (ed.) *Community Care*, Oxford: Basil Blackwell.
Weiss, C. (1986) 'Research and policy-making: a limited partnership', in F. Heller (ed.) *The Use and Abuse of Social Science*, London: Sage.
Wilkin, D. (1979) *Caring for the Mentally Handicapped Child*, Beckenham: Croom Helm.

18
The hidden curriculum: sexuality in professional education

Pam Carter and Tony Jeffs

Academic literature on higher education, like the bulk of writing on management and organizations, has opted for a 'booming silence' (Hearn and Parkin 1987: 4) on the issue of the sexual exploitation of women students. The campus novel has never displayed the same reticence. It has exploited to the full 'the glamour of the deviant and untypical, providing the novelist with a conveniently closed world marked by intellectual wrangling, political infighting and sexual intrigue' (Eagleton 1988: 94). Bradbury's *The History Man* and *Coming From Behind* by Howard Jacobson, when set beside the television series *A Very Peculiar Practice* and the film and play *Educating Rita*, have almost constructed afresh the social image of the contemporary university and polytechnic. All make great play of the 'comic' potential of snatched sexual liaisons between staff and student. Each creates a set of anti-heroes intent upon maximizing the opportunities available for the sexual exploitation of a seemingly inexhaustible supply of readily available students. The number of our interviewees who claimed to have encountered the 'history man' beggars the imagination. The list of names we might have drawn up reads like a scroll of honour for British sociology in the 1960s and 1970s. The image of higher education conveyed by this literature stands in stark contrast to that portrayed in 'official' documentation and studies. The chasm between the two cannot be easily explained away and it has to be asked if the former is merely the end product of writers artificially making use of the 'comic' potential of the campus environment or an exposé of a hidden culture. What the literature does confirm is that 'academic machismo at its worse is just a more rarified variety of the competitiveness, bravado and bullying which typifies men's behaviour generally' (Thompson 1987: 74). For very many women academic institutions offer little that approximates to an 'ivory tower'. Clearly on the basis of our, albeit limited, research it needs to be recognized that they are as likely to encounter sexual harassment and sexual exploitation on the campus as in any factory or office. Attempts by American writers to research and quantify the problem certainly suggest very high levels of sexual harassment and exploitation of students (Lott *et al*. 1982; Maihoff and Forrest 1983; Rutter 1989).

Lifting the lid

This chapter draws upon interviews with staff, students and ex-students from English universities and polytechnics. All were or had been involved in professional training, leading to qualifications in social work and youth and community work. When we commenced this research we asked ourselves the fairly obvious question – how widespread is the sexual exploitation of students? Our combined thirty plus years in HE, initially as students and then as lecturers, led us to believe that it was both common and pernicious in term of its impact on the learning experience of students and on relationships in institutions. Initial disquiet regarding the typicality of our observations and encounters rapidly evaporated. As we commenced our programme of interviews we were obliged to scale our estimates of the extent of the problem ever upwards. Subsequently and with growing frequency we have been contacted by individuals who, learning of our interest in this issue, are anxious to share their concerns and experiences with us. Obviously the furtive and secretive nature of so much sexual exploitation, linked to such feelings as anger and embarrassment on the part of many of the exploited, means that it will never be feasible to quantify the scale of the problem. Having made that proviso we nevertheless conclude that the problem is extensive, far more so than we, and we suspect most individuals, ever imagined.

Given the lengths to which institutions have been willing to go to hide instances of sexual exploitation of students and junior staff it is perhaps not surprising that it is the novel and television play that provide for outsiders a snapshot of reality. For some staff, 'fiction' may be the only professionally acceptable means by which they can 'tell it as it is' beyond the walls of the institution. However serious the offence, universities and polytechnics appear determined to ensure that their self-constructed external image and reputation are protected by 'dealing with it themselves'. This apparently applies even with regard to the most extreme cases:

> The worst example I have encountered certainly illustrates the extent to which the university was willing to go in order to sweep the problem under the carpet. One of my students, a third year, was offered a tutorial in the evening by a member of staff. He not only made uninvited advances but actually began what can only be described as an attempt to rape her. Fortunately her screams were heard by a porter who was checking the building. She was persuaded not to report the assault to the police, the condition being that the member of staff would have no further contact with her. That was achieved by granting him a sabbatical for the remainder of the year.
>
> (University lecturer, female)

The hidden curriculum: sexuality in professional education 233

Where sexual exploitation is referred to in relation to the position of women in higher education it is subsumed within the catch-all heading of sexual harassment. This often limits our awareness of the more complex patterns of sexual intimidation, exploitation and intrusion that occur. Wise and Stanley (1987) have drawn our attention to the dangers of sexual harassment policies that infer that such behaviour is extreme and limited to a few abnormal males. Instead they use the concept of 'the dripping tap' and describe sexual harassment as 'an unwanted and unsought intrusion by men into women's feelings, thoughts, behaviours, space, time, energies and bodies' (p. 71). Sexual harassment policies are increasingly being adopted in higher education. These are only as useful as the cultures, beliefs and practices that underpin them in any particular workplace allow. Unless policies are underpinned by a clear understanding of the complex linkages that exist between sexuality and power they will be ineffective. Worse, if they do not protect victims from further exploitation they will be self-defeating and often harmful in terms of impact.

For students in the majority of institutions the implementation procedures of sexual harassment policies expose complainants to a real and tangible risk of suffering victimization from the colleagues of the perpetrator. In case after case we found staff narrowly and unquestioningly identifying their pre-eminent loyalty as being owed to their colleague. Once the student had set the complaints procedure in motion she was transmuted into the role of aggressor and the perpetrator was sanitized into the victim. Without question any procedure that enables this to be the norm is fundamentally flawed. Our work suggests that narrow operational definitions of sexual harassment, together with policies being crudely elastoplasted on to sexually exploitative cultures, means that they have not even begun to tackle the serious problems we refer to here. Such policies, laudable as they may be, fundamentally relate to the control and identification of malpractice by staff towards colleagues. This ignores the different dynamics of staff–student harassment. It also opts to overlook the degree to which the sexual exploitation of students takes place within higher education, and condones it by a blanket refusal to acknowledge its existence. Trade union responses to sexual harassment between colleagues have now generally begun to recognize the importance of carefully weighing the different responsibilities in cases involving two of their own members. However, where the victim is a student, or for that matter a client, then unions, like the institutions where their members work, can and do more easily revert to an unquestioning defence of 'their own' against any complainant.

Within fictional accounts and much discourse concerning the sexual exploitation of students a picture emerges of experienced older men preying upon vulnerable young students fresh from the sixth form. Like the villain in Josephine Bell's novel *The Hunter and the Trapped*, almost invariably they teach in arts faculties and exploit not only the sexual inexperience of the students but their thirst for knowledge, insight and understanding. The behaviour of the men is often by implication partially excused on the grounds that they are initiating their students simultaneously into adulthood and an intellectual milieu. This attempt to portray sexual exploitation as a fair market exchange is simply the worst sort of patriarchal nonsense. First, it chooses to overlook the reality that the seduction takes place in an institutional setting that is 'dominated by gender-related values that bias organizational life in favour of one sex over another' (Morgan 1986: 178), values that negate from the onset any notion of equity between the participants. Second, such an account evades any recognition of another key factor. For as one respondent explained:

> It is all so dishonest because those who have sexual relationships with students choose to ignore the central fact that all staff student relationships and contact in an institution like this are taking place in a setting where staff from the beginning have power over students.
>
> (Youth and community lecturer, male)

Certainly we found scant evidence that any induction into an intellectual milieu ever takes place. Rather, the overwhelming majority of the liaisons are furtive and brief, and usually terminated by the member of staff, generally either before or shortly after the completion of the course. This was well illustrated in the following account:

> The affair started in the second year when he became my tutor. By mid-way through the second year I had moved into his flat. However, during the summer I went away with my parents on an end of course holiday they had promised me. When I returned there was a message from my friend waiting. He had actually turned up at her place and dumped my stuff there. Everyone knew what had happened yet one of the students in the following year actually still took up with him. She was much older than me and I believe they are still together. Her husband divorced her as a result of the affair so I guess that gave X a shock.
>
> (Youth and community worker, female)

The inherent authority of staff members ensures that they usually control not only the onset but also the cessation of the relationship. Whatever the reason given, the student victim, it emerges, is rarely introduced to the social world of the staff or even publicly acknowledged. Staff rarely seem to have any intention of keeping that side of the bargain. Indeed, what academic benefits may accrue can often be crudely negotiated. For example:

> X is hardly subtle in these matters. A friend of mine was invited to X's room to discuss her essay. She was told it was worth a B+ and was delighted. He then made a suggestion that they should go for a drink and then go back to his flat. She refused and left his room. When the essay was later returned it was given a C. She was angry and upset but given that her husband was less then whole-hearted about her attending college she decided that she would have to let the matter be.
>
> (Youth and community worker, female)

Given the concentration of women students in certain professional areas, such as nursing, social work, teaching and youth and community work, it is inevitable that exploitation by male staff of women students is unevenly spread throughout an institution. However, numbers alone do not account for the different rates of occurrence between courses and institutions. First, undergraduate courses tend to have higher proportions of younger students, who appear from our research less likely to be victims. Second, the organization of such courses into modules and options, the lecture format, often consisting of groups of fifty plus, and the infrequency of tutorials all reduce the opportunities available for staff to make the individual contact essential for applying pressure. Finally, the means of assessment by impersonal examination will tend to make it more problematic for staff to buy 'favours' either overtly or covertly. The professional courses, with their emphasis on tutor–tutee relationships, practice assessment, continuous assessment, individual and small group work, recruitment of older students with life or professional experience and a culture that places substantial emphasis on such matters as mutual support, sensitivity to the needs of others and awareness of self, all provide by comparison a far more fertile venue for sexual exploitation. They also more commonly include residential elements, which provide exploitative male staff with unique opportunities largely denied to colleagues on undergraduate programmes. Many respondents saw these as having only questionable educational value. To quote one ex-student:

> The course starts with a residential week. A couple of the male staff use it as a meat market. It is all mature students on the course, a lot of them are, as you would guess, very nervous and apprehensive about starting in higher education, they are really vulnerable. On my year at least a couple of them slept with staff during the residential. I think they regretted it later but at the time they probably thought that is how students behave. For those staff it was like a perk that goes with job.
> (Community worker, female)

Course cultures

The paradox within all this is that since undergraduate programmes only assess academic ability and therefore, although it is not excusable, the sexual exploitation of students does not imply any implicit message regarding subsequent behaviour in employment, it is on many of those courses seeking to prepare students for professional practice that exploitation appears to be most acute. For teachers the sexual exploitation of pupils is not deemed acceptable behaviour and is likely to lead to dismissal. Similar professional boundaries operate regarding client–worker relations in social work, therapy, nursing and youth work. Yet it is within the training of these professionals that we encountered many of the worst examples of sexual exploitation. An example of this is in the tutorial relationship, which is held to be at the core of social work and youth and community work training. Fundamental to this is the belief that it provides students with a model for future practice. 'It is in tutorials that tutor and student can relate, communicate and take stock, and here students can trace for themselves their own development and progress as potential professional social workers' (Hayward 1979: 14). To quote from a key official document, 'relationships between staff and students are one medium through which values are demonstrated' (CCETSW 1975).

Yet it is often in this setting that students are most vulnerable. Isolated and alone with the member of staff, they are expected to discuss the personal problems that impede their learning, to enter into a quasi-client–worker relationship wherein they learn from their tutor the value of counselling and case-working, while all the time being left in no doubt as to the power of the tutor. After all it is he or she who will often: determine whether they have an easy or difficult placement; participate in placement assessment; report on them to the final examination board; mark key pieces of work; and crucially judge their personal characteristics as being fit or otherwise to gain professional accreditation. Given that the overriding aim of any student is to pass the course it is only to be expected that he or she will 'assess the demands of tutors, develop strategies in relation to these demands and behave in ways which are felt to be compatible with what is required' (Heraud 1981:56). When Heraud's comments are placed in the context of the male member of staff who wishes to use the tutorial setting to exploit a student sexually the dangers hardly need to be spelt out.

> Lecturer Y never seems to fail to form at least one relationship with a student each intake. She is usually one of his tutees. He seems to have an unnerving ability to select vulnerable students.
>
> (Social work lecturer, male)

Although the tutorial may be private the results can, and often must spill over into the public arena. As another tutor explained:

> I am relatively new here and I know what is going on. I can't believe that the head of department and the other staff do not know. As far as I know he has had affairs with a couple of students and tried it on with a number of others. He should not be allowed female tutees but until someone makes an official complaint and produces evidence what can be done? Mind you it has been covered up in the past so why should they [students] expect anything to happen if they officially complained now.
>
> (Youth and community lecturer, female)

These supposedly clandestine relationships often disrupt relationships throughout the course. The student may well find that her capacity to work with other students is impeded and other members of staff who are aware of, or suspect, the liaison may be reluctant to engage openly with her. As the following illustrates, the student may be disadvantaged long after the relationship has ceased and learning opportunities may be lost that can never be recaptured.

> Within weeks of the course starting X had commenced an affair with one of the students in the group. She was highly flattered by his attention and made no secret of the relationship. It, however, made it very uncomfortable for the rest of us who were aware that in all probability our comments about the course as well as our dissatisfaction about the poor teaching of that lecturer were being carried back to him. The relationship continued until the end of the year when he selected a new student from the incoming first year. The student in our group after that felt both humiliated and

bitter. She never really had much to do with the rest of us after that and became a very irregular attender.

(Social worker, female)

Such behaviour results in the corruption of relationships between all staff and students. Innocent and perfectly acceptable social contact between staff and students becomes tainted with gossip and innuendo. The natural growth of friendship is curtailed and even ordinary discourse and collaboration becomes viewed by staff as professionally dangerous. Women students may well, with some degree of justification, come to view all male staff, innocent and guilty alike, as posing a threat, thus being denied access to learning that should arise in informal as well as formal settings. As one member of staff said:

> Given the behaviour of a fair number of my male colleagues you have no alternative but to put a fairly solid barrier up between you and the students. I now make it a rule never to socialize unless I am accompanied by my partner or an outside friend. It is a pity that one can't have informal contact with students.
>
> (Social work lecturer, male)

Although these aspects are sometimes discussed it is almost unknown for staff publicly to acknowledge the extent to which sexual exploitation can corrupt the assessment procedures within institutions. At one level liaisons can lead to over-generous marking and assessment of practice. For students this provides motivation and for staff a powerful form of leverage. We continually encountered anger and suspicion among students who perceived that members of their peer group had been given preferential treatment, or that they or others who had rejected the advances of staff had been unfairly treated as a consequence. Certain staff argued that on occasions the relationships had led to unprofessional conduct in examination boards:

> We had a particularly unpleasant case of a male student who was caught cheating by a woman member of staff. It emerged later that the student had been involved with a married woman student who was simultaneously having an affair with a male member of staff. That student not only learnt the content of all the discussions that had taken place about the incident but the names of the staff who had held that his behaviour was unacceptable. He even learnt how staff had voted at the examination board.
>
> (Social work lecturer, male)

In another instance an outsider became embroiled in the resulting conflict and abuse of academic authority:

> After the exam board this woman member of staff, absolutely furious, came up to me and asked if I knew why X had been so anxious that a particular student was passed without having to re-sit the failed element. I made a non-commital comment. . . . She then proceeded to tell me that he had had an affair with the student in her first year. It had ended but he was

now terrified that it would come out in an appeal. That was his agenda and he didn't care if that meant she got favourable treatment.

(External examiner, male)

In extreme cases whole courses and educational programmes can be damaged by the backwash emanating from the exploitation of an individual student. It can provide the hidden agenda of staff conflict, which can disrupt the delivery of teaching programmes and prevent staff exercising collective responsibility. In one case reported to us it even came to threaten the career of an innocent member of the academic staff.

I had to resign as course leader after the head of department who taught on the course started an affair with one of the students. She told me, and he must have found out that I knew. Later I saw them together miles from here by sheer accident. From then on it was difficult to put your finger on it but he was difficult to work with and obviously trying to catch me out. It got me down to the extent that I decided to leave but then thought better of it. Why should I move? Instead I resigned as course leader but working relationships are terrible.

(Social work lecturer, female)

Some of those who defend sexual relationships between staff and students as natural by-products of an adult learning environment choose to ignore the extent to which these liaisons impede the learning of the students concerned and, it should be noted, of their peers. For the overwhelming majority of those involved in liaisons with staff the disadvantages far outweigh any supposed benefits. Yet it has to be conceded that for some a tangible advantage is secured. Sexual exploiters after all will often seek out the vulnerable. Among these time and again we find those students whose academic and practice performance provides cause for concern. Consequently, marginal students pass who would otherwise have failed. In the context of placements it was clear that practice teachers exploit their power, endorsing poor performance and unprofessional conduct. This pattern of behaviour raises serious doubts as to the competency to practise of many students, for not only do individuals involved with staff, who should be referred or failed outright, pass but others are protected in order to give an impression of even-handedness. On some courses the culture of exploitation, according to a number of staff and ex-students we interviewed, meant that failure was virtually impossible. This benefit was recognized by many students outside the immediate circle of the exploited and exploiter, providing them with a powerful motive for condoning such behaviour. Perhaps worse, it de-motivates many among those who might ideologically be opposed to the sexual exploitation of students. For if it was stopped then standards and expectations might rise, making the collective life of the students less easy and the 'qualification at the end' less a foregone conclusion.

Professional training: the outside world

For all institutions of higher education sexual exploitation has a significance with regard to the outside world. All are anxious to convince parents and husbands that 'their women' are safe with us. Great play is often made of campus safety, bright lights, uniformed patrols, personal alarms, late night mini-bus services and security locks. The danger is always without. In lieu of any determination to confront sexual harassment and exploitation by their own staff they have no alternative but to sustain their image by suppressing all hint of danger in the classroom and study. Specifically in relation to professional training courses, universities and colleges must also seek to convey a picture of themselves as possessing the core values of the profession.

Ironically these professional groups are increasingly concerned with the management of social problems whose origins lie in the abuse of power through sexual behaviour. The reputation of a course or department will be damaged if it becomes known to students, practitioners and employers as one where sex is part of the hidden curriculum rather than responsibly dealt with in the formal syllabus. For example, one lecturer told us that she asked students in a formal teaching session about how sexuality had been addressed on the course. The students laughed and said that it had only been 'addressed' in the corridors. Asked what they meant, they said that there had been very little teaching about sexuality but that there was a lot of sexual chat and innuendo between staff and students outside the classroom. Many found this offensive but informal course culture did not allow it to be challenged. This is, of course, extremely damaging to the reputation of the course. For example:

> X Polytechnic social work department is notorious. I have always assumed that being a sexual harasser was a qualification for a job at that place.
> (Senior social worker, male)

Further, it feeds considerable cynicism in students and others involved with the training enterprise. Why bother to treat any of the course seriously when there is such hypocrisy at its heart? Core values and standards become easily disposable, often in the interests of natural justice. As one practice teacher noted:

> A student from Polytechnic X slept with one of the residents whilst she was on placement with us. I suppose I should have failed her but given the reputation of the male staff at the polytechnic it didn't seem fair to punish her for what they get up to all the time, so I warned her and let the matter rest.
> (CQSW practice teacher, female)

The condoning of behaviour such as this means that our collective knowledge about sexuality and power as well as how problems arising from them are best handled remains limited. Course cultures that support rather than question current social patterns of sex and power will not only prevent learning for individual students but also inhibit and damage the collective scholarship that ought to characterize academic life and professional training.

Although little consensus exists about the handling of the social problems of sex one conclusion shared by professional groups, judicial enquiries and media reportage is that more and better training is needed. More training is universally regarded as a Good Thing. It is likely that sex in a more sanitized form will start to find its way on to training programmes. The question is: what kind of agenda about sex is being shaped? While there is disagreement about curriculum content there is a shared assumption that 'rationality rules' in sex as in other areas of education. No awareness of the possibility of a hidden curriculum ever surfaces; no recognition that sex and power are inextricably linked for us professionals as well as for 'clients'; no understanding that if these issues are, or were, invisible 'out there' in the 'real world' they might be unspoken but ever present in training. That classrooms may not be safe, neutral places for sexuality to be explored. The silences about sex and power in training have much in common with the silences about sex and power in the home. Just as children and women have been forced to keep quiet about what goes on at home, so students and teachers keep quiet about what goes on at the college or in the practice placement. 'Naming the game' for students may be to risk failing the course, and for teaching staff to risk isolation and scapegoating. One lecturer told us that she was astonished that women colleagues whom she had seen as reasonably perceptive claimed not to have noticed fairly crude sexual harassment of students by their male colleagues.

Policy change

Attempting to change this picture through policy development and implementation is inherently problematic, requiring a formal and rational approach to a problem permeated with vested interests and alliances, silence and, almost always, dishonesty.

For example, CCETSW seems to have considerable faith in rational planning and policy-making. It appears to believe that if it makes regulations decreeing that all learning will take place in an environment where students can combat discrimination (CCETSW 1989) this will actually happen. Such naivity about power is particularly worrying in the case of sexuality. Social workers have been castigated for simply believing what they are told. Those who abuse children do not readily tell us that they have done so. There are major dilemmas for social workers about how and in what circumstances children are to be believed. But agency managers and heads of social work courses are, apparently, simply to be believed when they tell us that students are being educated in environments where they can tackle the sorts of power relationships that discrimination involves. As long as these responsible professionals tell us that they have so many hours of this and that on the timetable and that their staff are busy writing anti-discriminatory policy statements CCETSW officers apparently breathe a sigh of relief and go home.

If we have collectively learned anything about sexuality in the past few years it is that many apparently 'normal' situations are not what they seem. It is not only the poor and ignorant who sexually abuse their children. It is not only 'raving lunatics' on dark nights who rape and assault women. Sexual harassment at work is not rare abnormal behaviour. Sexuality is always about power and it is always about 'us' as well as 'them'. Rather than counting the hours devoted to child sexual abuse and reading the policy statements about discrimination, we need to ask other kinds of questions about training courses:

- Are sexual encounters between staff and students commonplace?
- Are such sexual relationships open and explicit or secret?
- Do staff use their position to curry sexual favours from students?
- Do sexual relationships influence the professional decision-making of tutors?
- Do some students use sexual attractiveness to secure advantage?
- Do other students struggle to succeed because they are perceived to be less attractive and/or because they refuse the sexual advances of their tutors?
- Do staff cover up the sexual harassment of their colleagues in order to keep the peace or advance their careers?
- Are those staff and students who raise the issue of sexual harassment victimized?

It seems unlikely that these questions will be asked through formal channels because of the existing conspiracy of silence. They need to be addressed by students and staff. Until validation processes and the inspection and monitoring procedures of professional bodies address these issues they can only be dealt with through other mechanisms. One is through the sexual harassment policies now widely adopted within higher education, the limitations of which we have already considered. The other is by the adoption within higher education of professional and ethical guidelines that exclude such behaviour; such guidelines clarify the nature of the professional relationship between staff and students and establish boundaries. We can already point to an example of this:

> No faculty member shall have an amorous relationship (consensual or otherwise) with a student who is enrolled in a course being taught by the faculty member or whose academic work (including work as a teaching assistant) is being supervised by the faculty member. Faculty members exercise power over students, whether in giving them praise or criticism, evaluating them, making recommendations for their further studies or their future employment, or conferring any other benefits on them. Amorous relationships between faculty members and students are wrong when the faculty member has professional responsibility for the student. Such situations greatly increase the chances that the faculty member will abuse his or her power and sexually exploit the student. Voluntary consent by the student in such a relationship is suspect given the fundamentally asymmetric nature of the relationship.
> (University of Iowa, quoted in Rutter 1989: 163)

We have surveyed HE institutions in the UK regarding existing policies and their willingness to adopt guidelines similar to the University of Iowa. Many claim that it is not possible to distinguish staff–student relationships from staff–staff relationships, which also involve power. Similarities do exist.

Certainly few would wish to ignore the sexual exploitation of a young secretary by a senior academic. Yet important differences remain:

- all workers are to some extent protected by contracts and employment law – inadequate as these are they exceed the legal rights of students;
- the temporary nature of the involvement of each student with the institution means that it is more difficult for them to pursue individual cases within the allotted timespan;
- the isolation of students, many of whom are part-time, means they have less access to mutual support and often little consciousness of the scale of the problem;
- management have an additional responsibility to protect students from harassment and exploitation because the brevity of their involvement with their institution will hinder their learning whom to avoid;
- uniquely, students are at risk from victimization within the assessment procedure – the essential confidentiality of this system means that only the institution can protect their interests within it;
- the educational reputation of an institution stands apart from its reputation as an employer and in the interests of all this cannot be comprised.

Another theme in these responses to our survey is the 'Mills and Boon' paradigm: 'people can't help falling in love'. We're very surprised that university and polytechnic personnel departments are so romantic! For example, one polytechnic maintained that a blanket policy would ignore the reality that 'some of these relationships may be loving, caring relationships which provide the spiritual, emotional and physical bond that for many people is an important part of being human'. From our research on sexual exploitation this picture does not accord with students and staff sleeping together in the first week of the course, nor with several affairs in a short period. It also sits rather oddly with our shared experience of doctor–patient or nurse–patient relationships. The fact that sex is not an expected part of these 'caring' relationships does not appear to be seen as coercive; rather it provides a sound basis for professional practice.

It is with some reluctance that we suggest an apparently authoritarian policy. For the prime objective is to secure a change in culture that enables the open discussion of sexuality and power. However, legislating such rules into existence will help to reconstruct sexual cultures by providing a known, understood and agreed boundary. At the heart of this debate are questions concerning the nature of the professional relationship between staff and students. At a time when management are obsessed with the rhetoric of quality it is ridiculous that they refuse to deal with practices that, perhaps more than any, help protect low teaching standards and incompetent staff, both of which survive in many cases because to do anything regarding either might entail the unwanted exposure of sexual exploitation and harassment. Time and again students and staff linked poor academic performance with the abuse of sexuality. Those staff most intent on exploiting students were all too often those who failed to meet professional criteria in relation to their teaching. Paradoxically it is those who engage in the sexual exploitation of students who are most comprehensively protected by management. Fearful of taking action regarding academic and administrative incompetence and indolence, they leave the bottle uncorked.

Making rules about behaviour is an extremely narrow way of handling the problem. We would not wish to propose solutions that are at best bureaucratic and at worst likely to enhance the power of management within HE. Broader solutions must rest in measures designed to reconstruct gender relations. We have suggested here that at present debate concerning these in this locale has avoided addressing a major dynamic: the abuse of staff power over students through sexual exploitation. In offering an account of this abuse of power we are aware that we have described students as 'victims' and that feminist discourse has forcefully questioned the use of victimology. It is a concept that inadequately confronts patriarchal power, feeding as a consequence images of feminine powerlessness and asserting individual responsibility. Our research sits uncomfortably beside notions of individual choice as a causal factor that leads students to be the object of sexual exploitation. Yet if allowance is made for the foregoing proviso then our research suggests that at present, sadly, 'victim' becomes an appropriate term capable of describing the experiences of some, perhaps many, women students in professional training. Those who become the object of sexual exploitation are isolated, sometimes with strong feelings of guilt and rarely with any feminist voice on hand to defend them or enable them to analyse their experiences as a dimension of patriarchy. Feminist staff, it seems, are just as likely as others to feign ignorance of the gross behaviour of male colleagues. As we have noted earlier, women (and indeed men) who do challenge such behaviour appear to run a greater risk of being isolated and scapegoated than the perpetrators. Such is the desire to protect corporate, departmental and professional cohesion. Our wish is to contribute to a debate whose existence must challenge the dominant sexual culture. The parameters of such a debate cannot be left for management to determine; rather it must be a collective endeavour that seeks to dismantle a culture which at present places women students in a position of such clear vulnerability.

References

CCETSW (1975) *Values in Social Work*, London. Central Council for Education and Training in Social Work.
CCETSW (1989) *Requirements and Regulations for the Diploma in Social Work*, London: Central Council for Education and Training in Social Work.
Eagleton, T. (1988) 'The campus novel', *New Left Review* 172: 93–105.
Hayward, C. (1979) *A Fair Assessment*, London: CCETSW.
Hearn, J. and Parkin, W. (1987) *Sex at Work: the Power and Paradox of Organisation Sexuality*, Brighton: Wheatsheaf.
Heraud, B. (1981) *Training For Uncertainty*, London: Routledge and Kegan Paul.
Lott, B., Reilly, M. and Howard, D. (1982) 'Sexual assault and harassment: a campus community case study', *Signs: Journal of Women in Culture and Society* 8, 2: 296–319.
Maihoff, N. and Forrest, L. (1983) 'Sexual harassment in higher education: an

assessment study', *Journal of the National Association for Women Deans, Administrators and Counselors* 46: 3–8.

Morgan, G. (1986) *Images of Organizations*, Beverly Hills: Sage.

Rutter, P. (1989) *Sex in the Forbidden Zone*, New York: Tarcher.

Thompson, J. L. (1987) 'The cost and value of higher education to working-class women', in S. Harrop *et al.* (eds) *Oxford and Working Class Education*, 2nd edn, Nottingham: Dept of Adult Education, University of Nottingham.

Wise, S. and Stanley, L. (1987) *Georgie Porgie: Sexual Harassment in Everyday Life*, London: Routledge and Kegan Paul.